I0120095

STUDIES

IN THE

PSYCHOLOGY OF SEX

BY

HAVELOCK ELLIS

STUDIES IN THE PSYCHOLOGY OF SEX.

(Complete in Six Volumes.)

I. The Evolution of Modesty, the Phenomena of Sexual Periodicity and Auto-erotism. $2.50, net.

II. Sexual Inversion. $2.00, net.

III. Analysis of the Sexual Impulse. $2.50, net.

IV. Sexual Selection in Man. $2.00, net.

V. Erotic Symbolism. The Mechanism of Detumescence. The Psychic State in Pregnancy. $2.00, net.

VI. Sex in Relation to Society. $3.00, net.

Each volume is sold separately, and is complete in itself.

This is the only edition in English published by the author's permission.

Havelock Ellis.

STUDIES

IN THE

PSYCHOLOGY OF SEX

EROTIC SYMBOLISM

THE MECHANISM OF DETUMESCENCE

THE PSYCHIC STATE IN PREGNANCY

BY

HAVELOCK ELLIS

PHILADELPHIA

F. A. DAVIS COMPANY, PUBLISHERS

1914

COPYRIGHT, 1906,

BY

F. A. DAVIS COMPANY

Philadelphia, Pa., U.S.A.:
Press of F. A. Davis Company
1916 Cherry Street.

PREFACE.

In this volume the terminal phenomena of the sexual process are discussed, before an attempt is finally made, in the concluding volume, to consider the bearings of the psychology of sex on that part of morals which may be called "social hygiene."

Under "Erotic Symbolism" I include practically all the aberrations of the sexual instinct, although some of these have seemed of sufficient importance for separate discussion in previous volumes. It is highly probable that many readers will consider that the name scarcely suffices to cover manifestations so numerous and so varied. The term "sexual equivalents" will seem preferable to some. While, however, it may be fully admitted that these perversions are "sexual equivalents"—or at all events equivalents of the normal sexual impulse—that term is merely a descriptive label which tells us nothing of the phenomena. "Sexual Symbolism" gives us the key to the process, the key that makes all these perversions intelligible. In all of them—very clearly in some, as in shoe-fetichism; more obscurely in others, as in exhibitionism—it has come about by causes congenital, acquired, or both, that some object or class of objects, some act or group of acts, has acquired a dynamic power over the psycho-physical mechanism of the sexual process, deflecting it from its normal adjustment to the whole of a beloved person of the opposite sex. There has been a transmutation of values, and certain objects, certain acts, have acquired an emotional value which for the normal person they do not possess. Such objects and acts are properly, it seems to me, termed symbols, and that term embodies the only justification that in most cases these manifestations can legitimately claim.

"The Mechanism of Detumescence" brings us at last to the final climax for which the earlier and more prolonged stage of tumescence, which has occupied us so often in these *Studies,* is the elaborate preliminary. "The art of love," a clever woman novelist has written, "is the art of preparation." That "preparation" is, on the physiological side, the production of tumescence, and all courtship is concerned in building up tumescence. But the final conjugation of two individuals in an explosion of detumescence, thus slowly brought about, though it is largely an involuntary act, is still not without its psychological implications and consequences; and it is therefore a matter for regret that so little is yet known about it. The one physiological act in which two individuals are lifted out of all ends that center in self and become the instrument of those higher forces which fashion the species, can never be an act to be slurred over as trivial or unworthy of study.

In the brief study of "The Psychic State in Pregnancy" we at last touch the point at which the whole complex process of sex reaches its goal. A woman with a child in her womb is the everlasting miracle which all the romance of love, all the cunning devices of tumescence and detumescence, have been invented to make manifest. The psychic state of the woman who thus occupies the supreme position which life has to offer cannot fail to be of exceeding interest from many points of view, and not least because the maternal instinct is one of the elements even of love between the sexes. But the psychology of pregnancy is full of involved problems, and here again, as so often in the wide field we have traversed, we stand at the threshold of a door it is not yet given us to pass.

HAVELOCK ELLIS.

Carbis Water, Lelant, Cornwall.

CONTENTS.

IV.

V.

VI.

THE MECHANISM OF DETUMESCENCE.

I.

APPENDIX.

EROTIC SYMBOLISM.

I.

The Definition of Erotic Symbolism—Symbolism of Act and Symbolism of Object—Erotic Fetichism—Wide extension of the symbols of Sex—The Immense Variety of Possible Erotic Fetiches—The Normal Foundations of Erotic Symbolism—Classification of the Phenomena—The Tendency to Idealize the Defects of a Beloved Person—Stendhal's "Crystallization."

By "erotic symbolism" I mean that tendency whereby the lover's attention is diverted from the central focus of sexual attraction to some object or process which is on the periphery of that focus, or is even outside of it altogether, though recalling it by association of contiguity or of similarity. It thus happens that tumescence, or even in extreme cases detumescence, may be provoked by the contemplation of acts or objects which are away from the end of sexual conjugation.[1]

In considering the phenomena of sexual selection in a previous volume,[2] it was found that there are four or five main factors in the constitution of beauty in so far as beauty determines sexual selection. Erotic symbolism is founded on the factor of individual taste in beauty; it arises as a specialized development of that factor, but it is, nevertheless, incorrect to merge it in sexual selection. The attractive characteristics of a beloved woman or man, from the point of view of sexual selection, are a complex but harmonious whole leading up to a desire for the complete possession of the person who displays them.

---

[1] The term "erotic symbolism" has already been employed by Eulenburg (*Sexuale Neuropathie*, 1895, p. 101). It must be borne in mind that this term, implying the specific emotion, is much narrower than the term "sexual symbolism," which may be used to designate a great variety of ritual and social practices which have played a part in the evolution of civilization.

[2] *Sexual Selection in Man*, iv, "Vision."

There is no tendency to isolate and dissociate any single character from the individual and to concentrate attention upon that character at the expense of the attention bestowed upon the individual generally. As soon as such a tendency begins to show itself, even though only in a slight or temporary form, we may say that there is erotic symbolism.

Erotic symbolism is, however, by no means confined to the individualizing tendency to concentrate amorous attention upon some single characteristic of the adult woman or man who is normally the object of sexual love. The adult human being may not be concerned at all, the attractive object or act may not even be human, not even animal, and we may still be concerned with a symbol which has parasitically rooted itself on the fruitful site of sexual emotion and absorbed to itself the energy which normally goes into the channels of healthy human love having for its final end the procreation of the species. Thus understood in its widest sense, it may be said that every sexual perversion, even homosexuality, is a form of erotic symbolism, for we shall find that in every case some object or act that for the normal human being has little or no erotic value, has assumed such value in a supreme degree; that is to say, it has become a symbol of the normal object of love. Certain perversions are, however, of such great importance on account of their wide relationships, that they cannot be adequately discussed merely as forms of erotic symbolism. This is notably the case as regards homosexuality, auto-erotism, and algolagnia, all of which phenomena have therefore been separately discussed in previous studies. We are now mainly concerned with manifestations which are more narrowly and exclusively symbolical.

A portion of the field of erotic symbolism is covered by what Binet (followed by Lombroso, Krafft-Ebing, and others) has termed "erotic fetichism," or the tendency whereby sexual attraction is unduly exerted by some special part or peculiarity of the body, or by some inanimate object which has become associated with it. Such erotic symbolism of object cannot, however, be dissociated from the even more important erotic symbolism of process, and the two are so closely bound together that we cannot attain a truly scientific view of them until we regard them broadly as related parts of a common psychic tendency. If, as Groos asserts,[1] a symbol has two chief meanings, one in which it indicates a physical process which stands for a psychic process, and another in which it indicates a part which represents the whole, erotic symbolism of act corresponds to the first of these chief meanings, and erotic symbolism of object to the other.

Although it is not impossible to find some germs of erotic symbolism in animals, in its more pronounced manifestations it is only found in the human species. It could not be otherwise, for such symbolism involves not only the play of fancy and imagination, the idealizing aptitude, but also a certain amount of power of concentrating the attention on a point outside the natural path of instinct and the ability to form new mental constructions around that point. There are, indeed, as we shall see, elementary forms of erotic symbolism which are not uncommonly associated with feeble-mindedness, but even these are still peculiarly human, and in its less crude manifestations erotic symbolism easily lends itself to every degree of human refinement and intelligence.

"It depends primarily upon an increase of the psychological process of representation," Colin Scott remarks of sexual symbolism generally, "involving greater powers of comparison and analysis as compared with the lower animals. The outer impressions come to be clearly distinguished as such, but at the same time are often treated as symbols of inner experiences, and a meaning read into them which they would not otherwise possess. Symbolism or fetichism is, indeed, just the capacity to see meaning, to emphasize something for the sake of other things which do not appear. In brain terms it indicates an activity of the higher centers, a sort of side-tracking or long-circuiting of the primitive energy; . . . Rosetti's poem, 'The Woodspurge,'

---

[1] K. Groos, *Der Æsthetische Genuss*, p. 122. The psychology of the associations of contiguity and resemblance through which erotic symbolism operates its transference is briefly discussed by Ribot in the *Psychology of the Emotions*, Part I, Chapter XII; the early chapters of the same author's *Logique des Sentiments* may also be said to deal with the emotional basis on which erotic symbolism arises.

gives a concrete example of the formation of such a symbol. Here the otherwise insignificant presentation of the three-cupped woodspurge, representing originally a mere side-current of the stream of consciousness, becomes the intellectual symbol or fetich of the whole psychosis forever after. It seems, indeed, as if the stronger the emotion the more likely will become the formation of an overlying symbolism, which serves to focus and stand in the place of something greater than itself; nowhere at least is symbolism a more characteristic feature than as an expression of the sexual instinct. The passion of sex, with its immense hereditary background, in early man became centered often upon the most trivial and unimportant features. . . . This symbolism, now become fetichistic, or symbolic in a bad sense, is at least an exercise of the increasing representative power of man, upon which so much of his advancement has depended, while it also served to express and help to purify his most perennial emotion." (Colin Scott, "Sex and Art," *American Journal of Psychology*, vol. vii, No. 2, p. 189.)

In the study of "Love and Pain" in a previous volume, the analysis of the large and complex mass of sexual phenomena which are associated with pain, gradually resolved them to a considerable extent into a special case of erotic symbolism; pain or restraint, whether inflicted on or by the loved person, becomes, by a psychic process that is usually unconscious, the symbol of the sexual mechanism, and hence arouses the same emotions as that mechanism normally arouses. We may now attempt to deal more broadly and comprehensively with the normal and abnormal aspects of erotic symbolism in some of their most typical and least mixed forms.

"When our human imagination seeks to animate artificial things," Huysmans writes in *Là-bas,* "it is compelled to reproduce the movements of animals in the act of propagation. Look at machines, at the play of pistons in the cylinders; they are Romeos of steel in Juliets of cast-iron." And not only in the work of man's hands but throughout Nature we find sexual symbols which are the less deniable since, for the most part, they make not the slightest appeal to even the most morbid human imagination. Language is full of metaphorical symbols of sex which constantly tend to lose their poetic symbolism and to become commonplace. Semen is but seed, and for the Latins especially the whole process of human sex, as well as the male and female organs, constantly presented itself in symbols derived from agricultural and horticultural life. The testicles were beans *(fabæ)* and fruit or apples *(poma* and *mala)*; the penis was a tree *(arbor)*, or a stalk *(thyrsus)*, or a root *(radix)*, or a sickle *(falx)*, or a ploughshare *(vomer)*. The semen, again, was dew *(ros)*. The labia majora or minora were wings *(alæ)*; the vulva and vagina were a field *(ager* and *campus)*, or a ploughed furrow *(sulcus)*, or a vineyard *(vinea)*, or a fountain *(fons)*, while the pudendal hair was herbage *(plantaria)*.[1] In other lanuages it is not difficult to trace similar and even identical imagery applied to sexual organs and sexual acts. Thus it is noteworthy that Shakespeare more than once applies the term "ploughed" to a woman who has had sexual intercourse. The Talmud calls the labia minora the doors, the labia majora hinges, and the clitoris the key. The Greeks appear not only to have found in the myrtle-berry, the fruit of a plant sacred to Venus, the image of the clitoris, but also in the rose an image of the feminine labia; in the poetic literature of many countries, indeed, this imagery of the rose may be traced in a more or less veiled manner.[2]

The widespread symbolism of sex arose in the theories and conceptions of primitive peoples concerning the function of generation and its nearest analogies in Nature; it was continued for the sake of the vigorous and expressive terminology which it furnished both for daily life and for literature; its final survivals were cultivated because they furnished a delicately æsthetic method of approaching matters which a growing refinement of sentiment made it difficult for lovers and poets to approach in a more crude and direct manner. Its existence is of interest to us now because it shows the objective validity of the basis on

---

[1] A number of synonyms for the female pudenda are brought together by Schurig—cunnus, hortus, concha, navis, fovea, larva, canis, annulus, focus, cymba, antrum, delta, myrtus, etc.—and he discusses many of them. *(Muliebria*, Section I, cap. I.)

[2] Kleinpaul, *Sprache Ohne Worte*, pp. 24-29; *cf.* K. Pearson, on the general and special words for sex, *Chances of Death*, vol. ii, pp. 112-245; a selection of the literature of the rose will be found in a volume of translations entitled *Ros Rosarum*.

which erotic symbolism, as we have here to understand it, develops. But from first to last it is a distinct phenomenon, having a more or less reasoned and intellectual basis, and it scarcely serves in any degree to feed the sexual impulse. Erotic symbolism is not intellectual but emotional in its origin; it starts into being, obscurely, with but a dim consciousness or for the most part none at all, either suddenly from the shock of some usually youthful experience, or more gradually through an instinctive brooding on those things which are most intimately associated with a sexually dsirable person.

The kind of soil on which the germs of erotic symbolism may develop is well seen in cases of sexual hyperæthesia. In such cases all the emotionally sexual analogies and resemblances, which in erotic symbolism are fixed and organized, may be traced in vague and passing forms, a single hyperæsthetic individual perhaps presenting a great variety of germinal symbolisms.

Thus it has been recorded of an Italian nun (whose sister became a prostitute) that from the age of 8 she had desire for coitus, from the age of 10 masturbated, and later had homosexual feelings, that the same feelings and practices continued after she had taken the veil, though from time to time they assumed religious equivalents. The mere contact, indeed, of a priest's hand, the news of the presentation of an ecclesiastic she had known to a bishopric, the sight of an ape, the contemplation of the crucified Christ, the figure of a toy, the picture of a demon, the act of defecation in the children entrusted to her care (whom, on this account, and against the regulations, she would accompany to the closets), especially the sight and the mere recollection of flies in sexual connection—all these things sufficed to produce in her a powerful orgasm. (*Archivio di Psichiatria*, 1902, fasc. II-III, p. 338.)

A boy of 15 (given to masturbation), studied by Macdonald in America, was similarly hyperæsthetic to the symbols of sexual emotion. "I like amusing myself with my comrades," he told Macdonald, "rolling ourselves into a ball, which gives one a funny kind of warmth. I have a special pleasure in talking about some things. It is the same when the governess kisses me on saying good night or when I lean against her breast. I have that sensation, too, when I see some of the pictures in the comic papers, but only in those representing a woman, as when a young man skating trips up a girl so that her clothes are raised a little. When I read how a man saved a young girl from drowning, so that they swam together, I had the same sensation. Looking at the statues of women in the museum produces the same effect, or when I see naked babies, or when a mother suckles a child. I have often had that sensation when reading novels I ought not to read, or when looking at a new-born calf, or seeing dogs and cows and horses mounting on each other. When I see a girl flirting with a boy, or leaning on his shoulder or with his arm round her waist, I have an erection. It is the same when I see women and little girls in bathing costume, or when boys talk of what their fathers and mothers do together. In the Natural History Museum I often see things which give me that sensation. One day when I read how a man killed a young girl and carried her into a wood and undressed her I had a feeling of enjoyment. When I read of men who were bastards the idea of a woman having a child in that way gives me this sensation. Some dances, and seeing young girls astride a horse, excited me, too, and so in a circus when a woman was shot out of a cannon and her skirts flew in the air. It has no effect on me when I see men naked. Sometimes I enjoy seeing women's underclothes in a shop, or when I see a lady or a girl buying them, especially if they are drawers. When I saw a lady in a dress which buttoned from top to bottom it had more effect on me than seeing underclothes. Seeing dogs coupling gives me more pleasure than looking at pretty women, but less than looking at pretty little girls." In order of increasing intensity he placed the phenomena that affected him thus: The coupling of flies, then of horses, then the sight of women's undergarments, then a boy and a girl flirting, then cows mounting on each other, the statues of women with naked breasts, then contact with the governess's body and breasts, finally coitus. (Arthur Macdonald, *Le Criminel-Type*, pp. 126 *et seq.*)

It is worthy of remark that the instinct of nutrition, when restrained, may exhibit something of an analogous symbolism, though in a minor degree, to that of sex. The ways in which a hyperæsthetic hunger may seek its symbols are illustrated in the case of a young woman called Nadia, who during several years was carefully studied by Janet. It is a case of obsession ("maladie du scrupule"), simulating hysterical anorexia, in which the patient, for fear of getting fat, reduced her nourishment to the smallest possible amount. "Nadia is generally hungry, even very hungry. One can tell this by her actions; from time to time she forgets herself to such an extent as to devour greedily anything she can put her hands on. At other times, when she cannot resist the desire to eat, she secretly takes a biscuit. She feels horrible remorse for the action, but, all the same, she does it again. Her confidences are very curious. She recognizes that a great effort is needed to avoid eating, and considers she is a heroine to resist so long. 'Sometimes I spent whole hours in thinking about food, I was so hungry; I swallowed my saliva, I bit my handkerchief, I rolled on the floor, I wanted to eat so badly. I would look in books for descriptions of meals and feasts, and tried to deceive my hunger by imagining that I was sharing all these good things.'" (P. Janet, "La Maladie du Scrupule," *Revue Philosophique,* May, 1901, p. 502.) The deviations of the instinct of nutrition are, however, confined within narrow limits, and, in the nature of things, hunger, unlike sexual desire, cannot easily accept a fetich.

"There is almost no feature, article of dress, attitude, act," Stanley Hall declares, "or even animal or perhaps object in nature, that may not have to some morbid soul specialized erogenic and erethic power."[1] Even a mere shadow may become a fetich. Goron tells of a merchant in Paris—a man with a reputation for ability, happily married and the father of a family, altogether irreproachable in his private life—who was returning home one evening after a game of billiards with a friend, when, on chancing to raise his eyes, he saw against a lighted window the shadow of a woman changing her chemise. He fell in love with that shadow and returned to the spot every evening for many months to gaze at the window. Yet—and herein lies the fetichism—he made no attempt to see the woman or to find out who she was; the shadow sufficed; he had no need of the realty.[2] It is even possible to have a negative fetich, the absence of some character being alone demanded, and the case has been recorded in Chicago of an American gentleman of average intelligence, education, and good habits who, having as a boy cherished a pure affection for a girl whose leg had been amputated, throughout life was relatively impotent with normal women, but experienced passion and affection for women who had lost a leg; he was found by his wife to be in extensive correspondence with one-legged women all over the country, expending no little money on the purchase of artificial legs for his various protegées.[3]

It is important to remember, however, that while erotic symbolism becomes fantastic and abnormal in its extreme mani-

[1] G. S. Hall, *Adolescence,* vol. i, p. 470.
[2] Goron, *Les Parias de l'Amour,* p. 45.
[3] A. R. Reynolds, *Medical Standard,* vol. x, cited by Kiernan, "Responsibility in Sexual Perversion," *American Journal of Neurology and Psychiatry,* 1882.

festations, it is in its essence absolutely normal. It is only in the very grossest forms of sexual desire that it is altogether absent. Stendhal described the mental side of the process of tumescence as a crystallization, a process whereby certain features of the beloved person present points around which the emotions held in solution in the lover's mind may concentrate and deposit themselves in dazzling brilliance. This process inevitably tends to take place around all those features and objects associated with the beloved person which have most deeply impressed the lover's mind, and the more sensitive and imaginative and emotional he is the more certainly will such features and objects crystallize into erotic symbols. "Devotion and love," wrote Mary Wollstonecraft, "may be allowed to hallow the garments as well as the person, for the lover must want fancy who has not a sort of sacred respect for the glove or slipper of his mistress. He would not confound them with vulgar things of the same kind." And nearly two centuries earlier Burton, who had gathered together so much of the ancient lore of love, clearly asserted the entirely normal character of erotic symbolism. "Not one of a thousand falls in love," he declares, "but there is some peculiar part or other which pleaseth most, and inflames him above the rest. . . . If he gets any remnant of hers, a busk-point, a feather of her fan, a shoe-tie, a lace, a ring, a bracelet of hair, he wears it for a favor on his arm, in his hat, finger, or next his heart; as Laodamia did by Protesilaus, when he went to war, sit at home with his picture before her: a garter or a bracelet of hers is more precious than any Saint's Relique, he lays it up in his casket (O blessed Relique) and every day will kiss it: if in her presence his eye is never off her, and drink he will where she drank, if it be possible, in that very place," etc.[1]

Burton's accuracy in describing the ways of lovers in his century is shown by a passage in Hamilton's *Mémoires de Gramont*. Miss Price, one of the beauties of Charles II's court, and Dongan were ten-

---

[1] R. Burton, *Anatomy of Melancholy*, Part III, Section II, Mem. II, Subs. II, and Mem. III, Subs. I.

derly attached to each other; when the latter died he left behind a casket full of all possible sorts of love-tokens pertaining to his mistress, including, among other things, "all kinds of hair." And as regards France, Burton's contemporary, Howell, wrote in 1627 in his *Familiar Letters* concerning the repulse of the English at Rhé: "A captain told me that when they were rifling the dead bodies of the French gentlemen after the first invasion they found that many of them had their mistresses' favors tied about their genitories."

Schurig (*Spermatologia*, p. 357) at the beginning of the eighteenth century knew a Belgian lady who, when her dearly loved husband died, secretly cut off his penis and treasured it as a sacred relic in a silver casket. She eventually powdered it, he adds, and found it an efficacious medicine for herself and others. An earlier example, of a lady at the French court who embalmed and perfumed the genital organs of her dead husband, always preserving them in a gold casket, is mentioned by Brantôme. Mantegazza knew a man who kept for many years on his desk the skull of his dead mistress, making it his dearest companion. "Some," he remarks, "have slept for months and years with a book, a garment, a trifle. I once had a friend who would spend long hours of joy and emotion kissing a thread of silk which *she* had held between her fingers, now the only relic of love." (Mantegazza, *Fisiologia dell' Amore*, cap. X.) In the same way I knew a lady who in old age still treasured in her desk, as the one relic of the only man she had ever been attracted to, a fragment of paper he had casually twisted up in a conversation with her half a century before.

The tendency to treasure the relics of a beloved person, more especially the garments, is the simplest and commonest foundation of erotic symbolism. It is without doubt absolutely normal. It is inevitable that those objects which have been in close contact with the beloved person's body, and are intimately associated with that person in the lover's mind, should possess a little of the same virtue, the same emotional potency. It is a phenomenon closely analogous to that by which the relics of saints are held to possess a singular virtue. But it becomes somewhat less normal when the garment is regarded as essential even in the presence of the beloved person.[1]

While an extremely large number of objects and acts may be found to possess occasionally the value of erotic symbols, such

[1] Numerous examples are given by Moll, *Konträre Sexualempfindung*, third edition, pp. 265-268.

symbols most frequently fall into certain well-defined groups. A vast number of isolated objects or acts may be exceptionally the focus of erotic contemplation, but the objects and acts which frequently become thus symbolic are comparatively few.

It seems to me that the phenomena of erotic symbolism may be most conveniently grouped in three great classes, on the basis of the objects or acts which arouse them.

I. PARTS OF THE BODY.—*A. Normal:* Hand, foot, breasts, nates, hair, secretions and excretions, etc.

B. Abnormal: Lameness, squinting, pitting of smallpox, etc. Paidophilia or the love of children, presbyophilia or the love of the aged, and necrophilia or the attraction for corpses, may be included under this head, as well as the excitement caused by various animals.

II. INANIMATE OBJECTS.[1]—*A. Garments:* Gloves, shoes and stockings and garters, caps, aprons, handkerchiefs, underlinen.

B. Impersonal Objects: Here may be included all the various objects that may accidentally acquire the power of exciting sexual feeling in auto-erotism. Pygmalionism may also be included.

III. ACTS AND ATTITUDES.—*A. Active:* Whipping, cruelty, exhibitionism. *B. Passive:* Being whipped, experiencing cruelty. Personal odors and the sound of the voice may be included under this head. *C. Mixoscopic:* The vision of climbing, swinging, etc. The acts of urination and defecation. The coitus of animals.

Although the three main groups into which the phenomena of erotic symbolism are here divided may seem fairly distinct, they are yet very closely allied, and indeed overlap, so that it

---

[1] Chevalier (*De l'Inversion*, 1885; *id. L'Inversion Sexuelle*, 1892, p. 52), followed by E. Laurent (*L'Amour Morbide*, 1891, Chapter X), separates this group from other fetichistic perversions, under the head of "azoöphilie." I see no adequate ground for this step. The various forms of fetichism are too intimately associated to permit of any group of them being violently separated from the others.

is possible, as we shall see, for a single complex symbol to fall into all three groups.

A very complete kind of erotic symbolism is furnished by Pygmalionism or the love of statues.[1] It is exactly analogous to the child's love of a doll, which is also a form of sexual (though not erotic) symbolism. In a somewhat less abnormal form, erotic symbolism probably shows itself in its simplest shape in the tendency to idealize unbeautiful peculiarities in a beloved person, so that such peculiarities are ever afterward almost or quite essential in order to arouse sexual attraction. In this way men have become attracted to limping women. Even the most normal man may idealize a trifling defect in a beloved woman. The attention is inevitably concentrated on any such slight deviation from regular beauty, and the natural result of such concentration is that a complexus of associated thoughts and emotions becomes attached to something that in itself is unbeautiful. A defect becomes an admired focus of attention, the embodied symbol of the lover's emotion.

Thus a mole is not in itself beautiful, but by the tendency to erotic symbolism it becomes so. Persian poets especially have lavished the richest imagery on moles (*Anis El-Ochchâq* in *Bibliothèque des Hautes Etudes*, fasc, 25, 1875); the Arabs, as Lane remarks (*Arabian Society in the Middle Ages*, p. 214), are equally extravagant in their admiration of a mole.

Stendhal long since well described the process by which a defect becomes a sexual symbol. "Even little defects in a woman's face," he remarked, "such as a smallpox pit, may arouse the tenderness of a man who loves her, and throw him into deep reverie when he sees them in another woman. It is because he has experienced a thousand feelings in the presence of that smallpox mark, that these feelings have been for the most part delicious, all of the highest interest, and that, whatever they may have been, they are renewed with incredible vivacity on the sight of this sign, even when perceived on the face of another woman. If in such a case we come to prefer and love *ugliness*, it is only because in such a case ugliness is beauty. A man loved a woman who

---

[1] This has already been considered as a perversion founded on vision, in discussing *Sexual Selection in Man.* IV.

was very thin and marked by smallpox; he lost her by death. Three years later, in Rome, he became acquainted with two women, one very beautiful, the other thin and marked by smallpox, on that account, if you will, rather ugly. I saw him in love with this plain one at the end of a week, which he had employed in effacing her plainness by his memories." (*De l'Amour*, Chapter XVII.)

In the tendency to idealize the unbeautiful features of a beloved person erotic symbolism shows itself in a simple and normal form. In a less simple and more morbid form it appears in persons in whom the normal paths of sexual gratification are for some reasons inhibited, and who are thus led to find the symbols of natural love in unnatural perversions. It is for this reason that so many erotic symbolisms take root in childhood and puberty, before the sexual instincts have reached full development. It is for the same reason also, that, at the other end of life, when the sexual energies are failing, erotic symbols sometimes tend to be substituted for the normal pleasures of sex. It is for this reason, again, that both men and women whose normal energies are inhibited sometimes find the symbols of sexual gratification in the caresses of children.

The case of a schoolmistress recorded by Penta instructively shows how an erotic symbolism of this last kind may develop by no means as a refinement of vice, but as the one form in which sexual gratification becomes possible when normal gratification has been pathologically inhibited. F. R., aged 48, schoolmistress; she was some years ago in an asylum with religious mania, but came out well in a few months. At the age of 12 she had first experienced sexual excitement in a railway train from the jolting of the carriage. Soon after she fell in love with a youth who represented her ideal and who returned her affection. When, however, she gave herself to him, great was her disillusion and surprise to find that the sexual act which she had looked forward to could not be accomplished, for at the first contact there was great pain and spasmodic resistance of the vagina. There was a condition of vaginismus. After repeated attempts on subsequent occasions her lover desisted. Her desire for intercourse increased, however, rather than diminished, and at last she was able to tolerate coitus, but the pain was so great that she acquired a horror of the sexual embrace and no longer sought it. Having much will power, she restrained all erotic impulses during many years. It was not until the period of the menopause that the long repressed desires broke out, and at last found a symbolical outlet that was no longer normal, but was felt to supply a complete gratification. She sought the close physical contact of the young children in her care. She would lie on her bed naked, with two or three naked children, make them suck her breasts and press them to every part of her body. Her conduct was discovered by means of other children who peeped through the keyhole, and she was placed under Penta for treatment. In this case the loss of moral and mental inhibition, due probably to troubles of the climacteric, led to indulgence, under abnormal conditions, in those primitive contacts which are normally the beginning of love, and these, supported by the ideal image of the early lover, constituted a complete and adequate symbol of natural love in a morbidly perverted individual. (P. Penta, *Archivio delle Pricopatie Sessuale*, January, 1896.)

II.

Foot-fetichism and Shoe-fetichism—Wide Prevalence and Normal Basis—Restif de la Bretonne—The Foot a Normal Focus of Sexual Attraction Among Some Peoples—The Chinese, Greeks, Romans, Spaniards, etc.—The Congenital Predisposition in Erotic Symbolism—The Influence of Early Association and Emotional Shock—Shoe-fetichism in Relation to Masochism—The Two Phenomena Independent Though Allied—The Desire to be Trodden On—The Fascination of Physical Constraint—The Symbolism of Self-inflicted Pain—The Dynamic Element in Erotic Symbolism—The Symbolism of Garments .

Of all forms of erotic symbolism the most frequent is that which idealizes the foot and the shoe. The phenomena we here encounter are sometimes so complex and raise so many interesting questions that it is necessary to discuss them somewhat fully.

It would seem that even for the normal lover the foot is one of the most attractive parts of the body. Stanley Hall found that among the parts specified as most admired in the other sex by young men and women who answered a *questionnaire* the feet came fourth (after the eyes, hair, stature and size).[1] Casanova, an acute student and lover of women who was in no degree a foot fetichist, remarks that all men who share his interest in women are attracted by their feet; they offer

---

[1] G. Stanley Hall, *Adolescence*, vol. ii, p. 113. It will be noted that the hand does not appear among the parts of the body which are normally of supreme interest. An interest in the hand is by no means uncommon (it may be noted, for instance, in the course of History XII in Appendix B to vol. iii of these *Studies*), but the hand does not possess the mystery which envelops the foot, and hand-fetichism is very much less frequent than foot-fetichism, while glove-fetichism is remarkably rare. An interesting case of hand-fetichism, scarcely reaching morbid intensity, is recorded by Binet, *Etudes de Psychologie Expérimentale,* pp. 13-19; and see Krafft-Ebing, *Op. cit.,* pp. 214 *et seq.*

the same interest, he considers, as the question of the particular edition offers to the book-lover.[2]

In a report of the results of a *questionnaire* concerning children's sense of self, to which over 500 replies were received, Stanley Hall thus summarizes the main facts ascertained with reference to the feet: "A special period of noticing the feet comes somewhat later than that in which the hands are discovered to consciousness. Our records afford nearly twice as many cases for feet as for hands. The former are more remote from the primary psychic focus or position, and are also more often covered, so that the sight of them is a more marked and exceptional event. Some children become greatly excited whenever their feet are exposed. Some infants show signs of fear at the movement of their own knees and feet covered, and still more often fright is the first sensation which signalizes the child's discovery of its feet. . . . Many are described as playing with them as if fascinated by strange, newly-discovered toys. They pick them up and try to throw them away, or out of the cradle, or bring them to the mouth, where all things tend to go. . . . Children often handle their feet, pat and stroke them, offer them toys and the bottle, as if they, too, had an independent hunger to gratify, an *ego* of their own. . . . Children often develop [later] a special interest in the feet of others, and examine, feel them, etc., sometimes expressing surprise that the pinch of the mother's toe hurts her and not the child, or comparing their own and the feet of others point by point. Curious, too, are the intensifications of foot-consciousness throughout the early years of childhood, whenever children have the exceptional privilege of going barefoot, or have new shoes. The feet are often apostrophized, punished, beaten sometimes to the point of pain for breaking things, throwing the child down, etc. Several children have habits, which reach great intensity, and then vanish, of touching or tickling the feet, with gales of laughter, and a few are described as showing an almost morbid reluctance to wear anything upon the feet, or even to having them touched by others. . . . Several almost fall in love with the great toe or the little one, especially admiring some crease or dimple in it, dressing it in some rag of silk or bit of ribbon, or cut-off glove fingers, winding it with string, prolonging it by tying on bits of wood. Stroking the feet of others, especially if they are shapely, often becomes almost a passion with young children, and several adults confess a survival of the same impulse which it is an exquisite pleasure to gratify. The interest of some mothers in babies' toes, the expressions of which are ecstatic and almost incredible, is a factor of great importance." (G. Stanley Hall, "Some Aspects of the

---

[2] *Mémoires*, vol. i, Chapter VII.

Early Sense of Self," *American Journal of Psychology*, April, 1898.) In childhood, Stanley Hall remarks elsewhere (*Adolescence*, vol. ii, p. 104), "a form of courtship may consist solely in touching feet under the desk." It would seem that even animals have a certain amount of sexual consciousness in the feet; I have noticed a male donkey, just before coitus, bite the feet of his partner.

At the same time it is scarcely usual for the normal lover, in most civilized countries to-day, to attach primary importance to the foot, such as he very frequently attaches to the eyes, though the feet play a very conspicuous part in the work of certain novelists.[1]

In a small but not inconsiderable minority of persons, however, the foot or the boot becomes the most attractive part of a woman, and in some morbid cases the woman herself is regarded as a comparatively unimportant appendage to her feet or her boots. The boots under civilized conditions much more frequently constitute the sexual symbol than do the feet themselves; this is not surprising since in ordinary life the feet are not often seen.

It is usually only under exceptionally favoring conditions that foot-fetichism occurs, as in the case recorded by Marandon de Montyel of a doctor who had been brought up in the West Indies. His mother had been insane and he himself was subject to obsessions, especially of being incapable of urinating; he had had nocturnal incontinence of urine in childhood. All the women of the people in the West Indies go about with naked feet, which are often beautiful. His puberty evolved under this influence, and foot-fetichism developed. He especially admired large, fat, arched feet, with delicate skin and large, regular toes. He masturbated with images of feet. At 15 he had relations with a colored chambermaid, but feared to mention his fetichism, though it was the touch of her feet that chiefly excited him. He now gave up masturbation, and had a succession of mistresses, but was always ashamed to confess his fancies until, at the age of 33, in Paris, a very intelligent woman who had become his mistress discovered his

---

[1] Among leading English novelists Hardy shows an unusual but by no means predominant interest in the feet and shoes of his heroines; see, *e.g.*, the observations of the cobbler in *Under the Greenwood Tree*, Chapter III. A chapter in Goethe's *Wahlverwandschaften* (Part I, Chapter II) contains an episode involving the charm of the foot and the kissing of the beloved's shoe.

mania and skillfully enabled him to yield to it without shock to his
modesty. He was devoted to this mistress, who had very beautiful feet
(he had been horrified by the feet of Europeans generally), until she
finally left him. (*Archives de Neurologie*, October, 1904.)

Probably the first case of shoe-fetichism ever recorded in any
detail is that of Restif de la Bretonne (1734-1806), publicist and novelist,
one of the most remarkable literary figures of the later eighteenth
century in France. Restif was a neurotic subject, though not to an
extreme degree, and his shoe-fetichism, though distinctly pronounced,
was not pathological; that is to say, that the shoe was not itself an
adequate gratification of the sexual impulse, but simply a highly important aid to tumescence, a prelude to the natural climax of detumescence; only occasionally, and *faute de mieux*, in the absence of
the beloved person, was the shoe used as an adjunct to masturbation.
In Restif's stories and elsewhere the attraction of the shoe is frequently
discussed or used as a motive. His first decided literary success, *Le Pied
de Fanchette,* was suggested by a vision of a girl with a charming foot,
casually seen in the street. While all such passages in his books are
really founded on his own personal feelings and experiences, in his
elaborate autobiography, *Monsieur Nicolas,* he has frankly set forth
the gradual evolution and cause of his idiosyncrasy. The first remembered trace dated from the age of 4, when he was able to recall having
remarked the feet of a young girl in his native place. Restif was a
sexually precocious youth, and at the age of 9, though both delicate in
health and shy in manners, his thoughts were already absorbed in the
girls around him. "While little Monsieur Nicolas," he tells us, "passed
for a Narcissus, his thoughts, as soon as he was alone, by night or by
day, had no other object than that sex he seemed to flee from. The
girls most careful of their persons were naturally those who pleased
him most, and as the part least easy to keep clean is that which touches
the earth it was to the foot-gear that he mechanically gave his chief
attention. Agathe, Reine, and especially Madeleine, were the most
elegant of the girls at that time; their carefully selected and kept shoes,
instead of laces or buckles, which were not yet worn at Sacy, had blue
or rose ribbon, according to the color of the skirt. I thought of these
girls with emotion; I desired—I knew not what; but I desired something, if it were only to subdue them." The origin Restif here assigns
to his shoe-fetichism may seem paradoxical; he admired the girls who
were most clean and neat in their dress, he tells us, and, therefore, paid
most attention to that part of their clothing which was least clean and
neat. But, however paradoxical the remark may seem, it is psychologically sound. All fetichism is a kind of not necessarily morbid
obsession, and as the careful work of Janet and others in that field has
shown, an obsession is a fascinated attraction to some object or idea

which gives the subject a kind of emotional shock by its contrast to his habitual moods or ideas. The ordinary morbid obsession cannot usually be harmoniously co-ordinated with the other experiences of the subject's daily life, and shows, therefore, no tendency to become pleasurable. Sexual fetichisms, on the other hand, have a reservoir of agreeable emotion to draw on, and are thus able to acquire both stability and harmony. It will also be seen that no element of masochism is involved in Restif's fetichism, though the mistake has been frequently made of supposing that these two manifestations are usually or even necessarily allied. Restif wishes to subject the girl who attracts him, he has no wish to be subjected by her. He was especially dazzled by a young girl from another town, whose shoes were of a fashionable cut, with buckles, "and who was a charming person besides." She was delicate as a fairy, and rendered his thoughts unfaithful to the robust beauties of his native Sacy. "No doubt," he remarks, "because, being frail and weak myself, it seemed to me that it would be easier to subdue her." "This taste for the beauty of the feet," he continues, "was so powerful in me that it unfailingly aroused desire and would have made me overlook ugliness. It is excessive in all those who have it." He admired the foot as well as the shoe: "The factitious taste for the shoe is only a reflection of that for pretty feet. When I entered a house and saw the boots arranged in a row, as is the custom, I would tremble with pleasure; I blushed and lowered my eyes as if in the presence of the girls themselves. With this vivacity of feeling and a voluptuousness of ideas inconceivable at the age of 10 I still fled, with an involuntary impulse of modesty, from the girls I adored."

We may clearly see how this combination of sensitive and precocious sexual ardor with extreme shyness, furnished the soil on which the germ of shoe-fetichism was able to gain a firm root and persist in some degree throughout a long life very largely given up to a pursuit of women, abnormal rather by its excessiveness than its perversity. A few years later, he tells us, he happened to see a pretty pair of shoes in a bootmaker's shop, and on hearing that they belonged to a girl whom at that time he reverently adored at a distance he blushed and nearly fainted.

In 1749 he was for a time attracted to a young woman very much older than himself; he secretly carried away one of her slippers and kept it for a day; a little later he again took away a shoe of the same woman which had fascinated him when on her foot, and, he seems to imply, he used it to masturbate with.

Perhaps the chief passion of Restif's life was his love for Colette Parangon. He was still a boy (1752), she was the young and virtuous wife of the printer whose apprentice Restif was and in whose house he lived. Madame Parangon, a charming woman, as she is described, was not happily married, and she evidently felt a tender affection for the boy whose excessive love and reverence for her were not always successfully concealed. "Madonna Parangon," he tells us, "possessed a charm which I could never resist, a pretty little foot; it is a charm which arouses more than tenderness. Her shoes, made in Paris, had that voluptuous elegance which seems to communicate soul and life. Sometimes Colette wore shoes of simple white drugget or with silver flowers; sometimes rose-colored slippers with green heels, or green with rose heels; her supple feet, far from deforming her shoes, increased their grace and rendered the form more exciting." One day, on entering the house, he saw Madame Parangon elegantly dressed and wearing rose-colored shoes with tongues, and with green heels and a pretty rosette. They were new and she took them off to put on green slippers with rose heels and borders which he thought equally exciting. As soon as she had left the room, he continues, "carried away by the most impetuous passion and idolizing Colette, I seemed to see her and touch her in handling what she had just worn; my lips pressed one of these jewels, while the other, deceiving the sacred end of nature, from excess of exaltation replaced the object of sex (I cannot express myself more clearly). The warmth which she had communicated to the insensible object which had touched her still remained and gave a soul to it; a voluptuous cloud covered my eyes." He adds that he would kiss with rage and transport whatever had come in close contact with the woman he adored, and on one occasion eagerly pressed his lips to her cast-off underlinen, *vela secretiora penetralium.*

At this period Restif's foot-fetichism reached its highest point of development. It was the aberration of a highly sensitive and very precocious boy. While the preoccupation with feet and shoes persisted throughout life, it never became a complete perversion and never replaced the normal end of sexual desire. His love for Madam Parangon, one of the deepest emotions in his whole life, was also the climax of his shoe-fetichism. She represented his ideal woman, an ethereal sylph with wasp-waist and a child's feet; it was always his highest praise for a woman that she resembled Madame Parangon, and he desired that her slipper should be buried with him. (Restif de la Bretonne, *Monsieur Nicolas,* vols. i-iv, vol. xiii, p. 5; *id, Mes Inscriptions,* pp. ci-cv.)

Shoe-fetichism, more especially if we include under this term all the cases of real or pseudo-masochism in which an attraction to the boots or slippers is the chief feature, is a not infrequent phenomenon, and is certainly the most frequently occurring form of fetichism. Many cases are brought together by Krafft-Ebing in his *Psychopathia Sexualis.* Every prostitute of any experience has known men who merely desire to gaze at her shoes, or possibly to lick them, and who are quite willing to pay for this privilege. In London such a person is known as a "bootman," in Germany as a "Stiefelfrier."

The predominance of the foot as a focus of sexual attraction, while among us to-day it is a not uncommon phenomenon, is still not sufficiently common to be called normal; the majority of even ardent lovers do not experience this attraction in any marked degree. But these manifestations of foot-fetichism which with us to-day are abnormal, even when they are not so extreme as to be morbid, may perhaps become more intelligible to us when we realize that in earlier periods of civilization, and even to-day in some parts of the world, the foot is generally recognized as a focus of sexual attraction, so that some degree of foot-fetichism becomes a normal phenomenon.

The most pronounced and the best known example of such normal foot-fetichism at the present day is certainly to be found among the Southern Chinese. For a Chinese husband his wife's foot is more interesting than her face. A Chinese woman is as shy of showing her feet to a man as a European woman her breasts; they are reserved for her husband's eyes alone, and to look at a woman's feet in the street is highly improper and indelicate. Chinese foot-fetichism is connected with the custom of compressing the feet. This custom appears to rest on the fact that Chinese women naturally possess a very small foot and is thus an example of the universal tendency in the search for beauty to accentuate, even by deformation, the racial characteristics. But there is more than this. Beauty is largely a name for sexual attractiveness, and the energy expended in the effort to make the Chinese woman's small foot still smaller is a measure of the sexual fascination which it exerts. The practice arose on the basis of the sexual attractiveness of the foot, though it has doubtless served to heighten that attractiveness, just as the small waist, which (if we may follow Stratz) is a characteristic beauty of the European woman, becomes to the average European man still more attractive when accentuated, even to the extent of deformity, by the compression of the corset.

Referring to the sexual fascination exerted by the foot in China, Matignon writes: "My attention has been drawn to this point by a large number of pornographic engravings, of which the Chinese are very fond. In all these lascivious scenes we see the male voluptuously fondling the woman's foot. When a Celestial takes into his hand a woman's foot, especially if it is very small, the effect upon him is precisely the same as is provoked in a European by the palpation of a young and firm bosom. All the Celestials whom I have interrogated on this point have replied unanimously: 'Oh, a little foot! You Europeans cannot understand how exquisite, how sweet, how exciting it is!' The contact of the genital organ with the little foot produces in the male an indescribable degree of voluptuous feeling, and women skilled in love know that to arouse the ardor of their lovers a better method than all Chinese aphrodisiacs—including 'giusen' and swallows' nests—is to take the penis between their feet. It is not rare to find Chinese Christians accusing themselves at confession of having had 'evil thoughts on looking at a woman's foot.'" (Dr. J. Matignon, "A propos d'un Pied de Chinoise," *Archives d'Anthropologie Criminelle*, 1898.)

It is said that a Chinese Empress, noted for her vice and having a congenital club foot, about the year 1100 B.C., desired all women to resemble her, and that the practice of compressing the foot thus arose. But this is only tradition, since, in 300 B.C., Chinese books were destroyed (Morache, Art. "Chine," *Dictionnaire Encyclopédique des Sciences Médicales*, p. 191). It is also said that the practice owes its origin to the wish to keep women indoors. But women are not secluded in China, nor does foot compression usually render a woman unable to walk. Many intelligent Chinese are of opinion that its object is to promote the development of the sexual parts and of the thighs, and so to aid both intercourse and parturition. There is no ground for believing that it has any such influence, though Morache found that the mons veneris and labia are largely developed in Chinese women, and not in Tartar women living in Pekin (who do not compress the foot). If there is any correlation between the feet and the pelvic regions, it is more probably congenital than due to the artificial compression of the feet. The ancients seem to have believed that a small foot indicated a small vagina. Restif de la Bretonne, who had ample opportunities for forming an opinion on a matter in which he took so great an interest, believed that a small foot, round and short, indicated a large vagina (*Monsieur Nicolas*, vol. i, reprint of 1883, p. 92). Even, however, if we admit that there is a real correlation between the foot and the vagina, that would by no means suffice to render the foot a focus of sexual attraction.

It remains the most reasonable view that the foot bandage must be regarded as strictly analogous to the waist bandage or corset which also tends to produce deformity of the constricted region. Stratz has ingeniously remarked (*Frauenkleidung*, third edition, p. 101) that the success of the Chinese in dwarfing trees may have suggested a similar attempt in regard to women's feet, and adds that in any case both dwarfed trees and bound feet bear witness in the Mongolian to the same love for small and elegant, not to say deformed, things. For a China-man the deformed foot is a "golden water-lily."

Many facts (together with illustrations) bearing on Chinese de-formation of the foot will be found in Ploss, *Das Weib*, vol. i, Section IV.

The significance of the sexual emotion aroused by the female foot in China and the origin of its compression begin to become clear when we realize that this foot-fetichism is merely an ex-treme development of a tendency which is fairly well marked among nearly all the peoples of yellow race. Jacoby, who has brought together a number of interesting facts bearing on the sexual significance of the foot, states that a similar tendency is to be found among the Mongol and Turk peoples of Siberia, and in the east and central parts of European Russia, among the Permiaks, the Wotiaks, etc. Here the woman, at all events when young, has always her feet, as well as head, covered, however little clothing she may otherwise wear.

"On hot nights or on baking days," Jacoby states, "you may see these women with uncovered breasts, or even entirely naked without embarrassment, but you will never see them with bare feet, and no male relations, except the husband, will ever see the feet and lower part of the legs of the women in the house. These women have their modesty in their feet, and also their coquetry; to unbind the feet of a woman is for a man a voluptuous act, and the touch of the bands produces the same effect as a corset still warm from a woman's body on a European man. A woman's beauty, that which attracts and excites a man, lies in her foot; in Mordvin love poems celebrating the beauty of women there is much about her attire, especially her embroidered chemise, but as regards the charms of her person the poet is content to state that 'her feet are beautiful;' with that everything is said. The young peasant woman of the central provinces as part of her holiday raiment puts on great woolen stockings which come up to the groin and are then folded over to below the knee. To uncover the feet of a person of the opposite sex is a sexual act, and has thus become the symbol of sexual possession, so that the stocking or foot-gear became the emblem of marriage, as later the ring. (It was so among the Jews, as we see in the book of *Ruth*, Chapter III, v. 4, and Chapter IV, vv. 7 and 8). St. Vladimir the Great asked in marriage the daughter of Prince Rogvold; as Vladimir's mother had been a serf, the princess proudly replied that she would not uncover the feet of a slave.' At the present time in the east of Russia when a young girl tries to find out by divination whom she will have as a husband the traditional formula is 'Come and take my stockings off.' Among the populations of the north and east, it is sometimes the bride who must do this for her husband on the wedding night, and sometimes the bridegroom for his wife, not as a token of love, but as a nuptial ceremony. Among the professional classes and small nobility in Russia parents place money in the stocking of their child at marriage as a present for the other partner, it being supposed that the couple mutually remove each other's foot raiment, as an act of sexual possession, the emblem of coitus." (Paul Jacoby, *Archives d'Anthropologie Criminelle*, December, 1903, p. 793.) The practice among ourselves of children hanging up their stockings at night for presents would seem to be a relic of the last-mentioned custom.

While we may witness the sexual symbolism of the foot, with or without an associated foot-fetichism, most highly developed in Asia and Eastern Europe, it has by no means been altogether unknown in some stages of western civilization, and traces of it may be found here and there even yet. Schinz refers to the connection between the feet and sexual pleasure as existing not only among the Egyptians and the Arabs, but among the ancient Germans and the modern Spaniards,[1] while Jacoby points out that among the Greeks, the Romans, and especially the Etruscans, it was usual to represent chaste and virgin goddesses with their feet covered, even though they might be otherwise nude. Ovid, again, is never weary of dwelling on the sexual charm of the feminine foot. He represents the chaste matron as wearing a weighted *stola* which always fell so as to cover her feet; it was only the courtesan, or the nymph who is taking part in an erotic festival, who appears with raised robes, revealing her feet.[2] So grave a historian as Strabo, as well as Ælian,

---

[1] Schinz, "Philosophie des Conventions Sociales," *Revue Philosophique*, June, 1903, p. 626. Mirabeau mentions in his *Erotika Biblion* that modern Greek women sometimes use their feet to provoke orgasm in their lovers. I may add that simultaneous mutual masturbation by means of the feet is not unknown to-day, and I have been told by an English shoe-fetichist that he at one time was accustomed to practice this with a married lady (Brazilian)—she with slippers on and he without—who derived gratification equal to his own.

[2] Jacoby (*loc. cit.* pp. 796-7) gives a large number of references to

refers to the story of the courtesan Rhodope whose sandal was carried off by an eagle and dropped in the King of Egypt's lap as he was administering justice, so that he could not rest until he had discovered to whom this delicately small sandal belonged, and finally made her his queen. Kleinpaul, who repeats this story, has collected many European sayings and customs (including Turkish), indicating that the slipper is a very ancient symbol of a woman's sexual parts.[1]

In Rome, Dufour remarks, "Matrons having appropriated the use of the shoe (*soccus*) prostitutes were not allowed to use it, and were obliged to have their feet always naked in sandals or slippers (*crepida* and *solea*), which they fastened over the instep with gilt bands. Tibullus delights to describe his mistress's little foot, compressed by the band that imprisoned it: *Ansaque compressos colligat arcta pedes.* Nudity of the foot in woman was a sign of prostitution, and their brilliant whiteness acted afar as a pimp to attract looks and desires." (Dufour, *Histoire de la Prostitution*, vol. II., ch. xviii.)

This feeling seems to have survived in a more or less vague and unconscious form in mediæval Europe. "In the tenth century," according to Dufour (*Histoire de la. Prostitution*, vol. VI., p. 11), "shoes *à la poulaine*, with a claw or beak, pursued for more than four centuries by the anathemas of popes and the invectives of preachers, were always regarded by mediæval casuists as the most abominable emblems of immodesty. At a first glance it is not easy to see why these shoes—terminating in a lion's claw, an eagle's beak, the prow of a ship, or other metal appendage—should be so scandalous. The excommunication inflicted on this kind of footgear preceded the impudent invention of some libertine, who wore *poulaines* in the shape of the phallus, a custom adopted also by women. This kind of *poulaine* was denounced as *mandite de Dieu* (Ducange's Glossary, at the word Poulainia) and prohibited by royal ordinances (see letter of Charles V., 17 October, 1367, regarding the garments of the women of Montpellier). Great lords and ladies continued, however, to wear *poulaines*." In Louis XI.'s court they were still worn of a quarter of an ell in length.

Spain, ever tenacious of ancient ideas, appears to have preserved

---

Ovid's works bearing on this point. "In reading him," he remarks, "one is inclined to say that the psychology of the Romans was closely allied to that of the Chinese."

[1] R. Kleinpaul, *Sprache ohne Worte*, p. 308. See also Moll, *Konträre Sexualempfindung*, third edition, pp. 306-308. Bloch brings together many interesting references bearing on the ancient sexual and religious symbolism of the shoe, *Beiträge zur Ätiologie der Psychopathia Sexualis*, Teil II, p. 324.

longer than other countries the ancient classic traditions in regard to
the foot as a focus of modesty and an object of sexual attraction. In
Spanish religious pictures it was always necessary that the Virgin's feet
should be concealed, the clergy ordaining that her robe should be long
and flowing, so that the feet might be covered with decent folds. Pacheco, the master and father-in-law of Velasquez, writes in 1649 in his
Arte de la Pintura: "What can be more foreign from the respect which
we owe to the purity of Our Lady the Virgin than to paint her sitting
down with one of her knees placed over 'the other, and often with her
sacred feet uncovered and naked. Let thanks be given to the Holy
Inquisition which commands that this liberty should be corrected!" It
was Pacheco's duty in Seville to see that these commands were obeyed.
At the court of Philip IV. at this time the princesses never showed
their feet, as we may see in the pictures of Velasquez. When a local
manufacturer desired to present that monarch's second bride, Mariana
of Austria, with some silk stockings the offer was indignantly rejected
by the Court Chamberlain: "The Queen of Spain has no legs!" Philip
V.'s queen was thrown from her horse and dragged by the feet; no one
ventured to interfere until two gentlemen bravely rescued her and then
fled, dreading punishment by the king: they were, however, graciously
pardoned. Reinach ("Pieds Pudiques," *Cultes, Mythes et Religions*, pp.
105-110) brings together several passages from the Countess D'Aulnoy's
account of the Madrid Court in the seventeenth century and from other
sources, showing how careful Spanish ladies were as regards their feet,
and how jealous Spanish husbands were in this matter. At this
time, when Spanish influence was considerable, the fashion of Spain
seems to have spread to other countries. One may note that in Van-
dyck's pictures of English beauties the feet are not visible, though in
the more characteristically English painters of a somewhat later age it
became usual to display them conspicuously, while the French custom
in this matter is the farthest removed from the Spanish. At the
present day a well-bred Spanish woman shows as little as possible of her
feet in walking, and even in some of the most characteristic Spanish
dances there is little or no kicking, and the feet may even be invisible
throughout. It is noteworthy that in numerous figures of Spanish
women (probably artists' models) reproduced in Ploss's *Das Weib* the
stockings are worn, although the women are otherwise, in most cases,
quite naked. Max Dessoir mentions ("Psychologie der Vita Sexualis,"
Zeitschrift für Psychiatrie, 1894, p. 954) that in Spanish pornographic photographs women always have their shoes on, and he considers this an indication of perversity. I have seen the statement (attributed to Gautier's *Voyage en Espagne*, where, however, it does not occur) that Spanish prostitutes uncover their feet in sign of assent, and
Madame d' Aulnoy stated that in her time to show her lover her feet
was a Spanish woman's final favor.

The tendency, which we thus find to be normal at some earlier periods of civilization, to insist on the sexual symbolism of the feminine foot or its coverings, and to regard them as a special sexual fascination, is not without significance for the interpretation of the sporadic manifestations of foot-fetichism among ourselves. Eccentric as foot-fetichism may appear to us, it is simply the re-emergence, by a pseudo-atavism or arrest of development, of a mental or emotional impulse which was probably experienced by our forefathers, and is often traceable among young children to-day.[1] The occasional reappearance of this bygone impulse and the stability which it may acquire are thus conditioned by the sensitive reaction of an abnormally nervous and usually precocious organism to influences which, among the average and ordinary population of Europe to-day, are either never felt, or quickly outgrown, or very strictly subordinated in the highly complex crystallizations which the course of love and the process of tumescence create within us.

It may be added that this is by no means true of foot-fetichism only. In some other fetichisms a seemingly congenital predisposition is even more marked. This is not only the case as regards hair-fetichism and fur-fetichism (see, *e.g.*, Krafft-Ebing, *Psychopathia Sexualis*, English translation of tenth edition, pp. 233, 255, 262). In many cases of fetichisms of all kinds not only is there no record of any commencement in a definite episode (an absence which may be accounted for by the supposition that the original incident has been forgotten), but it would seem in some cases that the fetichism developed very slowly.

In this sense, it will be seen, although it is hazardous to speak of foot-fetichism as strictly an atavism, it may certainly be said to arise on a congenital basis. It represents the rare development of an inborn germ, usually latent among ourselves, which in earlier stages of civilization frequently reached a normal and general fruition.

---

[1] Jacoby (*loc. cit.* p. 797) appears to regard shoe-fetichism as a true atavism: "The sexual adoration of feminine foot-gear," he concludes, "perhaps the most enigmatic and certainly the most singular of degenerative insanities, is thus merely a form of atavism, the return of the degenerate to the very ancient and primitive psychology which we no longer understand and are no longer capable of feeling."

It is of interest to emphasize this congenital element of foot symbolism, because more than any other forms of sexual perversion the fetichisms are those which are most vaguely conditioned by inborn states of the organism and most definitely aroused by seemingly accidental associations or shocks in early life. Inversion is sometimes so fundamentally ingrained in the individual's constitution that it arises and develops in spite of the very strongest influence in a contrary direction. But a fetichism, while it tends to occur in sensitive, nervous, timid, precocious individuals—that is to say, individuals of more or less neuropathic heredity—can usually, though not always, be traced to a definite starting point in the shock of some sexually emotional episode in early life.

A few examples of the influences of such association may here be given, referring miscellaneously to various forms of erotic symbolism. Magnan has recorded the case of a hair-fetichist, living in a district where the women wore their hair done up, who at the age of 15 experienced pleasurable feelings with erection at the sight of a village beauty combing her hair; from that time flowing hair became his fetich, and he could not resist the temptation to touch it and if possible sever it, thus becoming a hair-despoiler, for which he was arrested but not sentenced. (*Archives de l'Anthropologie Criminelle*, vol. v, No. 28.)

I have elsewhere recorded the history of a boy of 14, having already had imperfect connection with a grown-up woman, who associated much with a young married lady; he had no sexual relations with her, but one day she urinated in his presence, and he saw that her mons veneris was covered by very thick hair; from that time he worshiped this woman in secret and acquired a life-long fetichistic attraction to women whose pubic hair was similarly abundant (*Studies in the Psychology of Sex*, vol. iii, Appendix B, History V).

Roubaud reported the case of a general's son, sexually initiated at the age of 14 by a blonde young lady of 21 who, in order to avoid detection, always retained her clothing: gaiters, a corset and a silk dress; when the boy's studies were completed and he was sent to a garrison where he could enjoy freedom he found that his sexual desires could only be aroused by blonde women dressed like the lady who had first aroused his sexual desires; consequently he gave up all thoughts of matrimony, as a woman in nightclothes produced impotence (*Traité de l'Impuissance*, p. 439). Krafft-Ebing records the somewhat similar case of a nervous Polish boy of old family seduced at the age of 17 by a French governess, who during several months practiced mutual masturbation with him; in this way his attention bcame attracted by her very elegant boots, and in the end he became a coufirmed boot-fetichist (*Psychopathia Sexualis,* English translation, p. 249).

A boy of 7, of bad heredity, was taught to masturbate by a servant girl; on one occasion she practiced this on him with her foot without taking off her shoe; it was the first time the manœuvre gave him any pleasure, and an association was thus established which led to shoe-fetichism (Hammond, *Sexual Impotence,* p. 44). A government official whose first coitus in youth took place on a staircase; the sound of his partner's creaking shoes against the stairs, produced by her efforts to accelerate orgasm, formed an association which developed into an auditory shoe-fetichism; in the streets he was compelled to follow ladies whose shoes creaked, ejaculation being thus produced, while to obtain complete satisfaction he would make a prostitute, otherwise naked, sit in front of him in her shoes, moving her feet so that the shoes creaked. (Moraglia, *Archivio di Psichiatria,* vol. xiii, p. 568.)

Bechterew, in St. Petersburg, has recorded the case of a man who when a child used to fall asleep at the knees of his nurse with his head buried in the folds of her apron; in this position he first experienced erection and voluptuous sensations; when a youth he had no attraction to naked women, and in real life and in dreams was only excited sexually under conditions recalling his early experience; in his relations with women he preferred them dressed, and was excited by the rustling sound of their skirts; in this case there was no traceable neuropathic taint nor any other personal peculiarity. (Summarized in *Journal de Psychologie Normale et Pathologique,* January-February, 1904, p. 72.)

In a curious case recorded in detail by Moll, a philologist of sensitive temperament but sound heredity, who had always been fond of flowers, at the age of 21 became engaged to a young lady who wore large roses fastened in her jacket; from this time roses became to him a sexual fetich, to kiss them caused erection, and his erotic dreams were accompanied by visions of roses and the hallucination of their odor; the engagement was finally broken off and the rose-fetichism disappeared (*Untersuchungen über Libido Sexualis,* bd. i, p. 540).

Such associations may naturally occur in the early experiences of even the most normal persons. The degree to which they will influence the subsequent life and thought and feeling depends on the degree of the individual's morbid emotional receptivity, on the extent to which he is hereditarily susceptible of abnormal deviation. Precocity is undoubtedly a condition which favors such deviation; a child who is precociously and abnormally sensitive to persons of the opposite sex before puberty has established the normal channels of sexual desire, is peculiarly liable to become the prey of a chance symbolism. All degrees of such symbolism are possible. While the average insensitive person may fail to perceive them at all, for the more alert and imaginative lover they are a fascinating part of the highly charged crystallization of passion. A more nervously exceptional person, when once such a symbolism has become firmly implanted, may find it an absolutely essential element in the charm of a beloved and charming person. Finally, for the individual who is thoroughly unsound the symbol becomes generalized; a person is no longer desired at all, being merely regarded as an appendage of the symbol, or being dispensed with altogether; the symbol is alone desired, and is fully adequate to impart by itself complete sexual gratification. While it must be considered a morbid state to demand a symbol as an almost essential part of the charm of a desired person, it is only in the final condition, in which the symbol becomes all-sufficing, that we have a true and complete perversion. In the less complete forms of symbolism it is still the woman who is desired, and the ends of procreation may be served; when the woman is ignored and the mere symbol is an adequate and even preferred stimulus to detumescence the pathological condition becomes complete.

Krafft-Ebing regarded shoe-fetichism as, in large measure, a more or less latent form of masochism, the foot or the shoe being the symbol of the subjection and humiliation which the masochist feels in the presence of the beloved object. Moll is also inclined to accept such a connection.

"The very numerous class of boot-and-shoe-fetichists," Krafft-Ebing wrote, "forms the transition to the manifestations of another independent perversion, i.e., fetichism itself; but it stands in closer relationship to the former. . . . It is highly probable, and shown by a correct classification of the observed cases, that the majority, and perhaps all of the cases of shoe-fetichism, rest upon a basis of more or less conscious masochistic desire for self-humiliation. . . . The majority or all may be looked upon as instances of latent masochism (the motive remaining unconscious) in which the *female foot or shoe, as the masochist's fetich*, has acquired an independent significance." (*Psychopathia Sexualis*, English translation of tenth edition, pp. 159, *et seq.*) "Though Krafft-Ebing may not have cleared up the whole matter," Moll remarks, "I regard his deductions concerning the connection of foot-and-shoe fetichism to masochism as the most important progress that has been made in the theoretic study of sexual perversions. . . . In any case, the connection is very frequent." (*Konträre Sexualempfindung*, third edition, p. 306.)

It is quite easy to see that this supposed identity of masochism and foot-fetichism forms a seductive theory. It is also undoubtedly true that a masochist may very easily be inclined to find in his mistress's foot an aid to the ecstatic self-abnegation which he desires to attain.[1] But only confusion is attained by any general attempt to amalgamate masochism and foot-fetichism. In the broad sense in which erotic symbolism is here understood, both masochism and foot-fetichism may be coördinated as symbolisms; for the masochist his self-humiliating impulses are the symbol of ecstatic adoration; for the foot-fetichist his mistress's foot or shoe is the concentrated symbol of all that is most beautiful and elegant and feminine in her personality. But if in this sense they are coördinated, they remain entirely distinct and have not even any necessary tendency to become merged. Masochism merely simulates foot-fetichism; for the masochist the boot is not strictly a symbol, it is only an instrument which enables him to carry out his impulse; the true sexual symbol for him is not the boot, but the emotion of self-subjection. For the foot-fetichist, on the other hand, the foot or the shoe is not a mere instrument, but a true symbol; the focus of his worship, an idealized object which he is content to contemplate or reverently touch. He has no necessary impulse to any self-degrading action, nor any constant emotion of subjec-

---

[1] Moll has reported in detail (*Untersuchungen über die Libido Sexualis*, bd. i, Teil II, pp. 320-324) a case which both he and Krafft-Ebing regard as illustrative of the connection between boot-fetichism and masochism. It is essentially a case of masochism, though manifesting itself almost exclusively in the desire to perform humiliating acts in connection with the attractive person's boots.

tion. It may be noted that in the very typical case of foot-fetichism which is presented to us in the person of Restif de la Bretonne (*ante,* p. 18), he repeatedly speaks of "subjecting" the woman for whom he feels this fetichistic adoration, and mentions that even when still a child he especially admired a delicate and fairy-like girl in this respect because she seemed to him easier to subjugate. Throughout life Restif's attitude toward women was active and masculine, without the slightest trace of masochism.[1]

To suppose that a fetichistic admiration of his mistress's foot is due to a lover's latent desire to be kicked, is as unreasonable as it would be to suppose that a fetichistic admiration for her hand indicated a latent desire to have his ears boxed. In determining whether we are concerned with a case of foot-fetichism or of masochism we must take into consideration the whole of the subject's mental and emotional attitude. An act, however definite, will not suffice as a criterion, for the same act in different persons may have altogether different implications. To amalgamate the two is the result of inadequate psychological analysis and only leads to confusion.

It is, however, often very difficult to decide whether we are dealing with a case which is predominantly one of masochism or of foot-fetichism. The nature of the action desired, as we have seen, will not suffice to determine the psychological character of the perversion. Krafft-Ebing believed that the desire to be trodden on, very frequently experienced by masochists, is absolutely symptomatic of masochism.[2] This is scarcely the case. The desire to be trodden on may be fundamentally an

---

[1] Krafft-Ebing goes so far as to assert. (*Psychopathia Sexualis,* English translation of tenth edition, p. 174) that "when in cases of shoe-fetichism the female shoe appears alone as the excitant of sexual desire one is justified in presuming that masochistic motives have remained latent. . . . Latent masochism may always be assumed as the unconscious motive." In this way he hopelessly misinterprets some of his own cases.

[1] Krafft-Ebing goes so far as to assert (*Psychopathia Sexualis,* English translation, pp. 159 and 174). Yet some of the cases he brings forward (*e.g.,* Coxe's as quoted by Hammond) show no sign of masochism, since, according to Krafft-Ebing's own definition (p. 116), the idea of subjugation by the opposite sex is of the essence of masochism.

erotic symbolism, closely approaching foot-fetichism, and such slight indications of masochism as appear may be merely a parasitic growth on the symbolism, a growth perhaps more suggested by the circumstances involved in the gratification of the abnormal desire than inherent in the innate impulse of the subject. This may be illustrated by the interesting case of a very intelligent man with whom I am well acquainted.

C. P., aged 38. Heredity good. Parents both healthy and normal. Several children of the marriage, all sexually normal so far as is known. C. P. is the youngest of the family and separated from the others by an interval of many years. He was a seven-months' child. He has always enjoyed good health and is active and vigorous, both mentally and physically.

From the age of 9 or 10 to 14 he masturbated occasionally for the sake of physical relief, having discovered the act for himself. He was, however, quite innocent and knew nothing of sexual matters, never having been initiated either by servants or by other boys.

"When I encounter a woman who very strongly attracts me and whom I very greatly admire," he writes, "my desire is never that I may have sexual connection with her in the ordinary sense, but that I may lie down upon the floor on my back and be trampled upon by her. This curious desire is seldom present unless the object of my admiration is really a lady, and of fine proportions. She must be richly dressed— preferably in an evening gown, and wear dainty high-heeled slippers, either quite open so as to show the curve of the instep, or with only one strap or 'bar' across. The skirts should be raised sufficiently to afford me the pleasure of seeing her feet and a liberal amount of ankle, but in no case above the knee, or the effect is greatly reduced. Although I often greatly admire a woman's intellect and even person, sexually no other part of her has any serious attraction for me except the leg, from the knee downwards, and the foot, and these must be exquisitely clothed. Given this condition, my desire amounts to a wish to gratify my sexual sense by contact with the (to me) attractive part of the woman. Comparatively few women have a leg or foot sufficiently beautiful to my mind to excite any serious or compelling desire, but when this is so, or I suspect it, I am willing to spend any time or trouble to get her to tread upon me and am anxious to be trampled on with the greatest severity.

"The treading should be inflicted for a few minutes all over the chest, abdomen and groin, and lastly on the penis, which is, of course, lying along the belly in a violent state of erection, and consequently too hard for the treading to damage it. I also enjoy being nearly strangled by a woman's foot.

"If the lady finally stands facing my head and places her slipper upon my penis so that the high heel falls about where the penis leaves the scrotum, the sole covering most of the rest of it and with the other foot upon the abdomen, into which I can *see* as well as feel it sink as she shifts her weight from one foot to the other, orgasm takes place almost at once. Emission under these conditions is to me an agony of delight, during which practically the lady's whole weight should rest upon the penis.

"One reason for my special pleasure in this method seems to be that first the heel and afterwards the sole of the slipper as it treads upon the penis greatly check the passage of the semen and consequently the pleasure is considerably prolonged. There is also a curious mental side to the affair. I love to imagine that the lady who is treading upon me is my mistress and I her slave, and that she is doing it to punish me for some fault, or to give *herself* (not me) pleasure.

"It follows that the greater the contempt and severity with which I am 'punished,' the greater becomes my pleasure. The idea of 'punishment' or 'slavery' is seldom aroused except when I have great difficulty in accomplishing my desire and the treader is more than usually handsome and heavy and the trampling mercilessly inflicted. I have been trampled so long and so mercilessly several times, that I have flinched each time the slipper pressed its way into my aching body and have been black and blue for days afterwards. I take the greatest interest in leading ladies on to do this for me where I think I will not offend, and have been surprisingly successful. I must have lain beneath the feet of quite a hundred women, many of them of good social position, who would never dream of permitting any ordinary sexual intercourse, but who have been so interested or amused by the idea as to do it for me—many of them over and over again. It is perhaps needless to say that none of my own or the ladies' clothing is ever removed, or disarranged, for the accomplishment of orgasm in this manner. After a long and varied experience, I may say that my favorite weight is 10 to 11 stone, and that black, very high-heeled slippers, in combination with tan silk stockings, seem to give me the greatest pleasure and create in me the strongest desires.

"Boots, or outdoor shoes, do not attract me to anything like the same degree, although I have, upon several occasions, enjoyed myself fairly well by their use. Nude women repel me, and I find no pleasure in seeing a woman in tights. I am not averse to normal sexual connection and occasionally employ it. To me, however, the pleasure is far inferior to that of being trampled upon. I also derive keen pleasure—and usually have a strong erection—from seeing a woman, dressed as I have described, tread upon anything which yields under her foot—such as the seat of a carriage, the cushions of a punt, a footstool, etc., and I enjoy seeing her crush flowers by treading upon them. I have often strolled along in the wake of some handsome lady at a picnic or garden party, for the pleasure of seeing the grass upon which she has trodden rise slowly again after her foot has pressed it. I delight also to see a carriage sway as a woman leaves or enters it—anything which needs the pressure of the foot.

"To pass now to the origin of this direction of my feelings.

"Even in early childhood I admired pretty feminine foot-gear, and in the contemplation of it experienced vague sensations which I now recognize as sexual. When a lad of 14 or so, I stayed a good deal at the house of some intimate friends of my parents, the daughter of the house —an only child—a beautiful and powerful girl, about six years my senior, being my special chum. This girl was always daintily dressed, and having most lovely feet and ankles not unnaturally knew it. Whenever possible she dressed so as to show off their beauty to the best advantage—rather short skirts and usually little high-heeled slippers—and was not averse to showing them in a most distractingly coquettish manner. She seemed to have a passion for treading upon things which would scrunch or yield under her foot, such as flowers, little windfallen apples and pears, acorns, etc., or heaps of hay, straw or cut grass. As we wandered about the gardens—for we were left to do exactly as we liked—I got quite accustomed to seeing her hunt out and tread upon such things, and used to chaff her about it. At that time I was—as I am still—fond of lying at full length on a thick hearthrug before a good fire. One evening as I was lying in this way and we were alone, A. crossed the room to reach a bangle from the mantelpiece. Instead of reaching over me, she playfully stepped upon my body, saying that she would show me how the hay and straw felt. Naturally I fell in with the joke and laughed. After standing upon me a few moments she raised her skirt slightly and, holding on to the mantelpiece for support, stretched out one dainty foot in its brown silk stocking and high-heeled slipper to the blaze to warm, while looking down and laughing at my scarlet, excited face. She was a perfectly frank and charming girl, and I feel pretty certain that, although she evidently enjoyed my excitement and the feeling of my body yielding under her feet, she did not on this first occasion clearly understand my condition; nor can I remember that, though the desire for sexual gratification drove me nearly mad, it appeared to awaken in her any reciprocal feeling. I took hold of her raised foot and, after kissing it, guided it by an absolutely irresistible impulse on to my penis, which was as hard as wood and seemed almost bursting. Almost at the moment that her weight was thrown upon it, orgasm took place for the first time in my life thoroughly and effectively. No description can give any idea of what I felt—I only know that from that moment my distorted sexual focus was fixed forever. Numberless times, after that evening, I felt the weight of her dainty slippers, and nothing will ever cause the memory of the pleasure she thus gave me to fade. I know that A. came to enjoy treading upon me, as much as I enjoyed having her do it. She had a liberal dress allowance and, seeing the pleasure they gave me, she was always buying pretty stockings and ravishing slippers with the highest and most slender Louis heels she could find and would show them to me with the greatest glee, urging me to lie down that she might try them on me. She confessed that she loved to see and feel them sink into my body as she trod upon me and enjoyed the crunch of the muscles under her heel as she moved about. After some minutes of this, I always guided her slipper on to my penis, and she would tread carefully, but with her whole weight—probably about 9 stone—and watch me with flashing eyes, flushed cheeks, and quivering lips, as she felt—as she must have done plainly—the throbbing and swelling of my penis under her foot as emission took place. I have not the smallest doubt that orgasm took place simultaneously with her, though we never at any time spoke openly of it. This went on for several years on almost every favorable opportunity we had, and after a month or two of separation sometimes four or five times during a single day. Several times during A.'s absence I masturbated by getting her slipper and pressing it with all my strength against the penis while imagining that she was treading upon me. The pleasure was, of course, very inferior to her attentions. There was never at any time between us any question of normal sexual intercourse, and we were both well content to let things drift as they were.

"A little after 20 I went abroad, and on my return about three years later I found her married. Although we met often, the subject was never alluded to, though we remained firm friends. I confess I often, when I could do so without being seen, looked longingly at her feet and would have gladly accepted the pleasure she could have given me by an occasional resumption of our strange practice—but it never came.

"I went abroad again, and now neither she nor her husband are alive and leave no issue. From time to time I have had occasional relations with prostitutes, but always in this manner, though I much prefer to find some lady of or above my own social position who will do the treading for me. This is, however, interestingly difficult.

"Out of say a hundred women (which at home and abroad is what I should estimate must have stood upon my body) I should say quite 80 or 85 were *not* prostitutes. Certainly not more than 10 to 12 shared any *sexual* excitement, but while they were evidently excited they were not gratified. A. alone, so far as I know, had complete sexual satisfaction of it. I have never asked a woman in so many words to tread upon me for the purpose of gratifying my sexual desires (prostitutes excepted), but have always tempted them to do it in a jocular or teasing manner, and it is very doubtful if more than a few (married) women really understood, even after they had given me the extreme pleasure, that they had done so, because any flushing and movement on my part under their feet was not unnaturally put down to the trampling to which they were subjecting me, and it was easy for me to guide the foot as often as was necessary on to the penis till orgasm took place, and even to keep it there by laying hold of the other one to kiss it or on some other pretext during emission. Of course many understood after once doing it (most have done it only once) what I was at, and, although they did not ever discuss it nor did I, they were not unwilling to give me as many treadings as I cared to playfully suggest. I don't think they got any pleasure sexually out of it themselves, though they could see plainly that I did, and they did not object to give it me. I have spent as long as twelve months with some women working gradually nearer and nearer to my desire—often getting what I want in the end, but more often failing. I *never* risk it till I am certain it would be safe to ask it, and have never had a serious rebuff. In very many cases I should say the doing of what I want has simply been regarded by the woman as gratifying a silly and perhaps amusing whim, in which, beyond the novelty of treading on a man's body, she has taken but little interest.

"As in normal seduction, the endeavor to win the woman over to do what I want without arousing her antagonism is a great part of the charm to me, and naturally the better her social position the more difficult this becomes—and the more attractive. I have found that in three instances prostitutes have performed the same office for other men and knew all about it. It is not uninteresting to note that these three women were all of fine, massive build—one standing about 5 feet 10 inches and weighing nearly 14 stone—but with comparatively uninteresting faces. The weight, build and clothing count for a good deal in exciting me. I find that a sudden check to a man at the supreme moment of sexual pleasure tends to heighten and prolong the pleasure. My physical satisfaction is due to the fact that by getting the lady to stand with all her weight upon my penis (as it lies between her foot and the soft bed of my own body into which it is deeply pressed) the act of emission is enormously prolonged, with corresponding enjoyment. For this reason also I prefer a very high-heeled slipper. The seminal fluid has to be forced past two separate obstacles—the pressure of the heel close at the root of the penis and afterwards the ball of the foot which compresses the outer half, leaving a free portion between them under the arched sole of the slipper. I may add that the pleasure is greatly increased by the retention of the urine, and I always try to retain as much water as I dare. I have an unconquerable aversion to red in slippers or stockings; it will even cause impotence. Why, I know not. Strange as it may seem, although pain and bruising are often inflicted by a severe treading, I have never been in any way injured by the practice, and my pleasure in it seems not to diminish by constant repetition. The comparative difficulty of obtaining the pleasure from just the woman I want has a never-ending, if inexplicable, charm for me."

It will be observed that in this case special importance is attached to shoes with high heels, and the subject considers that the pressure of such shoes is for mechanical reasons most favorable for procuring ejaculation. Nearly all heterosexual shoe-fetichists seem, however, to be equally attracted by high heels. Restif de la Bretonne frequently referred to this point, and he gave a number of reasons for the attractiveness of high heels: (1) They are unlike men's boots and, therefore, have a sexual fascination; (2) they make the leg and foot look more charming; (3) they give a less bold and more sylph-like character to the walk; (4) they keep the feet clean. (Restif de la Bretonne, *Nuits de Paris*, vol. v, quoted in Preface to his *Mes Inscriptions*, p. ciii.) It is doubtless the first reason—the fact that high heels are a kind of secondary sexual character—which is most generally potent in this attraction.

The foregoing history, while it very distinctly brings before us a case of erotic symbolism, is not strictly an example of shoe-fetichism. The symbolism is more complex. The focus of beauty in a desirable woman is transferred and concentrated in the region below the knee; in that sense we have foot-fetichism. But the act of coitus itself is also symbolically transferred. Not only has the foot become the symbol of the vulva, but trampling has become the symbol of coitus; intercourse takes place symbolically *per pedem*. It is a result of this symbolization of the foot and of trampling that all acts of treading take on a new and symbolical sexual charm. The element of masochism—of pleasure in being a woman's slave—is a parasitic growth; that is to say, it is not founded in the subject's constitution, but chances to have found a favorable soil in the special circumstances under which his sexual life developed. It is not primary, but secondary, and remains an unimportant and merely occasional element.

It may be instructive to bring forward for comparison a case in which also we have a symbolism involving boot-fetichism, but extending beyond it. In this case there is a basis of inversion (as is not infrequent in erotic symbolisms), but from the present point of view the psychological significance of the case remains the same.

A. N., aged 29, unmarried, healthy, though not robust, and without any known hereditary taint. Has followed various avocations without taking great interest in them, but has shown some literary ability.

"I am an Englishman," his own narrative runs, "the third of three children. At my birth my father was 41 and my mother 34. My mother died of cancer when I was 15. My father is still alive, a reserved man, who still nurses his sorrow for his wife's death. I have no reason to believe my parents anything but normal and useful members of society. My sister is normal and happily married. My brother I have reason to believe to be an invert.

"A horoscope cast for me describes me in a way I think correct, and so do my friends: 'A mild, obliging, gentle, amiable person, with many fine traits of character; timid in nature, fond of society, loving peace and quietude, delighting in warm and close friendships. There is much that is firm, steadfast and industrious, some self-love, a good deal of diplomacy, a little that is subtle, or what is called finesse. You are reserved with those you dislike. There is a serious and sad side to your character; you are very thoughtful and contemplative when in these moods. But you are not pessimistic. You have superior abilities, for they are intuitively intellectual. There is a cold reticence which restrains generous impulses and which inclines to acquisitiveness; it will make you deliberate, inventive, adding self-esteem, some vanity.'

"At an early age I was left much alone in the nursery and there contracted the habit of masturbation long before the age of puberty. I use the word 'masturbation' for want of a better, though it may not quite describe my case. I have never used my hand to the penis. As far back as I can remember I have had what a Frenchman has described as 'le fetichisme de la chaussure,' and in those early days, before I was 6 years old, I would put on my father's boots, taken from a cupboard at hand, and then tying or strapping my legs together would produce an erection, and all the pleasurable feelings experienced, I suppose, by means of masturbation. I always did this secretly, but couldn't tell why. I continued this practice on and off all my boyhood and youth. When I discovered the first emission I was much surprised. I always did this thing without loosening my trousers. As to how these feelings arose I am totally unable to say. I can't remember being without such feelings, and they seem to me perfectly normal. The sight, or even thought, of high boots, or leggings, especially if well polished or in patent leather, would set all my sexual passions aflame, and does yet. As a boy my great desire was to wear these things. A soldier in boots and spurs, a groom in tops, or even an errand-boy in patent leather leggings, fascinated me, and to this day, despite reason and everything else. The sight of such things produced an erection. An emission I could always produce by tightly tying my legs together, but only when wearing boots, and preferably leggings, which when I had pocket money

I bought for this purpose. (At the present moment I have five pairs in the house and two pairs of high boots, quite unjustified by ordinary use.) This habit I lapse into yet at times. The smell of leather affects me, but I never know how far this may be due to association with boots; the smell suggests the image. Restraint by a leather strap is more exciting than by cords. Erotic dreams always take the form of restraint on the limbs when booted.

"Uniforms and liveries have a great temptation for me, but only when of a tight-fitting nature and smart, as soldiers', grooms', etc., but not sailors'; most powerfully when the person is in boots or leggings and breeches.

"I was a quiet, sensitive boy, taking no part in games or sports. Have always been indifferent to them. I made few friends, but didn't want them. The craving for friendship came much later, after I was 21. I was a day boy at a private school, and never had any conversation with any boy on sexual matters, though I was dimly aware of much 'nastiness' about the school. I knew nothing of sodomy. But all these things were repulsive to me, notwithstanding my secret practices. I was a 'good boy.'

"Up to the age of 21 I was perfectly satisfied with my own society, something of a prig, fond of books and reading, etc. I was and ever have been absolutely insensible to the influence of the other sex. I am not a woman hater, and take intellectual pleasure in the society of certain ladies, but they are nearly all much older than myself. I have a strong repulsion from sexual relations with women. I should not mind being married for the sake of companionship and for the sake of having boys of my own. But the sexual act would frighten me. I could not in my present frame of mind go to bed with a woman. Yet I feel an immense envy of my married friends in that they are able to give out, and find satisfaction for, their affection in a way that is quite impossible for me. I picture certain boys in the place of the wife.

"I am now only happy in the society of men younger than myself, age 17 to (say) 23 or 24, youths with smooth faces, or first sign of hair on lip, well groomed, slightly effeminate in feature, of sympathetic, perhaps weak nature. I feel I want to help them, do something for them, devote myself entirely to their welfare.

"With such there is no fixed line between friendship and love. I ⎡rn for intimacy with particular friends, but never dare express it. ⎡nd so many people object to any strong expression of feeling that I ⎡are not run the risk of appearing ridiculous in the eyes of these desired intimates.

"I have no desire for *paedicatio*, but the idea itself does not repulse me or seem unnatural, though personally it repels me a little. But I think this to be mere prejudice on my part, which might be broken down if the loved person showed a willingness to act a passive part. I should never dare to make an advance, however.

"I am restrained by moral and religious considerations from making my real feelings known, and I feel I should sink in my own estimation if I gave way, though my natural desire is to do so. In the face of opportunities (not I mean of *paedicatio*, but of expression of excessive affection, etc.), or what might be such, I always fail to speak lest I should forfeit the esteem of the other person. I have a feeling of surprise when any one I like evinces a liking for me. I feel that those I love are immeasurably my superiors, though my reason may tell me it is not so. I would grovel at their feet, do anything to win a smile from them, or to make them give me their company.

"Ordinary bodily contact with the boy I love gives me most exquisite pleasure, and I never lose an opportunity of bringing such contact about when it can be done naturally. I feel an immense desire to embrace, kiss, squeeze, etc., the person, to generally maul him, and say nice things—the kind of things a man usually says to a woman. A handshake, the mere presence of the person, makes me happy and content.

"I can say with the Albanian: 'If I find myself in the presence of the beloved, I rest absorbed in gazing on him. Absent, I think of nought but him. If the beloved unexpectedly appears I fall into confusion. My heart beats faster. I have eyes and ears only for the beloved.'

"I feel that my capacity of affection is finer and more spiritual than that which commonly subsists between persons of different sexes. And so, while trying to fight my instincts by religion, I find my natural feeling to be part of my religion, and its highest expression. In this sense I can speak from experience in my own case, and more especially in that of my brother, that what you have said about philanthropic activity resulting from repressed homosexuality is very true indeed. I can say with one of your female cases: 'Love is to me a religion. The very nature of my affection for my friends precludes the possibility of any element entering into it which is not absolutely pure and sacred.' I am, however, madly jealous. I want entire possession, and I can't bear for a moment that any one I do not care for should know the person I love.

"I am never attracted by men older than myself. The youths who attract me may be of any class, though preferably, I think, of a class a little lower than myself. I am not quite sure of this, however, as circumstances may have contributed more than deliberate choice to bring certain youths under my notice. Those who have exercised the most powerful influence on me have been an Oxford undergraduate, a barber's assistant, and a plumber's apprentice. Though naturally fond of intellectual society, I do not ask for intellect in those I love. It goes for nothing. I always prefer their company to that of the most educated persons. This preference has alienated me to some extent from more refined and educated circles that formerly I was intimate with.

"I have been led entirely out of my old habits by association with younger friends, and now do things which before I should never have dreamed of doing. My thoughts now are always with certain youths, and if they speak of leaving the town, or in any way talk of a future that I cannot share, I suffer horrid sinkings of the heart and depression of spirits."

This case, while it concerns a person of quite different temperament, with a more innate predisposition to specific perversions, is yet in many respects analogous to the previous case. There is boot-fetichism; nothing is felt to be so attractive as the foot-gear, and there is also at the same time more than this; there is the attraction of repression and constraint developed into a sexual symbol. In C. P.'s case that symbolism arises from the experience of an abnormal heterosexual relationship; in A. N.'s case it is founded on auto-erotic experiences associated with inversion; in both alike the entire symbolism has become diffused and generalized.

In the two cases just brought forward we have an erotic symbolism of act founded on, and closely associated with, an erotic symbolism of object. It may be instructive to bring forward another case in which no fetichistic feeling toward an object can be traced, but an erotic symbolism still clearly exists. In this case pain, even when self-inflicted, has acquired a symbolic value as a stimulus to tumescence, without any element of masochism. Such a case serves to indicate how the sexual attraction of pain is really a special case of the erotic symbolism with which we are here concerned.

A. W., aged 50, a writer and lecturer, physically and mentally energetic and enjoying good health. He is, however, very emotional and of nervous temperament, but self-controlled. Though physically well developed, the sexual organs are small. He is married to an attractive woman, to whom he is much attached, and has two healthy children.

At 10 or 12 years of age he had a frequent desire to be whipped, his parents never having struck him, and on one occasion he asked a brother to go with him to the closet to get him to whip him on the posterior; but on arrival he was too shy to make the request. He did not recognize the cause of these desires, knowing nothing of such things except from the misinformation of his schoolfellows' talk. As far as he can remember, he was an entirely normal, healthy boy up to the age of about 15, when his attention was arrested by an advertisement of a quack medicine for the results of "youthful excesses."

Being a city boy, he was unfamiliar with the coupling even of animals, had never had a conscious erection and did not know of frictional excitement. Experiment, however, resulted in an orgasm, and, though believing that it was wicked or at least weak and degrading, he indulged in masturbation at intervals, usually about six times a month, and has continued even up to the present.

He had an abnormally small opening in the prepuce, making the uncovering of the glans almost impossible. (At the age of about 37, he himself slit the prepuce by three or four cuts of a scissors at intervals of about ten days. This was followed by a marked decrease in desire, especially as he shortly afterwards learned the importance of local cleanliness.) While in college at about the age of 19 he began to have nocturnal emissions occasionally and once or twice a week when at stool. Alarmed by these, he consulted a physician, who warned him of the danger, gave him bromide and prescribed cold bathing of the parts, with a hard, cool bed. These stopped the emissions.

He never had connection with women until the age of about 25, and then only three times until his marriage at 30 years of age, being deterred partly by conscientious scruples, but more by shyness and convention, and deriving very little pleasure from these instances. Even since marriage he has derived more pleasure from sexual excitement than from coitus, and can maintain erection for as long as two hours.

He has always been accustomed to torture himself in various ingenious ways, nearly always connected with sex. He would burn his skin deeply with red hot wire in inconspicuous places. These and similar acts were generally followed by manual excitation nearly always brought to a climax.

He considers that he is attracted to refined and intellectual women. But he is without very ardent desires, having several times gone to bed with attractive women who stripped themselves naked, but without attempting any sexual intercourse with them. He became interested in the "Karezza" theory and has tried to practice it with his wife, but could never entirely control the emission.

He has hired a masseur to whip him, as children are whipped, with a heavy dog whip, which caused pleasurable excitement. During this time he had relations with his wife generally about once a week without any great ecstasy. She was cold and sexually slow, owing to conventional sex repression and to an idea that the whole thing was "like animals" and to fear of child-bearing, usually necessitating the use of a cover or withdrawal. It was only eight years after their marriage that she desired and obtained a child. During these years he would often stick pins through his mammæ and tie them together by a string round the pins drawn so short as to cause great pain and then indulge himself in the sexual act. He used strong wooden clips with a tack fixed in them, so as to pierce and pinch the mammæ, and once he drove a pin entirely through the penis itself, then obtaining orgasm by friction. He was never able to get an automatic emission in this way, though he often tried, not even by walking briskly during an erection.

In another class of cases a purely ideal symbolism may be present by means of a fetich which acts as a powerful stimulus without itself being felt to possess any attraction. A good illustration of this condition is furnished by a case which has been communicated to me by a medical correspondent in New Zealand.

"The patient went out to South Africa as a trooper with the contingent from New Zealand, throwing up a good position in an office to do so. He had never had any trouble as regards connection with women before going out to South Africa. While in active service at the front he sustained a nasty fall from his horse, breaking his leg. He was unconscious for four days, and was then invalided down to Cape Town. Here he rapidly got well, and his accustomed health returning to him he started having what he terms 'a good time.' He repeatedly went to brothels, but was unable to have more than a temporary erection, and no ejaculation would take place. In one of these places he was in company with a drunken trooper, who suggested that they should perform the sexual act with their boots and spurs (only) on. My patient, who was also drunk, readily assented, and to his surprise was enabled to perform the act of copulation without any difficulty at all. He has repeatedly tried since to perform the act without any spurs, but is quite unable to do so; with the spurs he has no difficulty at all in obtaining all the gratification he desires. His general health is good. His mother was an extremely nervous woman, and so is his sister. His father died when he was quite young. His only other relation in the colony is a married sister, who seems to enjoy vigorous health."

The consideration of the cases here brought forward may suffice to show that beyond those fetichisms which find their satisfaction in the contemplation of a part of the body or a garment, there is a more subtle symbolism. The foot is a center of force, an agent for exerting pressure, and thus it furnishes a point of departure not alone for the merely static sexual fetich, but for a dynamic erotic symbolization. The energy of its movements becomes a substitute for the energy of the sexual organs themselves in coitus, and exerts the same kind of fascination. The young girl (page 35) "who seemed to have a passion for treading upon things which would scrunch or yield under her foot," already possessed the germs of an erotic symbolism which, under the influence of circumstances in which she herself took an active part, developed into an adequate method of sexual gratification.[1] The youth who was her partner learned, in the same way, to find an erotic symbolism in all the pressure reactions of attractive feminine feet, the swaying of a carriage beneath their weight, the crushing of the flowers on which they tread, the slow rising of the grass which they have pressed. Here we have a symbolism which is altogether different from that fetichism which adores a definite object; it is a dynamic symbolism finding its gratification in the spectacle of movements which ideally recall the fundamental rhythm and pressure reactions of the sexual process.

We may trace a very similar erotic symbolism in an absolutely normal form. The fascination of clothes in the lover's eyes is no doubt a complex phenomenon, but in part it rests on the aptitudes of a woman's garments to express vaguely a dynamic symbolism which must always remain indefinite and elusive, and on that account always possess fascination. No one has so acutely described this symbolism as Herrick, often an admirable psychologist in matters of sexual attractiveness. Especially instructive in this respect are his poems, "Delight in Disorder," "Upon Julia's Clothes," and notably "Julia's Petticoat." "A sweet disorder in the dress," he tells us, "kindles in clothes a wantonness;" it is not on the garment itself, but on the

---

[1] Her actions suggest that there is often a latent sexual consciousness in regard to the feet in women, atavistic or pseudo-atavistic, and corresponding to the sexual attraction which the feet formerly aroused, almost normally, in men. This is also suggested by the case, referred to by Shufeldt, of an unmarried woman, belonging to a family exhibiting in a high degree both erotic and neurotic traits, who had "a certain uncontrollable fascination for shoes. She delights in new shoes, and changes her shoes all day long at regular intervals of three hours each. She keeps this row of shoes out in plain sight in her apartment." (R. W. Shufeldt, "On a Case of Female Impotency," 1896, p. 10.)

character of its movement that he insists; on the "erring lace," the "winning wave" of the "tempestuous petticoat;" he speaks of the "liquefaction" of clothes, their "brave vibration each way free," and of Julia's petticoat he remarks with a more specific symbolism still,

> "Sometimes 'twould pant and sigh and heave,
>   As if to stir it scarce had leave;
>   But having got it, thereupon,
>   'Twould make a brave expansion.''

In the play of the beloved woman's garment, he sees the whole process of the central act of sex, with its repressions and expansions, and at the sight is himself ready to "fall into a swoon."

III.

Scatalogic Symbolism—Urolagnia—Coprolagnia—The Ascetic Attitude Towards the Flesh—Normal basis of Scatalogic Symbolism—Scatalogic Conceptions Among Primitive Peoples—Urine as a Primitive Holy Water—Sacredness of Animal Excreta—Scatalogy in Folk-lore—The Obscene as Derived from the Mythological—The Immature Sexual Impulse Tends to Manifest Itself in Scatalogic Forms—The basis of Physiological Connection Between the Urinary and Genital Spheres—Urinary Fetichism Sometimes Normal in Animals—The Urolagnia of Masochists—The Scatalogy of Saints—Urolagnia More Often a Symbolism of Act Than a Symbolism of Object—Only Occasionally an Olfactory Fetichism—Comparative Rarity of Coprolagnia—Influence of Nates Fetichism as a Transition to Coprolagnia—Ideal Coprolagnia—Olfactory Coprolagnia—Urolagnia and Coprolagnia as Symbols of Coitus.

WE meet with another group of erotic symbolisms—alike symbolisms of object and of act—in connection with the two functions adjoining the anatomical sexual focus: the urinary and alvine excretory functions. These are sometimes termed the scatalogical group, with the two subdivisions of urolagnia and coprolagnia.[1] *Inter fæces et urinam nascimur* is an ancient text which has served the ascetic preachers of old for many discourses on the littleness of man and the meanness of that reproductive power which plays so large a part in man's life. "The stupid bungle of Nature," a correspondent writes, "whereby the generative organs serve as a means of relieving the bladder, is doubtless responsible for much of the disgust which those organs excite in some minds."

At the same time, it is necessary to point out, such reflex influence may act not in one direction only, but also in the reverse

---

[1] Fuchs (*Das Erotische Element in der Karikatur*, p. 26), distinguishing sharply between the "erotic" and the "obscene," reserves the latter term exclusively for the representation of excretory organs and acts. He considers that this is etymologically the most exact usage. However that may be, it seems to me that, in any case, "obscene" has become so vague a term that it is now impracticable to give it a restricted and precise sense.

direction. From the standpoint of ascetic contemplation eager to belittle humanity, the excretory centers may cast dishonor upon the genital center which they adjoin. From the more ecstatic standpoint of the impassioned lover, eager to magnify the charm of the woman he worships, it is not impossible for the excretory centers to take on some charm from the irradiating center of sex which they enclose.

Even normally such a process is traceable. The normal lover may not idealize the excretory functions of his mistress, but the fact that he finds no repulsion in the most intimate contacts and feels no disgust at the proximity of the excretory orifices or the existence of their functions, indicates that the idealization of love has exerted at all events a neutralizing influence; indeed, the presence of an acute sensibility to the disturbing influence of this proximity of the excretory orifices and their functions must be considered abnormal; Swift's "Strephon and Chloe"—with the conviction underlying it that it is an easy matter for the excretory functions to drown the possibilities of love—could only have proceeded from a morbidly sensitive brain.[1]

A more than mere neutralizing influence, a positively idealizing influence of the sexual focus on the excretory processes adjoining it, may take place in the lover's mind without the normal variations of sexual attraction being over-passed, and even without the creation of an excretory fetichism.

Reflections of this attitude may be found in the poets. In the *Song of Songs* the lover says of his mistress, "Thy navel is like a round goblet, wherein no mingled wine is wanting;" in his lyric "To Dianeme," Herrick says with clear reference to the mons veneris:—

> "Show me that hill where smiling love doth sit,
>   Having a living fountain under it;"

and in the very numerous poems in various languages which have more

---

[1] In this connection we may profitably contemplate the hand and recall the vast gamut of functions, sacred and profane, which that organ exercises. Many savages strictly reserve the left hand to the lowlier purposes of life; but in civilization that is not considered necessary, and it may be wholesome for some of us to meditate on the more humble uses of the same hand which is raised in the supreme gesture of benediction and which men have often counted it a privilege to kiss.

or less obscurely dealt with the rose as the emblem of the feminine pudenda there are occasional references to the stream which guards or presides over the rose. It may, indeed, be recalled that even in the name *nymphæ* anatomists commonly apply to the *labia minora* there is generally believed to be a poetic allusion to the Nymphs who presided over streams, since the *labia minora* exert an influence on the direction of the urinary stream.

In *Wilhelm Meister* (Part I, Chapter XV), Goethe, on the basis of his own personal experiences, describes his hero's emotions in the humble surroundings of Marianne's little room as compared with the stateliness and order of his own home. "It seemed to him when he had here to remove her stays in order to reach the harpsichord, there to lay her skirt on the bed before he could seat himself, when she herself with unembarrassed frankness would make no attempt to conceal from him many natural acts which people are accustomed to hide from others out of decency—it seemed to him, I say, that he became bound to her by invisible bands." We are told of Wordsworth (Findlay's *Recollections of De Quincey*, p. 36) that he read *Wilhelm Meister* till "he came to the scene where the hero, in his mistress's bedroom, becomes sentimental over her dirty towels, etc., which struck him with such disgust that he flung the book out of his hand, would never look at it again, and declared that surely no English lady would ever read such a work." I have, however, heard a woman of high intellectual distinction refer to the peculiar truth and beauty of this very passage.

In one of his latest novels, *Les Rencontres de M. de Bréot*, Henri de Régnier, one of the most notable of recent French novelists, narrates an episode bearing on the matter before us. A personage of the story is sitting for a moment in a dark grotto during a night fête in a nobleman's park, when two ladies enter and laughingly proceed to raise their garments and accomplish a natural necessity. The man in the background, suddenly overcome by a sexual impulse, starts forward; one lady runs away, the other, whom he detains, offers little resistance to his advances. To M. de Bréot, whom he shortly after encounters, he exclaims, abashed at his own actions: "Why did I not flee? But could I imagine that the spectacle of so disgusting a function would have any other effect than to give me a humble opinion of human nature?" M. de Bréot, however, in proceeding to reproach his interlocutor for his inconsiderate temerity, observes: "What you tell me, sir, does not entirely surprise me. Nature has placed very various instincts within us, and the impulse that led you to what you have just now done is not so peculiar as you think. One may be a very estimable man and yet love women even in what is lowliest in their bodies." In harmony with this passage from Régnier's novel are the remarks of a correspondent who writes to me of the function of urination that it "appeals sexually to most normal individuals. My own observations and inquiries prove this. Women themselves instinctively feel it. The secrecy surrounding the matter lends, too, I think, a sexual interest."

The fact that scatalogic processes may in some degree exert an attraction even in normal love has been especially emphasized by Bloch (*Beiträge zur Ætiologie der Psychopathia Sexualis*, Teil II, pp. 222, *et seq.*): "The man whose intellect and æsthetic sense has been 'clouded by the sexual impulse' sees these things in an entirely different light from him who has not been overcome by the intoxication of love. For him they are idealized (sit venia verbo) since they are a part of the beloved person, and in consequence associated with love." Bloch quotes the *Memoiren einer Sängerin* (a book which is said to be, though this seems doubtful, genuinely autobiographical) in the same sense: "A man who falls in love with a girl is not dragged out of his poetic sphere by the thought that his beloved must relieve certain natural necessities every day. It seems, indeed, to him to be just the opposite. If one loves a person one finds nothing obscene or disgusting in the object that pleases me." The opposite attitude is probably in extreme cases due to the influence of a neurotic or morbidly sensitive temperament. Swift possessed such a temperament. The possession of a similar temperament is doubtless responsible for the little prose poem, "L'Extase," in which Huysmans in his first book, *Le Drageloir à Epices*, has written an attenuated version of "Strephon and Chloe" to express the disillusionment of love; the lover lies in a wood clasping the hand of the beloved with rapturous emotion; "suddenly she rose, disengaged her hand, disappeared in the bushes, and I heard as it were the rustling of rain on the leaves." His dream has fled.

In estimating the significance of the lover's attitude in this matter, it is important to realize the position which scatologic conceptions took in primitive belief. At certain stages of early culture, when all the emanations of the body are liable to possess mysterious magic properties and become apt for sacred uses, the excretions, and especially the urine, are found to form part of religious ritual and ceremonial function. Even among savages the excreta are frequently regarded as disgusting, but under the influence of these conceptions such disgust is inhibited, and those emanations of the body which are usually least honored become religious symbols.

Urine has been regarded as the original holy water, and many customs which still survive in Italy and various parts of Europe, involving the use of a fluid which must often be yellow and sometimes salt, possibly indicate the earlier use of urine. (The Greek water of aspersion, according to Theocritus, was mixed with salt, as is sometimes the modern Italian holy water. J. J. Blunt, *Vestiges of Ancient Manners and Customs*, p. 173.) Among the Hottentots, as Kolbein and others have recorded, the medicine man urinated alternately on bride and bridegroom, and a successful young warrior was sprinkled in the same way. Mungo Park mentions that in Africa on one occasion a bride sent a bowl of her urine which was thrown over him as a special mark of honor to a distinguished guest. Pennant remarked that the Highlanders sprinkled their cattle with urine, as a kind of holy water, on the first Monday in every quarter. (Bourke, *Scatalogic Rites*, pp. 228, 239; Brand, *Popular Antiquities*, "Bride-Ales.")

Even the excreta of animals have sometimes been counted sacred. This is notably so in the case of the cow, of all animals the most venerated by primitive peoples, and especially in India. Jules Bois (*Visions de l'Inde*, p. 86) describes the spectacle presented in the temple of the cows at Benares: "I put my head into the opening of the holy stables. It was the largest of temples, a splendor of precious stones and marble, where the venerated heifers passed backwards and forwards. A whole people adored them. They take no notice, plunged in their divine and obscure unconsciousness. And they fulfil with serenity their animal functions; they chew the offerings, drink water from copper vessels, and when they are filled they relieve themselves. Then a stercoraceous and religious insanity overcomes these starry-faced women and venerable men; they fall on their knees, prostrate themselves, eat the droppings, greedily drink the liquid, which for them is miraculous and sacred." (*Cf.* Bourke, *Scatalogic Rites*, Chapter XVII.)

Among the Chevsurs of the Caucasus, perhaps an Iranian people, a woman after her confinement, for which she lives apart, purifies herself by washing in the urine of a cow and then returns home. This mode of purification is recommended in the Avesta, and is said to be used by the few remaining followers of this creed.

We have not only to take into account the frequency with which among primitive peoples the excretions possess a religious significance. It is further to be noted that in the folk-lore of modern Europe we everywhere find plentiful evidence of the earlier prevalence of legends and practices of a scatalogical character. It is significant that in the majority of cases it is easy to see a sexual reference in these stories and customs. The legends have lost their earlier and often mythical significance, and frequently take on a suggestion of obscenity, while the scatalogical practices have become the magical devices of lovelorn maidens or forsaken wives practiced in secrecy. It has happened to scatalogical rites to be regarded as we may gather from the *Clouds* of Aristophanes, that the sacred leathern phallus borne by the women in the Bacchanalia was becoming in his time, an object to arouse the amusement of little boys.

Among many primitive peoples throughout the world, and among the lower social classes of civilized peoples, urine possesses magic properties, more especially, it would seem, the urine of women and that of people who stand, or wish to stand, in sexual relationship to each other. In a legend of the Indians of the northwest coast of America, recorded by Boas, a woman gives her lover some of her urine and says: "You can wake the dead if you drop some of my urine in their ears and nose." *(Zeitschrift für Ethnologie*, 1894, Heft IV, p. 293.) Among the same Indians there is a legend of a woman with a beautiful white skin who found on bathing every morning in the river that the fish were attracted to her skin and could not be driven off even by magical solutions. At last she said to herself: "I will make water on them and then they will leave me alone." She did so, and henceforth the fish left her. But shortly after fire came from Heaven and killed her. (*Ib.*, 1891, Heft V, p. 640.) Among both Christians and Mohammedans a wife can attach an unfaithful husband by privately putting some of her urine in his drink. (B. Stern, *Medizin in der Türkei*, vol. ii, p. 11.) This practice is world-wide; thus among the aborigines of Brazil, according to Martius, the urine and other excretions and secretions are potent for aphrodisiacal objects. (Bourke's *Scatalogic Rites of All Nations* contains many references to the folk-lore practices in this matter; a study of popular beliefs in the magic power of urine, published in Bombay by Professor Eugen Wilhelm in 1889, I have not seen.)

The legends which narrate scatalogic exploits are numerous in the literature of all countries. Among primitive peoples they often have a purely theological character, for in the popular mythologies of all countries (even, as we learn from Aristophanes, among the Greeks) natural phenomena such as the rain, are apt to be regarded as divine excretions, but in course of time the legends take on a more erotic or a more obscene character. In the Irish *Book of Leinster* (written down somewhere about the twelfth century, but containing material of very much older date) we are told how a number of princesses in Emain Macha, the seat of the Ulster Kings, resolved to find out which of them could by urinating on it melt a snow pillar which the men had made, the woman who succeeded to be regarded as the best among them. None of them succeeded, and they sent for Derbforgaill, who was in love with Cuchullain, and she was able to melt the pillar; whereupon the other women, jealous of the superiority she had thus shown, tore out her eyes. (Zimmer, "Keltische Beiträge," *Zeitschrift für Deutsche Alterthum*, vol.

xxxii, Heft II, pp. 216-219.) Rhys considers that Derbforgaill was really a goddess of dawn and dusk, "the drop glistening in the sun's rays," as indicated by her name, which means a drop or tear. (J. Rhys, *Lectures on the Origin and Growth of Religion as Illustrated by Celtic Heathendom*, p. 466.) It is interesting to compare the legend of Derbforgaill with a somewhat more modern Picardy folk-lore *conte* which is clearly analogous but no longer seems to show any mythologic element, "La Princesse qui pisse par dessus les Meules." This princess had a habit of urinating over hay-cocks; the king, her father, in order to break her of the habit, offered her in marriage to anyone who could make a hay-cock so high that she could not urinate over it. The young men came, but the princess would merely laugh and at once achieve the task. At last there came a young man who argued with himself that she would not be able to perform this feat after she had lost her virginity. He therefore seduced her first and she then failed ignobly, merely wetting her stockings. Accordingly, she became his bride. (Κρυπτάδια, vol. i. p. 333.) Such legends, which have lost any mythologic elements they may originally have possessed and have become merely *contes*, are not uncommon in the folk-lore of many countries. But in their earlier more religious forms and in their later more obscene forms, they alike bear witness to the large place which scatalogic conceptions play in the primitive mind.

It is a notable fact in evidence of the close and seemingly normal association with the sexual impulse of the scatalogic processes, that an interest in them, arising naturally and spontaneously, is one of the most frequent channels by which the sexual impulse first manifests itself in young boys and girls.

Stanley Hall, who has made special inquiries into the matter, remarks that in childhood the products of excretion by bladder and bowels are often objects of interest hardly less intense for a time than eating and drinking. ("Early Sense of Self," *American Journal of Psychology*, April, 1898, p. 361.) "Micturitional obscenities," the same writer observes again, "which our returns show to be so common before adolescence, culminate at 10 or 12, and seem to retreat into the background as sex phenomena appear." They are, he remarks, of two classes: "Fouling persons or things, secretly from adults, but openly with each other," and less often "ceremonial acts connected with the act or the product that almost suggest the scatalogical rites of savages, unfit for description here, but of great interest and importance." (G. Stanley Hall, *Adolescence*, vol. i, p. 116.) The nature of such scatalogical phenomena in childhood—which are often clearly the instinctive manifestations of an erotic symbolism—and their wide prevalence among both boys and girls, are very well illustrated in a narrative which I include in Appendix B, History II.

In boys as they approach the age of puberty, this attraction to the scatalogic, when it exists, tends to die out, giving place to more normal sexual conceptions, or at all events it takes a subordinate and less serious place in the mind. In girls, on the other hand, it often tends to persist. Edmond de Goncourt, a minute observer of the feminine mind, refers in *Chérie* to "those innocent and triumphant gaieties which scatalogic stories have the privilege of arousing in women who have remained still children, even the most distinguished women." The extent to which innocent young women, who would frequently be uninterested or repelled in presence of the sexually obscene are sometimes attracted by the scatalogically obscene, becomes intelligible, however, if we realize that a symbolism comes here into play. In women the more specifically sexual knowledge and experience of life frequently develop much later than in men or even remains in abeyance, and the specifically sexual phenomena cannot therefore easily lend themselves to wit, or humor, or imagination. But the scatalogic sphere, by the very fact that in women it is a specially intimate and secret region which is yet always liable to be unexpectedly protruded into consciousness, furnishes an inexhaustible field for situations which have the same character as those furnished by the sexually obscene. It thus happens that the sexually obscene which in men tends to overshadow the scatalogically obscene, in women—partly from inexperience and partly, it is probable, from their almost physiological modesty—plays a part subordinate to the scatalogical. In a somewhat analogous way scatalogical wit and humor play a considerable part in the work of various eminent authors who were clergymen or priests

In addition to the anatomical and psychological associations which contribute to furnish a basis on which erotic symbolisms may spring up, there are also physiological connections between the genital and urinary spheres which directly favor such symbolisms. In discussing the analysis of the sexual impulse in a previous volume of these *Studies,* I have pointed out the remarkable relationship—sometimes of transference, sometimes of compensation—which exists between genital tension and vesical tension, both in men and women. In the histories of normal sexual development brought together at the end of that and subsequent volumes the relationship may frequently be traced, as also in the case of C. P. in the present study (p. 37). Vesical power is also commonly believed to be in relation with sexual potency, and the inability to project the urinary stream in a normal manner is one of the accepted signs of sexual impotency.[1] Féré, again, has recorded the history of a man with periodic crises of sexual desire, and subsequently sexual obsession without desire, which were always accompanied by the impulse to urinate and by increased urination.[2] In the case, recorded by Pitres and Régis, of a young girl who, having once at the sight of a young man she liked in a theater been overcome by sexual feeling accompanied by a strong desire to urinate, was afterward tormented by a groundless fear of experiencing an irresistible desire to urinate at inconvenient times,[3] we have an example of what may be called a physiological scatalogic symbolism of sex, an emotion which was primarily erotic becoming transferred to the bladder and then remaining persistent. From such a physiological symbolism it is but a step to the psychological symbolisms of scatalogic fetichism.

It is worthy of note, as an indication that such phenomena are scarcely abnormal, that a urinary symbolism, and even a strictly sexual fetichism, are normal among many animals.

---

[1] See, *e.g.,* Morselli, *Una Causa di Nullità del Matrimonio,* 1902, p. 39.

[2] Féré, *Comptes-Rendus Société de Biologie,* July 23, 1904.

[3] Transactions of the International Medical Congress, Moscow, vol. iv, p. 19. A similar symbolism may be traced in many of the cases in which the focus of modesty becomes in modest women centered in the excretory sphere and sometimes exaggerated to the extent of obsession. It must not be supposed, however, that every obsession in this sphere has a symbolical value of an erotic kind. In the case, for instance, which has been recorded by Raymond and Janet (*Les Obsessions,* vol. ii, p. 306) of a woman who spent much of her time in the endeavor to urinate perfectly, always feeling that she failed in some respect, the

The most familiar example of this kind is furnished by the dog, who is sexually excited in this manner by traces of the bitch and himself takes every opportunity of making his own path recognizable. "This custom," Espinas remarks (*Des Sociétés Animales*, p. 228), "has no other aim than to spread along the road recognizable traces of their presence for the benefit of individuals of the other sex, the odor of these traces doubtless causing excitement."

It is noteworthy, also, that in animals as well as in man, sexual excitement may manifest itself in the bladder. Thus Daumas states (*Chevaux de Sahara*, p. 49) that if the mare urinates when she hears the stallion neigh it is a sign that she is ready for connection.

It is in masochism, or passive algolagnia, that we may most frequently find scatalogic symbolism in its fully developed form. The man whose predominant impulse is to subjugate himself to his mistress and to receive at her hands the utmost humiliation, frequently finds the climax of his gratification in being urinated on by her, whether in actual fact or only in imagination.

In many such cases, however, it is evident that we have a mixed phenomenon; the symbolism is double. The act becomes desirable because it is the outward and visible sign of an inwardly experienced abject slavery to an adored person. But it is also desirable because of intimately sexual associations in the act itself, as a symbolical detumescence, a simulacrum of the sexual act, and one which proceeds from the sexual focus itself.

Krafft-Ebing records various cases of masochism in which the emission of urine on to the body or into the mouth formed the climax of sexual gratification, as, for instance (*Psychopathia Sexualis*, English translation, p. 183) in the case of a Russian official who as a boy had fancies of being bound between the thighs of a woman, compelled to sleep beneath her nates and to drink her urine, and in later life experienced the greatest excitement when practicing the last part of this early imagination.

In another case, recorded by Krafft-Ebing and by him termed "ideal masochism" (*Op. cit.*, pp. 127-130), the subject from childhood indulged in voluptuous day-dreams in which he was the slave of a beautiful mistress who would compel him to obey all her caprices, stand over him with one foot on his breast, sit on his face and body, make him

---

obsession seems to have risen fortuitously on a somewhat neurotic basis without reference to the sexual life.

wait on her in her bath, or when she urinated, and sometimes insist on doing this on his face; though a highly intellectual man, he was always too timid to attempt to carry any of his ideas into execution; he had been troubled by nocturnal enuresis up to the age of 20.

Neri, again (*Archivio delle Psicopatie Sessuali*, vol. i, fasc. 7 and 8, 1896), records the case of an Italian masochist who experienced the greatest pleasure when both urination and defecation were practiced in this manner by the woman he was attached to.

In a previous volume of these *Studies* ("Sexual Inversion," History XXVI) I have recorded the masochistic day-dreams of a boy whose impulses were at the same time inverted; in his reveries "the central fact," he states, "became the discharge of urine from my lover over my body and limbs, or, if I were very fond of him, I let it be in my face." In actual life the act of urination casually witnessed in childhood became the symbol, even the reality, of the central secret of sex: "I stood rooted and flushing with downcast eyes till the act was over, and was conscious for a considerable time of stammering speech and bewildered faculties. . . . I was overwhelmed with emotion and could barely drag my feet from the spot or my eyes from the damp herbage where he had deposited the waters of secrecy. Even to-day I cannot dissociate myself from the shuddering charm that moment had for me."

It is not only the urine and the fæces which may thus acquire a symbolic fascination and attractiveness under the influence of masochistic deviations of sexual idealization. In some cases extreme rapture has been experienced in licking sweating feet. There is, indeed, no excretion or product of the body which has not been a source of ecstasy: the sweat from every part of the body, the saliva and menstrual fluid, even the wax from the ears.

Krafft-Ebing very truly points out (*Psychopathia Sexualis*, English translation, p 178) that this sexual scatalogic symbolism is precisely paralleled by a religious scatalogic symbolism. In the excesses of devout enthusiasm the ascetic performs exactly the same acts as are performed in these excesses of erotic enthusiasm. To mix excreta with the food, to lick up excrement, to suck festering sores—all these and the like are acts which holy and venerated women have performed.

Not only the saint, but also the prophet and medicine-man have been frequently eaters of human excrement; it is only necessary to refer to the instance of the prophet Ezekiel, who declared that he was commanded to bake his bread with human dung, and to the practices of medicine-men at Torres Straits, in whose training the eating of human excrement takes a recognized part. (Deities, notably Baal-Phegor, were sometimes supposed to eat excrement, so that it was natural that their messengers and representatives among men should do so. As regards Baal-Phegor, see Dulaure, *Des Divinités Génératrices*, Chapter IV, and J. G. Bourke, *Scatalogic Rites of All Nations*, p. 241. See also Ezekiel, Chapter IV, v. 12, and *Reports Anthropological Expedition to Torres Straits*, vol. v, p. 321.)

It must be added, however, that while the masochist is overcome by sexual rapture, so that he sees nothing disgusting in his act, the medicine-man and the ascetic are not so invariably overcome by religious rapture, and several ascetic writers have referred to the horror and disgust they experienced, at all events at first, in accomplishing such acts, while the medicine-men when novices sometimes find the ordeal too severe and have to abandon their career. Brénier de Montmorand, while remarking, not without some exaggeration, that "the Christian ascetics are almost all eaters of excrement" ("Ascétisme et Mysticisme," *Revue Philosophique*, March, 1904, p. 245), quotes the testimonies of Marguerite-Marie and Madame Guyon as to the extreme repugnance which they had to overcome. They were impelled by a merely intellectual symbolism of self-mortification rather than by the profoundly felt emotional symbolism which moves the masochist.

Coprophagic acts, whether under the influences of religious exaltation or of sexual rapture, inevitably excite our disgust. We regard them as almost insane, fortified in that belief by the undoubted fact that coprophagia is not uncommon among the insane. It may, therefore, be proper to point out that it is not so very long since the ingestion of human excrement was carried out by our own forefathers in the most sane and deliberate manner. It was administered by medical practitioners for a great number of ailments, apparently with entirely satisfactory results. Less than two centuries ago, Schurig, who so admirably gathered together and arranged the medical lore of his own and the immediately preceding ages, wrote a very long and detailed chapter, "De Stercoris Humani Usu Medico" (*Chylologia*, 1725, cap. XIII; in the Paris *Journal de Médecine* for February 19, 1905, there appeared an article, which I have not seen, entitled "Médicaments oubliées: l'urine et la fiente humaine.") The classes of cases in which the drug was found beneficial would seem to have been extremely various. It must not be supposed that it was usually ingested in the crude form. A common method was to take the fæces of boys, dry them, mix them with the best honey, and administer an an electuary. (At an earlier period such drugs appear to have met with some opposition from the Church, which seems to have seen in them only an application of magic; thus I note that in Burchard's remarkable Penitential of the fourteenth century, as reproduced by Wasserschleben, 40 days' penance is prescribed for the use of human urine or excrement as a medicine. Wasserschleben *Die Bussordnungen der Abendländlicher Kirche*, p. 651.)

The urolagnia of masochism is not a simple phenomenon; it embodies a double symbolism: on the one hand a symbolism of self-abnegation, such as the ascetic feels, on the other hand a symbolism of transferred sexual emotion. Krafft-Ebing was disposed to regard all cases in which a scatalogical sexual attraction existed as due to "latent masochism." Such a point of view is quite untenable. Certainly the connection is common, but in the majority of cases of slightly marked scatalogical fetichism no masochism is evident. And when we bear in mind the various considerations, already brought forward, which show how widespread and clearly realized is the natural and normal basis furnished for such symbolism, it becomes quite unnecessary to invoke any aid from masochism. There is ample evidence to show that, either as a habitual or more usually an occasional act, the impulse to bestow a symbolic value on the act of urination in a beloved person, is not extremely uncommon; it has been noted of men of high intellectual distinction; it occurs in women as well as men; when existing in only a slight degree, it must be regarded as within the normal limits of variation of sexual emotion.

The occasional cases in which the urine is drunk may possibly suggest that the motive lies in the properties of the fluid acting on the system. Support for this supposition might be found in the fact that urine actually does possess, apart altogether from its magic virtues embodied in folk-lore, the properties of a general stimulant. In composition (as Masterman first pointed out) "beef-tea differs little from healthy urine," containing exactly the same constituents, except that in beef-tea there is less urea and uric acid. Fresh urine—more especially that of children and young women—is taken as a medicine in nearly all parts of the world for various disorders, such as epistaxis, malaria and hysteria, with benefit, this benefit being almost certainly due to its qualities as a general stimulant and restorative. William Salmon's *Dispensatory*, 1678 (quoted in *British Medical Journal*, April 21, 1900, p. 974), shows that in the seventeenth century urine still occupied an important place as a medicine, and it frequently entered largely into the composition of Aqua Divina. Its use has been known even in England in the nineteenth century. (Masterman, *Lancet*, October 2, 1880; R. Neale, "Urine as a Medicine," *Practitioner*, November, 1881; Bourke brings together a great deal of evidence as to the therapeutic uses of urine in his *Scatalogic Rites*, especially pp. 331-335; Lusini has shown that normal urine invariably increases the frequency of the heart beats, *Archivio di Farmacologia*, fascs. 19-21, 1893.)

But it is an error to suppose that these facts account for the urolagnic drinking of urine. As in the gratification of a normal sexual impulse, the intense excitement of gratifying a scatalogic sexual impulse itself produces a degree of emotional stimulation far greater than the ingestion of a small amount of animal extractives would be adequate to effect. In such cases, as much as in normal sexuality, the stimulation is clearly psychic.

When, as is most commonly the case, it is the process of urination and not the urine itself which is attractive, we are clearly concerned with a symbolism of act and not with the fetichistic attraction of an excretion. When the excretion, apart from the act, provides the attraction, we seem usually to be in the presence of an olfactory fetichism. These fetichisms connected with the excreta appear to be experienced chiefly by individuals who are somewhat weak-minded, which is not necessarily the case in regard to those persons for whom the act, rather than its product apart from the beloved person, is the attractive symbol.

The sexually symbolic nature of the act of urination for many people is indicated by the existence, according to Bloch, who enumerates various kinds of indecent photographs, of a group which he terms "the notorious *pisseuses.*" It is further indicated by several of the reproductions in Fuch's *Erotsiche Element in der Karikatur*, such as Delorme's "La Necessité n'a point de Loi." (It should be added that such a scene by no means necessarily possesses any erotic symbolism, as we may see in Rembrandt's etching commonly called "Le Femme qui Pisse," in which the reflected lights on the partly shadowed stream furnish an artistic motive which is obviously free from any trace of obscenity.) In the case which Krafft-Ebing quotes from Maschka of a young man who would induce young girls to dance naked in his room, to leap, and to urinate in his presence, whereupon seminal ejaculation would take place, we have a typical example of urolagnic symbolism in a form adequate to produce complete gratification. A case in which the urolagnic form of scatalogic symbolism reached its fullest development as a sexual perversion has been described in Russia by Sukhanoff (summarized in *Archives d'Anthropologie Criminelle*, November, 1900, and *Annales Medico-psychologiques*, February, 1901), that of a young man of 27, of neuropathic temperament, who when he once chanced to witness a woman urinating experienced voluptuous sensations. From that moment he sought close contact with women urinating, the maximum of gratification being reached when he could place himself in such a position that a woman, in all innocence, would urinate into his mouth. All his amorous adventures were concerned with the search for opportunities for procuring this difficult gratification. Closets in which he was able to hide, winter weather and dull days he found most favorable to success. (A somewhat similar case is recorded in the *Archives de Neurologie*, 1902, p. 462.)

In the case of a robust man of neuropathic heredity recorded by Pelanda some light is shed on the psychic attitude in these manifestations; there was masturbation up to the age of 16, when he abandoned the practice, and up to the age of 30 found complete satisfaction in drinking the still hot urine of women. When a lady or girl in the house went to her room to satisfy a need of this kind, she had hardly left it but he hastened in, overcome by extreme excitement, culminating in spontaneous ejaculation. The younger the woman the greater the transport he experienced. It is noteworthy that in this, as possibly in all similar cases, there was no sensory perversion and no morbid attraction of taste or smell; he stated that the action of his senses was suspended by his excitement, and that he was quite unable to perceive the odor or taste of the fluid. (Pelenda, "Pornopatice," *Archivio di Psichiatria*, facs. iii-iv, 1889, p. 356.) It is in the emotional symbolism that the fascination lies and not in any sensory perversion.

Magnan records the spontaneous development of this sexual symbolism in a girl of 11, of good intellectual development but alcoholic heredity, who seduced a boy younger than herself to mutual masturbation, and on one occasion, lying on the ground and raising her clothes, asked him to urinate on her. (*International Congress of Criminal Anthropology*, 1889.) This case (except for the early age of the subject) illustrates sporadically occurring urolagnic symbolism in a woman, to whom such symbolism is fairly obvious on account of the close resemblance between the emission of urine and the ejaculation of semen In the man, and the fact that the same conduit serves for both fluids. (A urolagnic day-dream of this kind is recorded in the history of a lady contained in the third volume of these *Studies*, Appendix B, History VIII.) The natural and inevitable character of this symbolism is shown by the fact that among primitive peoples urine is sometimes supposed to possess the fertilizing virtues of semen. J. G. Frazer in his edition of Pausanias (vol. iv, p. 139) brings together various stories of women impregnated by urine. Hartland also (*Legend of Perseus*, vol. i, pp. 76, 92) records legends of women who were impregnated by accidentally or intentionally drinking urine.

The symbolic sexual significance of urolagnia has hitherto usually been confused with the fetichistic and mainly olfactory perversion by which the excretion itself becomes a source of sexual excitement. Long since Tardieu referred, under the name of "renifleurs," to persons who were said to haunt the neighborhood of quiet passages, more especially in the neighborhood of theatres, and who when they perceived a woman emerge after urination, would hasten to excite themselves by the odor of the excretion. Possibly a fetichism of this kind existed in a case recorded by Belletrud and Mercier (*Annales d'Hygiène Publique*, June, 1904, p. 48). A weak-minded, timid youth, who was very sexual but not attractive to women, would watch for women who were about to urinate and immediately they had passed on would go and lick the spot they had moistened, at the same time masturbating. Such a fetichistic perversion is strictly analogous to the fetichism by which women's handkerchiefs, aprons or underlinen become capable of affording sexual gratification. A very complete case of such urolagnic fetichism—complete because separated from association with the person accomplishing the act of urination—has been recorded by Moraglia in a woman. It is the case of a beautiful and attractive young woman of 18, with thick black hair, and expressive vivacious eyes, but sallow complexion. Married a year previously, but childless, she experienced a certain amount of pleasure in coitus, but she preferred masturbation, and frankly acknowledged that she was highly excited by the odor of fermented urine. So strong was this fetichism that when, for instance, she passed a street urinal she was often obliged to go aside and masturbate; once she went for this purpose into the urinal itself and was almost discovered in the act, and on another occasion into a church. Her perversion caused her much worry because of the fear of detection. She preferred, when she could, to obtain a bottle of urine—which must be stale and a man's (this, she said, she could detect by the smell)—and to shut herself up in her own room, holding the bottle in one hand and repeatedly masturbating with the other. (Moraglia, "Psicopatie Sessuali," *Archivio di Psichiatria*, vol. xiii, fasc. 6, p. 267, 1892.) This case is of especial interest because of the great rarity of fully developed fetichism in women. In a slight and germinal degree I believe that cases of fetichism are not uncommon in women, but they are certainly rare in a well-marked form, and Krafft-Ebing declared, even in the late editions of his *Psychopathia Sexualis*, that he knew of no cases in women.

So far we have been concerned with the urolagnic rather than the coprolagnic variety of scatalogical symbolism. Although the two are sometimes associated there is no necessary connection, and most usually there is no tendency for the one to involve the other. Urolagnia is certainly much the more frequently found; the act of urination is far more apt to suggest erotically symbolical ideas than the idea of defecation. It is not difficult to understand why this should be so. The act of urination lends itself more easily to sexual symbolism; it is more intimately associated with the genital function; its repetition is necessary at more frequent intervals so that it is more in evidence; moreover, its product, unlike that of the act of defecation, is not offensive to the senses. Still coprolagnia occurs and not so very infrequently. Burton remarked that even the normal lover is affected by this feeling: "immo nec ipsum amicæ stercus foetet."[1]

Of Caligula who, however, was scarcely sane, it was said "et quidem stercus uxoris degustavit."[2] In Parisian brothels (according to Taxil and others) provision is made for those who are sexually excited by the spectacle of the act of defecation (without reference to contact or odor) by means of a "tabouret de verre," from under the glass floor of which the spectacle of the defecating women may be closely observed. It may be added that the erotic nature of such a spectacle is referred to in the Marquis de Sade's novels.

There is one motive for the existence of coprolagnia which must not be passed over, because it has doubtless frequently served as a mode of transition to what, taken by itself, may well seem the least æsthetically attractive of erotic symbols. I refer to the tendency of the nates to become a sexual fetich. The nates have in all ages and in all parts of the world been frequently regarded as one of the most æsthetically beautiful parts of the feminine body.[3] It is probable that on the basis of this entirely normal attraction more than one form of erotic sym-

[1] *Anatomy of Melancholy*, Part III, Section II, Mem. III, Subs. I.

[2] It may be remarked here that while the eating of excrement (apart from its former use as a magic charm and as a therapeutic agent) is in civilization now confined to sexual perverts and the insane, among some animals it is normal as a measure of hygiene in relation to their young. Thus, as, *e.g.*, the Rev. Arthur East writes, the mistle thrush swallows the droppings of its young. (*Knowledge*, June 1, 1899, p. 133.) In the dog I have observed that the bitch licks her puppies shortly after birth as they urinate, absorbing the fluid.

[3] See, *e.g.*, the previous volume of these *Studies*, "Sexual Selection in Man," pp. 165 *et seq.*, and Dühren, *Geschlectsleben in England*, bd. ii, pp. 258, *et seq.*

bolism is at all events in part supported. Dühren and others have considered that the æsthetic charm of the nates is one of the motives which prompt the desire to inflict flagellation on women. In the same way—certainly in some and probably in many cases—the sexual charm of the nates progressively extends to the anal region, to the act of defecation, and finally to the feces.

In a case of Krafft-Ebing's (*Op. cit.*, p. 183) the subject, when a child of 6, accidentally placed his hand in contact with the nates of the little girl who sat next to him in school, and experienced so great a pleasure in this contact that he frequently repeated it; when he was 10 a nursery governess, to gratify her own desires, placed his finger in her vagina; in adult life he developed urolagnic tendencies.

In a case of Moll's the development of a youthful admiration for the nates in a coprolagnic direction may be clearly traced. In this case a young man, a merchant, in a good position, sought to come in contact with women defecating; and with this object would seek to conceal himself in closets; the excretal odor was pleasurable to him, but was not essential to gratification, and the sight of the nates was also exciting and at the same time not essential to gratification; the act of defecation appears, however, to have been regarded as essential. He never sought to witness prostitutes in this situation; he was only attracted to young, pretty and innocent women. The coprolagnia here, however, had its source in a childish impression of admiration for the nates. When 5 or 6 years old he crawled under the clothes of a servant girl, his face coming in contact with her nates, an impression that remained associated in his mind with pleasure. Three or four years later he used to experience much pleasure when a young girl cousin sat on his face; thus was strengthened an association which developed naturally into coprolagnia. (Moll, *Untersuchungen über die Libido Sexualis*, bd. i, p. 837.)

It is scarcely necessary to remark that an admiration for the nates, even when reaching a fetichistic degree, by no means necessarily involves, even after many years, any attraction to the excreta. A correspondent for whom the nates have constituted a fetich for many years writes: "I find my craving for women with profuse pelvic or posterior development is growing and I wish to copulate from behind; but I would feel a sickening feeling if any part of my person came in contact with the female anus. It is more pleasing to me to see the nates than the mons, yet I loathe everything associated with the anal region."

Moll has recorded in detail a case of what may be described as "ideal coprolagnia"—that is to say, where the symbolism, though fully developed in imagination, was not carried into real life—which is of great interest because it shows how, in a very intelligent subject, the deviated symbolism may become highly developed and irradiate all the views of life in the same way as the normal impulse. (The subject's desires were also inverted, but from the present point of view the psychological interest of the case is not thereby impaired.) Moll's case was one of symbolism of act, the excreta offering no attraction apart from the process of defecation. In a case which has been communicated to me there was, on the other hand, an olfactory fetichistic attraction to the excreta even in the absence of the person.

In Moll's case, the patient, X., 23 years of age, belongs to a family which he himself describes as nervous. His mother, who is anæmic, has long suffered from almost periodical attacks of excitement, weakness, syncope and palpitation. A brother of the mother died in a lunatic asylum, and several other brothers complain much of their nerves. The mother's sisters are very good-natured, but liable to break out in furious passions; this they inherit from their father. There appears to be no nervous disease on the patient's father's side. X.'s sisters are also healthy.

X. himself is of powerful undersized build and enjoys good health, injured by no excesses. He considers himself nervous. He worked hard at school and was always the first in his class; he adds, however, that this is due less to his own abilities than the laziness of his schoolfellows. He is, as he remarks, very religious and prays frequently, but seldom goes to church.

In regard to his psychic characters he says that he has no specially prominent talent, but is much interested in languages, mathematics, physics and philosophy, in fact, in abstract subjects generally. "While I take a lively interest in every kind of intellectual work," he says, "it is only recently that I have been attracted to real life and its requirements. I have never had much skill in physical exercises. For external things until recently I have only had contempt. I have a delicately constituted nature, loving solitude, and only associating with a few select persons. I have a decided taste for fiction, poetry and music; my temperament is idealistic and religious, with strict conceptions of duty and morality, and aspirations towards the good and beautiful. I detest all that is common and coarse, and yet I can think and act in the way you will learn from the following pages."

Regarding his sexual life, X. made the following communication: "During the last two years I have become convinced of the perversion of my sexual instinct. I had often previously thought that in me the impulse was not quite normal, but it is only lately that I have become convinced of my complete perversion. I have never read or heard of any case in which the sexual feelings were of the same kind. Although I can feel a lively inclination towards superior representatives of the female sex, and have twice felt something like love, the sight or the recollection even of a beautiful woman have never caused sexual excitement." In the two exceptional instances mentioned it appears that X. had an inclination to kiss the women in question, but that the thought of coitus had no attraction. "In my voluptuous dreams, connected with the emission of semen, women in seductive situations have never appeared. I have never had any desire to visit a *puella publica*. The love-stories of my fellow-students seemed very silly, dances and balls were a horror to me, and only on very rare occasions could I be persuaded to go into society. It will be easy to guess the diagnosis in my case: I suffer from the sexual attraction of my own sex, I am a lover of boys.

"You cannot imagine what a world of thoughts, wishes, feelings and impulses the words 'knabe,' 'παις,' 'garcon,' 'boy,' 'ragazzo' have for me; one of these words, even in an unmeaning clause of a translation-book, calls before me the whole sum of associations which in course of time have become bound up with this idea, and it is only with an effort that I can scare away the wild band. This group of thoughts shows a wonderful mixture of warm sensuality and ideal love, it unites my lowest and highest impulses, the strength and the weakness of my nature, my curse and my blessing. My inclination is especially towards boys of the age of 12 to 15; though they may be rather younger or older. That I should prefer beautiful and intelligent boys is comprehensible. I do not want a prostitute, but a friend or a son, whose soul I love, whom I can help to become a more perfect man, such as I myself would willingly be.

"When I myself belonged to that happy age (*i.e.*, below 15) I had no dearer wish than to possess a friend of similar tastes. I have sought, hoped, waited, grieved, and been at last disillusioned, overcome by desire and despair, and have not found that friend. Even later the hope often reappeared, but always in vain, and I cannot boast of that sure recognition which one reads of in the autobiographies of Urnings. I do not know personally a single fellow-sufferer. It is also doubtful whether such an acquaintanceship would greatly help me, for I have a very peculiar conception of homosexuality. As you will see, I have little more in common with what are called pæderasts than sexual indifference to the female sex, and I often ask myself: 'Does any other man in the whole world feel like you? Are you alone in the earth with your morbid desires? Are you a pariah of pariahs, or is there, perhaps, another soul with similar longings living near you? How often in summer have I gone to the lakes and streams outside cities to seek boys bathing; but I always came back unsatisfied, whether I found any or not. And in winter I have been irresistibly impelled to return to the same spots, as if it were sanctified by the boys, but my darlings had vanished and cold winds blew over the icy floods, so that I would return feeling as though I had buried all my happiness.

"It must be borne in mind, therefore, that what I have to say regarding my sexual impulses only refers to fancies and never to their practical realization. My sensual impulses are not connected with the sexual organs; all my voluptuous ideas are not in the least connected with these parts. For this reason I have never practiced onanism and *immissio membri in anum* is as repulsive to me as to a normal man. Even every imitation of coitus is, for me, without attraction. In a boy's body two things specially excite me: *his belly and his nates*, the first as containing the digestive tract, the second as holding the opening of the bowels. Of the vegetable processes of life in the boy none interest me nearly so much as the progress of his digestion and the process of defecation. It is incredible to what an extent this part of physiology has occupied me from youth. If as a boy I wanted to read something of a piquantly exciting character I sought in my father's encyclopædia for articles like: Obstruction, Constipation, Hæmorrhoids, Fæces, etc. No function of the body seemed to be so significant as this, and I regarded its disturbances as the most important in the whole mechanism of life. The description of other disorders I could read in cold blood, but intussusception of the bowels makes me ill even to-day. I am always extremely pleased to hear that the digestion of the people around me is in good condition. A man who did not sufficiently watch over his digestion aroused distrust in me, and I imagined that wicked men must be horribly indifferent regarding this weighty matter. Even more than in ordinary persons was I interested in the digestion of more mysterious beings, like magicians in legends, or men of other nations. I would willingly have made an anthropological study of my favorite subject, only to my annoyance books nearly always pass over the matter in silence. In history and fiction I regretted the absence of information concerning the state of my heroes' digestion when they languished in prison or in some unaccustomed or unhealthy spot. For this reason I held no book more precious than one which describes how a young man after being shipwrecked lived for a long time in a narrow snow-hut, and it was conscientiously stated that he became aware of digestive disturbances. No immorality angers me more than the foolish practice of ladies who in society neglect the satisfaction of their natural needs from misplaced motives of modesty. On a railway journey I suffer horribly from the thought that one of my fellow-travelers may be prevented from fulfilling some imperative natural necessity.

"I naturally devote the greatest attention to my own digestion. With painful conscientiousness I go to stool every day at the same

hour; if the operation does not come off to my satisfaction I feel not
so much physical as mental discomfort. To this quite useful hygienic
interest became associated at puberty a sensual interest. Since my fourteenth year I have had no greater enjoyment than to defecate undressed
(I do not do so now) after having first carefully examined the disten-
sion of my abdomen. In summer I would go into the woods, undress
myself in a secluded spot and indulge in the voluptuous pleasures of
defecation. I would sometimes combine with this a bath in a stream.
I would exhaust my imagination in the effort to invent specially enjoy-
able variations, longed for a desert island where I could go about naked,
fill my body with much nourishing food, hold in the excrement as long
as possible and then discharge it in some subtly-thought-out spot. These
practices and ideas often caused erections and later on emissions, but
the genitals played no part in my conceptions; their movements were
uncomfortable and gave no pleasure.

"I soon longed to be associated in these orgies with some boy of the
same age, but I wanted not only a companion in my passion, but also a
real friend. Since there could be no question of masturbation or pæder-
asty, our love would have been limited to kisses, embraces, and—as a
compensation for coitus—defecation together. That would have been
perfect bliss to me. I will spare you the unæsthetic contents of my
voluptuous dreams. But I remained without a companion, and, therefore, without real enjoyment. [He has, however, on various occasions
experienced erections, and even emissions, on seeing, by chance, men or
boys defecate.] Hinc illæ lacrimæ; the excitement over my own defecation only took place *faute de mieux.*

"I knew very well that my thoughts and practices were impure and
contemptible. Ah! how often, when the intoxication was over, have
I thrown myself remorsefully on my knees, praying to God for pardon!
For some weeks I repressed my longing; but at last it was too strong
for me, I tried to justify myself and fell into my vice anew. That I was
guilty of licentiousness and loved boys sexually first became clear to me
later on, when I knew the significance of erection as a sign of sexual
excitement.

"No one can imagine with what demoniacal joy I am possessed at
the thought of a beautiful naked boy whose abdomen is filled as the
result of long abstinence from stool. The thought powerfully excites
me, a flood of passion goes through my blood and my limbs tremble. I
would never grow tired of feeling that belly and looking at it. My
passion would express itself in tempestuous caresses, and the boy would
have to assume various positions in order to show off the beauty of
his form, *i.e.,* to bring the parts in question into better view. To observe
defecation would still further increase this peculiar enjoyment. If the
boy's bowels were not sufficiently filled I would feed him with all sorts

of food which produces much excrement, such as potatoes, coarse bread, etc. If possible I would seek to delay defecation for two or three days, so that it might be as copious as possible. When at last it occurred it would be an unspeakable joy for me to watch the fæces—which would have to be fairly firm—emerging from the anus."

X. would like to be a teacher and thinks he could exert a beneficial influence on boys. In spite of the pain he has suffered he does not think he would like to be cured of his perverse inclinations, for they have given him joy as well as pain, and the pain has chiefly been owing to the fact that he could not gratify his inclinations. X. smokes and drinks in moderation, and has no feminine habits. (The foregoing is a condensed summary of the case which is fully reported by Moll, *Konträre Sexualempfindung*, third edition, pp. 295-305.)

The case of coprolagnia communicated to me is that of a married man, normal in all other respects, intellectually brilliant and filling successfully a very responsible position. When a child the women of his household were always indifferent as to his presence in their bed-rooms, and would satisfy all natural calls without reserve before him. He would dream of this with erections. His sexual interests became slowly centered in the act of defecation, and this fetich throughout life never appealed to him so powerfully as when associated with the particular type of household furniture which was used for this purpose in his own house. The act of defecation in the opposite sex or anything pertaining to or suggesting the same caused uncontrollable sexual excitement; the nates also exerted a great attraction. The alvine excreta exerted this influence even in the absence of the woman; it was, however, necessary that she should be a sexually desirable person. The perversion in this case was not complete; that is to say, that the excitement produced by the act of defecation or the excretion itself was not actually preferred to coitus; the sexual idea was normal coitus in the normal manner, but preceded by the visual and olfactory enjoyment of the exciting fetich. When coitus was not possible the enjoyment of the fetich was accompanied by masturbation (as in the analogous case of urolagnia in a woman summarized on p. 62.) On one occasion he was discovered by a friend in a bedroom belonging to a woman, engaged in the act of masturbation over a vessel containing the desired fetich. In an agony of shame he begged the mercy of silence concerning this episode, at the same time revealing his life-history. He has constantly been haunted by the dread of detection, as well as by remorse and the consciousness of degradation, also by the fear that his unconquerable obsession may lead him to the asylum.

The scatalogic groups of sexual perversions, urolagnia and coprolagnia, as may be sufficiently seen in this brief summary, are not merely olfactory fetiches. They are, in a larger proportion of cases, dynamic symbols, a preoccupation with physiological acts which, by associations of contiguity and still more of resemblance, have gained the virtue of stimulating in slight cases, and replacing in more extreme cases, the normal preoccupation with the central physiological act itself. We have seen that there are various considerations which amply suffice to furnish a basis for such associations. And when we reflect that in the popular mind, and to some extent in actual fact, the sexual act itself is, like urination and defecation, an excretory act, we can understand that the true excretory acts may easily become symbols of the pseudo-excretory act. It is, indeed, in the muscular release of accumulated pressures and tensions, involved by the act of liberating the stored-up excretion, that we have the closest simulacrum of the tumescence and detumescence of the sexual process.[1]

In this way the erotic symbolism of urolagnia and coprolagnia is completely analogous with that dynamic symbolism of the clinging and swinging garments which Herrick has so accurately described, with the complex symbolism of flagellation and its play of the rod against the blushing and trembling nates, with the symbols of sexual strain and stress which are embodied in the foot and the act of treading.

---

[1] In the study of *Love and Pain* in a previous volume (p. 130) I have quoted the remarks of a lady who refers to the analogy between sexual tension and vesical tension—"Cette volupté que ressentent les bords de la mer, d'être toujours pleins sans jamais déborder"—and its erotic significance.

IV.

Animals as Sources of Erotic Symbolism—Mixoscopic Zoophilia—The Stuff-fetichism—Hair-fetichism—The Stuff-fetichisms Mainly on a Tactile Base—Erotic Zoophilia—Zooerastia—Bestiality—The Conditions that Favor Bestiality—Its Wide Prevalence Among Primitive Peoples and Among Peasants—The Primitive Conception of Animals—The Goat—The Influence of Familiarity with Animals—Congress Between Women and Animals—The Social Reaction Against Bestiality.

THE erotic symbols with which we have so far been concerned have in every case been portions of the body, or its physiological processes, or at least the garments which it has endowed with life. The association on which the symbol has arisen has in every case been in large measure, although not entirely, an association of contiguity. It is now necessary to touch on a group of sexual symbols in which the association of contiguity with the human body is absent: the various methods by which animals or animal products or the sight of animal copulation may arouse sexual desire in human persons. Here we encounter a symbolism mainly founded on association by resemblance; the animal sexual act recalls the human sexual act; the animal becomes the symbol of the human being.

The group of phenomena we are here concerned with includes several sub-divisions. There is first the more or less sexual pleasure sometimes experienced, especially by young persons, in the sight of copulating animals. This I would propose to call Mixoscopic Zoophilia; it falls within the range of normal variation. Then we have the cases in which the contact of animals, stroking, etc., produces sexual excitement or gratification; this is a sexual fetichism in the narrow sense, and is by Krafft-Ebing termed *Zoophilia Erotica.* We have, further, the class of cases in which a real or simulated sexual intercourse with animals is desired. Such cases are not regarded as fetichism by Krafft-

Ebing,[1] but they come within the phenomena of erotic symbolism as here understood. This class falls into two divisions: one in which the individual is fairly normal, but belongs to a low grade of culture; the other in which he may belong to a more refined social class, but is affected by a deep degree of degeneration. In the first case we may properly apply the term bestiality; in the second case it may perhaps be better to use the term *zooerastia,* proposed by Krafft-Ebing.[2]

Among children, both boys and girls, it is common to find that the copulation of animals is a mysteriously fascinating spectacle. It is inevitable that this should be so, for the spectacle is more or less clearly felt to be the revelation of a secret which has been concealed from them. It is, moreover, a secret of which they feel intimate reverberations within themselves, and even in perfectly innocent and ignorant children the sight may produce an obscure sexual excitement.[3] It would seem that this occurs more frequently in girls than in boys. Even in adult age, it may be added, women are liable to experience the same kind of emotion in the presence of such spectacles. One lady recalls, as a girl, that on several occasions an element of physical excitement entered into the feelings with which she watched the coquetry of cats. Another lady mentions that at the age of about 25, and when still quite ignorant of sexual matters, she saw from a window some boys tickling a dog and inducing sexual excitement in the animal; she vaguely divined what they were doing, and though feeling disgust at their conduct she at the same time experienced in a strong degree what she now knows was sexual excitement. The coupling of the larger animals is

---

[1] For Krafft-Ebing's discussion of the subject see *Op. cit.,* pp. 530-539.

[2] In England it is not uncommon to use the term "unnatural offence;" this is an awkward and possibly misleading practice which should not be followed. In Germany a similar confusion is caused by applying the term "sodomy" to these cases as well as to pederasty. Krafft-Ebing considers that this error is due to the jurists, while the theologians have always distinguished correctly. In this matter, he adds, science must be *ancilla theologiæ* and return to the correct usage of words.

[3] This childish interest, with later abnormal developments, may be seen in History I of the Appendix to this volume.

often an impressive and splendid spectacle which is far, indeed, from being obscene, and has commended itself to persons of intellectual distinction;[1] but in young or ill-balanced minds such sights tend to become both prurient and morbid. I have already referred to the curious case of a sexually hyperæsthetic nun who was always powerfully excited by the sight or even the recollection of flies in sexual connection, so that she was compelled to masturbate; this dated from childhood. After becoming a nun she recorded having had this experience, followed by masturbation, more than four hundred times.[2] Animal spectacles sometimes produce a sexual effect on children even when not specifically sexual; thus a correspondent, a clergyman, informs me that when a young and impressionable boy, he was much affected by seeing a veterinary surgeon insert his hand and arm into a horse's rectum, and dreamed of this several times afterward with emissions.

While the contemplation of animal coitus is an easily intelligible and in early life, perhaps, an almost normal symbol of sexual emotion, there is another sub-division of this group of animal fetichisms which forms a more natural transition from the fetichisms which have their center in the human body: the stuff-fetichisms, or the sexual ·attraction exerted by various tissues, perhaps always of animal origin. Here we are in the presence of a somewhat complicated phenomenon. In part we have,

---

[1] The Countess of Pembroke, Sir Philip Sidney's sister, appears to have found sexual enjoyment in the contemplation of the sexual prowess of stallions. Aubrey writes that she "was very salacious and she had a contrivance that in the spring of the year . . . the stallions . . . were to be brought before such a part of the house where she had a vidette to look on them." (*Short Lives*, 1898, vol. i, p. 311.) Although the modern editor's modesty has caused the disappearance of several lines from this passage, the general sense is clear. In the same century Burchard, the faithful secretary of Pope Alexander VI, describes in his invaluable diary how four race horses were brought to two mares in a court of the Vatican, the horses clamorously fighting for the possession of the mares and eventually mounting them, while the Pope and his daughter Lucrezia looked on from a window "cum magno risu et delectatione." (*Diarium*, ed Thuasne, vol. III, p. 169.)

[2] *Archivio di Psichiatria*, 1902, fasc. ii-iii, p. 338. In the case of pathological sexuality in a boy of 15, reported by A. MacDonald, and already summarized, the sight of copulating flies is also mentioned among many other causes of sexual excitation.

in a considerable number of such cases, the sexual attraction of
feminine garments, for all such tissues are liable to enter into
the dress. In part, also, we have a sexual perversion of tactile
sensibility, for in a considerable proportion of these cases it is
the touch sensations which are potent in arousing the erotic
sensations. But in part, also, it would seem, we have here the
conscious or sub-conscious presence of an animal fetich, and it
is notable that perhaps all these stuffs, and especially fur, which
is by far the commonest of the groups, are distinctively animal
products. We may perhaps regard the fetich of feminine hair—
a much more important and common fetich, indeed, than any
of the stuff fetichisms—as a link of transition. Hair is at once
an animal and a human product, while it may be separated from
the body and possesses the qualities of a stuff. Krafft-Ebing
remarks that the senses of touch, smell, and hearing, as well as
sight, seem to enter into the attraction exerted by hair.

The natural fascination of hair, on which hair-fetichism is founded,
begins at a very early age. "The hair is a special object of interest with
infants," Stanley Hall concludes, "which begins often in the latter part
of the first year. . . . The hair, no doubt, gives quite unique tactile
sensations, both in its own roots and to hands, and is plastic and yielding to the motor sense, so that the earliest interest may be akin to that
in fur, which is a marked object in infant experience. Some children
develop an almost fetichistic propensity to pull or later to stroke the
hair or beard of every one with whom they come in contact." (G.
Stanley Hall, "The Early Sense of Self," *American Journal of Psychology*,
April, 1898, p. 359.)

It should be added that the fascination of hair for the infantile and
childish mind is not necessarily one of attraction, but may be of repulsion. It happens here, as in the case of so many characteristics which
are of sexual significance, that we are in the presence of an object which
may exert a dynamic emotional force, a force which is capable of
repelling with the same energy that it attracts. Féré records the instructive case of a child of 3, of psychopathic heredity, who when he
could not sleep was sometimes taken by his mother into her bed. One
night his hand came in contact with a hairy portion of his mother's
body, and this, arousing the idea of an animal, caused him to leap out
of the bed in terror. He became curious as to the cause of his terror
and in time was able to observe "the animal," but the train of feelings
which had been set up led to a life-long indifference to women and a
tendency to homosexuality. It is noteworthy that he was attracted to

men in whom the hair and other secondary sexual characters were well developed. (Féré, *L'Instinct Sexuel*, second edition, pp. 262-267.)

As a sexual fetich hair strictly belongs to the group of parts of the body; but since it can be removed from the body and is sexually effective as a fetich in the absence of the person to whom it belongs, it is on a level with the garments which may serve in a similar way, with shoes or handkerchiefs or gloves. Psychologically, hair-fetichism presents no special problem, but the wide attraction of hair—it is sexually the most generally noted part of the feminine body after the eyes—and the peculiar facility with which when plaited it may be removed, render hair-fetichism a sexual perversion of specially great medico-legal interest.

The frequency of hair-fetichism, as well as of the natural admiration on which it rests, is indicated by a case recorded by Laurent. "A few years ago," he states, "one constantly saw at the Bal Bullier, in Paris, a tall girl whose face was lean and bony, but whose black hair was of truly remarkable length. She wore it flowing down her shoulders and loins. Men often followed her in the street to touch or kiss the hair. Others would accompany her home and pay her for the mere pleasure of touching and kissing the long black tresses. One, in consideration of a relatively considerable sum, desired to pollute the silky hair. She was obliged to be always on her guard, and to take all sorts of precautions to prevent any one cutting off this ornament, which constituted her only beauty as well as her livelihood. (E. Laurent, *L'Amour Morbide*, 1891, p. 164; also the same author's *Fétichistes et Erotomanes*, p. 23.)

The hair despoiler (*Coupeur des Nattes* or *Zopfabschneider*) may be found in any civilized country, though the most carefully studied cases have occurred in Paris. (Several medico-legal histories of hair-despoilers are summarized by Krafft-Ebing, *Op. cit.*, pp. 329-334). Such persons are usually of nervous temperament and bad heredity; the attraction to hair occasionally develops in early life; sometimes the morbid impulse only appears in later life after fever. The fetich may be either flowing hair or braided hair, but is usually one or the other, and not both. Sexual excitement and ejaculation may be produced in the act of touching or cutting off the hair, which is subsequently, in many cases, used for masturbation. As a rule the hair-despoiler is a pure fetichist, no element of sadistic pleasure entering into his feelings. In the case of a "capillary kleptomaniac" in Chicago—a highly intelligent and athletic married young man of good family—the impulse to cut off girls' braids appeared after recovery from a severe fever. He would gaze admiringly at the long tresses and then clip them off with great rapidity; he did this in some fifty cases before he was caught and imprisoned. He usually threw the braids away before he reached home. (*Alienist and Neurologist*, April, 1889, p. 325.) In this case there is no history of sexual excitement, probably because no proper medico-legal examination was made. (It may be added that hair-despoilers have been specially studied by Motet, "Les Coupeurs de Nattes," *Annales d'Hygiène*, 1890.)

The stuff-fetiches are most usually fur and velvet; feathers, silk, and leathers also sometimes exert this influence; they are all, it will be noted, animal substances.[1] The most interesting is probably fur, the attraction of which is not uncommon in association with passive algolagnia. As Stanley Hall has shown, the fear of fur, as well as the love of it, is by no means uncommon in childhood; it may appear even in infancy and in children who have never come in contact with animals.[2] It is noteworthy that in most cases of uncomplicated stuff-fetichism the attraction apparently arises on a congenital basis, as it appears in persons of nervous or sensitive temperament at an early age and without being attached to any definite causative incident. The sexual excitation is nearly always produced by the touch rather than by the sight. As we found, when dealing with the sense of touch in the previous volume, the specific sexual sensations may be regarded as a special modification of ticklishness. The erotic symbolism in the case of these stuff-fetichisms would seem to be a more or less congenital perversion of ticklishness in relation to specific animal contacts.

A further degree of perversion in this direction is reached in a case of erotic *zoophilia,* recorded by Krafft-Ebing.[3] In this case a congenital neuropath, of good intelligence but delicate and anæmic, with feeble sexual powers, had a great love of domestic animals, especially dogs and cats, from an early age; when petting them he experienced sexual emotions, although he was innocent in sexual matters. At puberty he realized the nature of his feelings and tried to break himself of his habits. He succeeded, but then began erotic dreams accompanied by images of

---

[1] Krafft-Ebing presents or quotes typical cases of all these fetiches, *Op. cit.*, pp. 255-266.

[2] G. Stanley Hall, "A study of Fears," *American Journal of Psychology*, 1897, pp. 213-215.

[3] *Op. cit.*, p. 268.

animals, and these led to masturbation associated with ideas of a similar kind. At the same time he had no wish for any sort of sexual intercourse with animals, and was indifferent as to the sex of the animals which attracted him; his sexual ideals were normal. Such a case seems to be fundamentally one of fetichism on a tactile basis, and thus forms a transition between the stuff-fetichisms and the complete perversions of sexual attraction toward animals.

In some cases sexually hyperæsthetic women have informed me that sexual feeling has been produced by casual contact with pet dogs and cats. In such cases there is usually no real perversion, but it seems probable that we may here have an occasional foundation for the somewhat morbid but scarcely vicious excesses of affection which women are apt to display towards their pet dogs or cats. In most cases of this affection there is certainly no sexual element; in the case of childless women, it may rather be regarded as a maternal than as an erotic symbolism. (The excesses of this non-erotic zoophilia have been discussed by Féré, *L'Instinct Sexuel*, second edition, pp. 166-171.)

Krafft-Ebing considers that complete perversion of sexual attraction toward animals is radically distinct from erotic *zoophilia*. This view cannot be accepted. Bestiality and *zooerastia* merely present in a more marked and profoundly perverted form a further degree of the same phenomenon which we meet with in erotic *zoophilia;* the difference is that they occur either in more insensitive or in more markedly degenerate persons.

A fairly typical case of *zooerastia* has been recorded in America by Howard, of Baltimore. This was the case of a boy of 16, precociously mature and fairly bright. He was, however, indifferent to the opposite sex, though he had ample opportunity for gratifying normal passions. His parents lived in the city, but the youth had an inordinate desire for the country and was therefore sent to school in a village. On the second day after his arrival at school a farmer missed a sow which was found secreted in an outhouse on the school grounds. This was the first of many similar incidents in which a sow always took part. So strong was his passion that on one occasion force had to be used to take him away from the sow he was caressing. He did not masturbate, and even when restrained from approaching sows he had no sexual inclination for other animals. His nocturnal pollutions, which were frequent, were always accompanied by images of wallowing swine. Notwithstanding careful treatment no cure was effected; mental and physical vigor failed, and he died at the age of 23.[1]

It is, however, somewhat doubtful whether we can always or even usually distinguish between zooerastia and bestiality. Dr. G. F. Lydston, of Chicago, has communicated to me a case (in which he was consulted) which seems fairly typical and is instructive in this respect. The subject was a young man of 21, a farmer's son, not very bright intellectually, but very healthy and strong, of great assistance on the farm, very capable and industrious, such a good farm hand that his father was unwilling to send him away and to lose his services. There was no history of insanity or neurosis in the family, and no injury or illness in his own history. He had spells of moroseness and irritability, however, and had also been a masturbator. Women had no attraction for him, but he would copulate with the mares upon his father's farm, and this without regard to time, place, or spectators. Such a case would seem to stand midway between ordinary bestiality and pathological zooerastia as defined by Krafft-Ebing, yet it seems probable that in most cases of ordinary bestiality some slight traces of mental anomaly might be found, if such cases always were, as they should be, properly investigated.[2]

---

[1] W. Howard, "Sexual Perversion," *Alienist and Neurologist*, January, 1896. Krafft-Ebing (*op. cit.*, p. 532) quotes from Boeteau the somewhat similar case of a gardener's boy of 16—an illegitimate child of neuropathic heredity and markedly degenerate—who had a passion, of irresistible and impulsive character, for rabbits. He was declared irresponsible. Moll (*Untersuchungen über die Libido Sexualis*, bd. i, pp. 431-433) presents the case of a neurotic man who from the age of 15 had been sexually excited by the sight of animals or by contact with them. He had repeatedly had connection with cows and mares; he was also sexually excited by sheep, donkeys, and dogs, whether female or male; the normal sexual instinct was weak and he experienced very slight attraction to women.

[2] Moll also remarks ("Perverse Sexualempfindung," in Senator's and Kaminer's *Krankheiten und Ehe*) that in this matter it is often hardly possible to draw a sharp line between vice and disease.

We have here reached the grossest and most frequent perversion in this group; bestiality, or the impulse to attain sexual gratification by intercourse, or other close contact, with animals. In seeking to comprehend this perversion it is necessary to divest ourselves of the attitude toward animals which is the inevitable outcome of refined civilization and urban life. Most sexual perversions, if not in large measure the actual outcome of civilized life, easily adjust themselves to it. Bestiality (except in one form to be noted later) is, on the other hand, the sexual perversion of dull, insensitive, and unfastidious persons. It flourishes among primitive peoples and among peasants. It is the vice of the clodhopper, unattractive to women or inapt to court them.

Three conditions have favored the extreme prevalence of bestiality: (1) primitive conceptions of life which built up no great barrier between man and the other animals; (2) the extreme familiarity which necessarily exists between the peasant and his beasts, often combined with separation from women; (3) various folk-lore beliefs such as the efficacy of intercourse with animals as a cure for venereal disease, etc.[1]

The beliefs and customs of primitive peoples, as well as their mythology and legends, bring before us a community of man and animals altogether unlike anything we know in civilization. Men may become animals and animals may become men; animals and men may communicate with each other and live on terms of equality; animals may be the ancestors of human tribes; the sacred totems of savages are most usually animals. There is no shame or degradation in the notion of a sexual relationship between men and animals, because in primitive conceptions animals are not inferior beings separated from man by a great gulf. They are much more like men in disguise, and in some respects possess powers which make them superior to men.

---

[1] Instances of this widespread belief—found among the Tamils of Ceylon as well as in Europe—are quoted from various authors by Bloch, *Beiträge zur Ætiologie der Psychopathia Sexualis*, Teil II, p. 278, and Moll, *Untersuchungen über die Libido Sexualis*, bd. i, p. 700. On the frequency of bestiality, from one cause or another, in the East, see, *e.g.*, Stern, *Medizin und Geschlechtsleben in der Türkei*, bd. ii, p. 219.

This is recognized in those plays, festivals, and religious dances, so common among primitive peoples, in which animal disguises are worn.[1] When men admire and emulate the qualities of animals and are proud to believe that they descend from them, it is not surprising that they should sometimes see nothing derogatory in sexual intercourse with them.[2]

A significant relic of primitive conceptions in this matter may perhaps be found in the religious rites connected with the sacred goat of Mendes described by Herodotus. After telling how the Mendesians reverence the goat, especially the he-goat, out of their veneration for Pan, whom they represent as a goat ("the real motive which they assign for this custom I do not choose to relate"), he adds: "It happened in this country, and within my remembrance, and was indeed universally notorious, that a goat had indecent and public communication with a woman."[3] The meaning of the passage evidently is that in the ordinary intercourse of women with the sacred goat, connection was only simulated or incomplete on account of the natural indifference of the goat to the human female, but that in rare cases the goat proved sexually excitable with the woman and capable of connection.[4] The goat has always been a kind of sacred emblem of lust. In the middle ages it became associated with the Devil as one of the favorite forms he assumed. It is significant of a primitively religious sexual association between men and animals, that witches constantly confessed, or were made to confess, that they had had intercourse with the Devil in the shape of an animal, very frequently a dog. The figures

---

[1] Sometimes (as among the Aleuts) the animal pantomime dances of savages may represent the transformation of a captive bird into a lovely woman who falls exhausted into the arms of the hunter. (H. H. Bancroft, *Native Races of the Pacific*, vol. i, p. 93.) A system of beliefs which accepts the possibility that a human being may be latent in an animal obviously favors the practice of bestiality.

[2] For an example of the primitive confusion between the intercourse of women with animals and with men see, *e.g.*, Boas, "Sagen aus British-Columbia," *Zeitschrift für Ethnologie*, heft V, p. 558.

[3] Herodotus, Book II, Chapter 46.

[4] Dulare (*Des Divinités Génératrices*, Chapter II) brings together the evidence showing that in Egypt women had connection with the sacred goat, apparently in order to secure fertility.

of human beings and animals in conjunction carved on temples in India, also seem to indicate the religious significance which this phenomenon sometimes presents. There is, indeed, no need to go beyond Europe even in her moments of highest culture to find a religious sanction for sexual union between human beings, or gods in human shape, and animals. The legends of Io and the bull, of Leda and the swan, are among the most familiar in Greek mythology, and in a later pictorial form they constitute some of the most cherished works of the painters of the Renaissance.

As regards the prevalence of occasional sexual intercourse between men or women and animals among primitive peoples at the present time, it is possible to find many scattered references by travelers in all parts of the world. Such references by no means indicate that such practices are, as a rule, common, but they usually show that they are accepted with a good-humored indifference.[1]

Bestiality is very rarely found in towns. In the country this vice of the clodhopper is far from infrequent. For the peasant, whose sensibilities are uncultivated and who makes but the most elementary demands from a woman, the difference between an animal and a human being in this respect scarcely seems to be very great. "My wife was away too long," a German peasant explained to the magistrate, "and so I went with my sow." It is certainly an explanation that to the uncultivated peasant, ignorant of theological and juridical conceptions, must often seem natural and sufficient.

Bestiality thus resembles masturbation and other abnormal manifestations of the sexual impulse which may be practiced merely *faute de mieux* and not as, in the strict sense, perversions of the impulse. Even necrophily may be thus practiced. A young man who when assisting the grave-digger conceived and carried out the idea of digging up the bodies of young girls to satisfy his passions with, and whose case

---

[1] Various facts and references bearing on this subject are brought together by Blumenbach, *Anthropological Memoirs*, translated by Bendyshe, p. 80; Block, *Bitrage zur Ætiologie der Psychopathia Sexualis*, Teil II, pp. 276-283; also Ploss and Bartels, *Das Weib*, seventh edition, p. 520.

has been recorded by Belletrud and Mercier, said: "I could find no young girl who would agree to yield to my desires; that is why I have done this. I should have preferred to have relations with living persons. I found it quite natural to do what I did: I saw no harm in it, and I did not think that any one else could. As living women felt nothing but repulsion for me, it was quite natural I should turn to the dead, who have never repulsed me. I used to say tender things to them like 'my beautiful, my love, I love you.'" (Belletrud and Mercier "Perversion de l'Instinct Genésique," *Annales d'Hygiène Publique*, June, 1903.) But when so highly abnormal an act is felt as natural we are dealing with a person who is congenitally defective so far as the finer developments of intelligence are concerned. It was so in this case of necrophily; he was the son of a weak-minded woman of unrestrainable sexual inclinations, and was himself somewhat feeble-minded; he was also, it is instructive to observe, anosmic.

But it is by no means only their dulled sensibility or the absence of women, which accounts for the frequency of bestiality among peasants. A highly important factor is their constant familiarity with animals. The peasant lives with animals, tends them, learns to know all their individual characters; he understands them far better than he understands men and women; they are his constant companions, his friends. He knows, moreover, the details of their sexual lives, he witnesses the often highly impressive spectacle of their coupling. It is scarcely surprising that peasants should sometimes regard animals as being not only as near to them as their fellow human beings, but even nearer.

The significance of the factor of familiarity is indicated by the great frequency of bestiality among shepherds, goatherds, and others whose occupation is exclusively the care of animals. Mirabeau, in the eighteenth century, stated, on the evidence of Basque priests, that all the shepherds in the Pyrenees practice bestiality. It is apparently much the same in Italy.[1] In South

---

[1] Mantegazza mentions (*Gli Amori degli Uomini*, cap V) that at Rimini a young goatherd of the Apennines, troubled with dyspepsia and nervous symptoms, told him this was due to excesses with the goats in his care. A finely executed marble group of a satyr having connection with a goat, found at Herculaneum and now in the Naples Museum (reproduced in Fuchs's *Erotische Element in der Karikatur*), perhaps symbolizes a traditional and primitive practice of the goatherd.

Italy and Sicily, especially, bestiality among goatherds and peasants is said to be almost a national custom.[1] In the extreme north of Europe, it is reported, the reindeer, in this respect, takes the place of the goat.

The importance of the same factor is also shown by the fact that when among women in civilization animal perversions appear, the animal is nearly always a pet dog. Usually in these cases the animal is taught to give gratification by *cunnilinctus*. In some cases, however, there is really sexual intercourse between the animal and the woman.

Moll mentions that in a case of *cunnilinctus* by a dog in Germany there was a difficulty as to whether the matter should be considered an unnatural offence or simply an offence against decency; the lower court considered it in the former light, while the higher court took the more merciful view. (Moll, *Untersuchungen über die Libido Sexualis*, bd. i, p. 697.) In a case reported by Pfaff and mentioned by Moll, a country girl was accused of having sexual intercourse with a large dog. On examination Pfaff found in the girl's thick pubic hair a loose hair which under the microscope proved to belong to the dog. (*Loc. cit.*, p. 698.) In such a case it must be noted that while this evidence may be held to show sexual contact with the dog, it scarcely suffices to show sexual intercourse. This has, however, undoubtedly occurred from time to time, even more or less openly. Bloch (*Op. cit.*, pp. 277 and 282) remarks that this is not an infrequent exhibition given by prostitutes in certain brothels. Maschka has referred to such an exhibition between a woman and a bull-dog, which was given to select circles in Paris. Rosse refers to a case in which a young unmarried woman in Washington was surprised during intercourse with a large English mastiff, who in his efforts to get loose caused such severe injuries that the woman died from hæmorrhage in about an hour. Rosse also mentions that some years ago a performance of this kind between a prostitute and a Newfoundland dog could be witnessed in San Francisco by paying a small sum; the woman declared that a woman who had once copulated with a dog would ever afterwards prefer this animal to a man. Rosse adds that he was acquainted with a similar performance between a woman

---

[1] Bayle (*Dictionary*, Art, Bathyllus) quotes various authorities concerning the Italian auxiliaries in the south of France in the sixteenth century and their custom of bringing and using goats for this purpose. Warton in the eighteenth century was informed that in Sicily priests in confession habitually inquired of herdsmen if they had anything to do with their sows. In Normandy priests are advised to ask similar questions.

and a donkey, which used to take place in Europe (Irving Rosse, "Sexual Hypochondriasis and Perversion of the Genesic Instinct," *Virginia Medical Monthly*, October, 1892, p. 379). Juvenal mentions such relations between the donkey and woman (vi, 332). Krauss (quoted by Bloch, *Bitrâge zur Ætiologie der Psychopathia Sexualis*, Teil 11, p. 276) states that in Bosnia women sometimes carry on these practices with dogs and also—as he would not have believed had he not on one occasion observed it—with cats. "It seems to me," writes Dr. Kiernan, of Chicago, (private letter) "that what Rosse says of the animal exhibitions in San Francisco is true of all great cities. The animal employed in such exhibitions here has usually been a donkey, and in one instance death occurred from the animal trampling the girl partner. The practice described occurs in country regions quite frequently. Thus in a case reported in the suburbs of Omaha, Nebraska, a sixteen-year-old boy engaged in rectal coitus with a large dog. In attempting to extricate his swollen penis from the boy's rectum the dog tore through the *sphincter ani* an inch into the gluteus muscles. (*Omaha Clinic*, March, 1893.) In a Missouri case, which I verified, a smart, pretty, well-educated country girl was found with a profuse offensive vaginal discharge which had been present for about a week, coming on suddenly. After washing the external genitals and opening the labia three rents were discovered, one through the fourchette and two through the left nymphæ. The vagina was excessively congested and covered with points bleeding on the slightest irritation. The patient confessed that one day while playing with the genitals of a large dog she became excited and thought she would have slight coitus. After the dog had made an entrance she was unable to free herself from him, as he clasped her so firmly with his fore legs. The penis became so swollen that the dog could not free himself, although for more than an hour she made persistent efforts to do so. (*Medical Standard*, June, 1903, p. 184). In an Indiana case, concerning which I was consulted, the girl was a hebephreniac who had resorted to this procedure with a Newfoundland dog at the instance of another girl, seemingly normal as regards mentality, and had been badly injured; a discharge resulted which resembled gonorrhœa, but contained no gonococci. These cases are probably more frequent than is usually assumed."

Women are known to have had intercourse with various other animals, occasionally or habitually, in various parts of the world. Monkeys have been mentioned in this connection. Moll remarks that it seems to be an indication of an abnormal interest in monkeys that some women are observed by the attendants in the monkey-house of zoölogical gardens to be very frequent visitors. Near the Amazon the traveler Castelnau saw an enormous Coati monkey belonging to an Indian woman and tried to purchase it; though he offered a large sum, the woman only laughed. "Your efforts are useless," remarked an

Indian in the same cabin, "he is her husband." (So far as the early literature of this subject is concerned, a number of facts and fables regarding the congress of women with dogs, goats and other animals was brought together at the beginning of the eighteenth century by Schurig in his *Gynæcologia*, Section II, cap. VII; I have not drawn on this collection.)

In some cases women, and also men, find gratification in the sexual manipulation of animals without any kind of congress. This may be illustrated by an observation communicated to me by a correspondent, a clergyman. "In Ireland, my father's house adjoined the residence of an archdeacon of the established church. I was then about 20 and was still kept in religious awe of evil ways. The archdeacon had two daughters, both of whom he brought up in great strictness, resolved that they should grow up examples of virtue and piety. Our stables adjoined, and were separated only by a thin wall in which was a doorway closed up by some boards, as the two stables had formerly been one. One night I had occasion to go to our stable to search for a garden tool I had missed, and I heard a door open on the other side, and saw a light glimmer through the cracks of the boards. I looked through to ascertain who could be there at that late hour, and soon recognized the stately figure of one of the daughters, F. F. was tall, dark and handsome, but had never made any advances to me, nor had I to her. She was making love to her father's mare after a singular fashion. Stripping her right arm, she formed her fingers into a cone, and pressed on the mare's vulva. I was astonished to see the beast stretching her hind legs as if to accommodate the hand of her mistress, which she pushed in gradually and with seeming ease to the elbow. At the same time she seemed to experience the most voluptuous sensation, crisis after crisis arriving." My correspondent adds that, being exceedingly curious in the matter, he tried a somewhat similar experiment himself with one of his father's mares and experienced what he describes as "a most powerful sexual battery" which produced very exciting and exhausting effects. Näcke (*Psychiatrische en Neurologische Bladen*, 1899, No. 2) refers to an idiot who thus manipulated the vulva of mares in his charge. The case has been recorded by Guillereau (*Journal de Médicine Vétérinaire et de Zootechnie*, January, 1899) of a youth who was accustomed to introduce his hand into the vulva of cows in order to obtain sexual excitement.

The possibility of sexual excitement between women and animals involves a certain degree of sexual excitability in animals from contact with women. Darwin stated that there could be no doubt that various quadrumanous animals could distinguish women from men—in the first place probably by smell and secondarily by sight—and be thus liable to sexual excitement. He quotes the opinions on this point of Youatt,

Brehm, Sir Andrew Smith and Cuvier (*Descent of Man,* second edition, p. 8). Moll quotes the opinion of an experienced observer to the same effect (*Untersuchungen über die Libido Sexualis,* Bd. i, p. 429). Hufeland reported the case of a little girl of three who was playing, seated on a stool, with a dog placed between her thighs and locked against her. Seemingly excited by this contact the animal attempted a sort of copulation, causing the genital parts of the child to become inflamed. Bloch (*Op. cit.,* p. 280, *et seq.)* discusses the same point; he does not consider that animals will of their own motion sexually cohabit with women, but that they may be easily trained to it. There can be no doubt that dogs at all events are sometimes sexually excited by the presence of women, perhaps especially during menstruation, and many women are able to bear testimony to the embarrassing attentions they have sometimes received from strange dogs. There can be no difficulty in believing that, so far as *cunnilinctus* is concerned dogs would require no training. In a case recorded by Moll (*Konträre Sexualempfindung,* third edition, p. 560) a lady states that this was done to her when a child, as also to other children, by dogs who, she said, showed signs of sexual excitement. In this case there was also sexual excitement thus produced in the child, and after puberty mutual *cunnilinctus* was practiced with girl friends. Guttceit (*Dreissig Jahre Praxis,* Theil I, p. 310) remarks that some Russian officers who were in the Turkish campaign of 1828 told him that from fear of veneral infection in Wallachia they refrained from women and often used female asses which appeared to show signs of sexual pleasure.

A very large number of animals have been recorded as having been employed in the gratification of sexual desire at some period or in some country, by men and sometimes by women. Domestic animals are naturally those which most frequently come into question, and there are few if any of these which can altogether be excepted. The sow is one of the animals most frequently abused in this manner.[1] Cases in which mares, cows, and donkeys figure constantly occur, as well as goats and sheep. Dogs, cats, and rabbits are heard of from time to time. Hens, ducks, and, especially in China, geese, are not uncommonly employed. The Roman ladies were said to have had an abnormal

---

[1] It is worth noting that in Greek the work χοῖρος means both a sow and a woman's pudenda; in the *Acharnians* Aristophanes plays on this association at some length. The Romans also (as may be gathered from Varro's *De Re Rustica*) called the feminine pudenda *porcus.*

affection for snakes. The bear and even the crocodile are also mentioned.[1]

The social and legal attitude toward bestiality has reflected in part the frequency with which it has been practiced, and in part the disgust mixed with mystical and sacrilegious horror which it has aroused. It has sometimes been met merely by a fine, and sometimes the offender and his innocent partner have been burnt together. In the middle ages and later its frequency is attested by the fact that it formed a favorite topic with preachers of the fifteenth and sixteenth centuries. It is significant that in the Penitentials,—which were criminal codes, half secular and half spiritual, in use before the thirteenth century, when penance was relegated to the judgment of the confessor,—it was thought necessary to fix the periods of penance which should be undergone respectively by bishops, priests and deacons who should be guilty of bestiality.

In Egbert's Penitential, a document of the ninth and tenth centuries, we read (V. 22): "Item Episcopus cum quadrupede fornicans VII annos, consuetudinem X, presbyter V, diaconus III, clerus II." There was a great range in the penances for bestiality, from ten years to (in the case of boys) one hundred days. The mare is specially mentioned (Haddon and Stubbs, *Councils and Ecclesiastical Documents*, vol. iii, p. 422). In Theodore's Penitential, another Anglo-Saxon document of about the same age, those who habitually fornicate with animals are adjudged ten years of penance. It would appear from the *Penitentiale Pseudo-Romanum* (which is earlier than the eleventh century) that one year's penance was adequate for fornication with a mare when committed by a layman (exactly the same as for simple fornication with a widow or virgin), and this was mercifully reduced to half a year if he had no wife. (Wasserschleben, *Die Bussordnungen der Abendländlichen Kirche*, p 366). The *Penitentiale Hubertense* (emanating from the monastery of St. Hubert in the Ardennes) fixes ten years' penance for sodomy, while Fulbert's Penitential (about the eleventh century) fixes seven years for either sodomy or bestiality. Burchard's Penitential,

---

[1] Schurig, *Gynæocologia*, pp. 280-387; Bloch, *op. cit.*, 270-277. The Arabs, according to Kocher, chiefly practice bestiality with goats, sheep and mares. The Annamites, according to Mondière, commonly employ sows and (more especially the young women) dogs. Among the Tamils of Ceylon bestiality with goats and cows is said to be very prevalent.

which is always detailed and precise, specially mentions the mare, the cow and the ass, and assigns forty days bread and water and seven years penance, raised to ten years in the case of married men. A woman having intercourse with a horse is assigned seven years penance in Burchard's Penitential. (Wasserschleben, *ib.*, pp. 651, 659.)

The extreme severity which was frequently exercised toward those guilty of this offense, was doubtless in large measure due to the fact that bestiality was regarded as a kind of sodomy, an offense which was frequently viewed with a mystical horror apart altogether from any actual social or personal injury it caused. The Jews seem to have felt this horror; it was ordered that the sinner and his victim should both be put to death (Exodus, Ch. 22, v. 19; Leviticus, Ch. 20, v. 15). In the middle ages, especially in France, the same rule often prevailed. Men and sows, men and cows, men and donkeys were burnt together. At Toulouse a woman was burnt for having intercourse with a dog. Even in the seventeenth century a learned French lawyer, Claude Lebrun de la Rochette, justified such sentences.[1] It seems probable that even to-day, in the social and legal attitude toward bestiality, sufficient regard is not paid to the fact that this offense is usually committed either by persons who are morbidly abnormal or who are of so low a degree of intelligence that they border on feeble-mindedness. To what extent, and on what grounds, it ought to be punished is a question calling for serious reconsideration.

---

[1] Mantegazza (*Gli Amori degli Uomini,* cap. V) brings together some facts bearing on this matter.

V.

Exhibitionism—Illustrative Cases—A Symbolic Perversion of Courtship—The Impulse to Defile—The Exhibitionist's Psychic Attitude—The Sexual Organs as Fetichs—Phallus Worship—Adolescent Pride in Sexual Development—Exhibitionism of the Nates—The Classification of the Forms of Exhibitionism—Nature of the Relationship of Exhibitionism to Epilepsy.

THERE is a remarkable form of erotic symbolism—very definite and standing clearly apart from all other forms—in which sexual gratification is experienced in the simple act of exhibiting the sexual organ to persons of the opposite sex, usually by preference to young and presumably innocent persons, very often children. This is termed exhibitionism.[1] It would appear to be a not very infrequent phenomenon, and most women, once or more in their lives, especially when young, have encountered a man who has thus deliberately exposed himself before them.

The exhibitionist, though often a young and apparently vigorous man, is always satisfied with the mere act of self-exhibition and the emotional reaction which that act produces; he makes no demands on the woman to whom he exposes himself; he seldom speaks, he makes no effort to approach her; as a rule, he fails even to display the signs of sexual excitation. His desires are completely gratified by the act of exhibition and by the emotional reaction it arouses in the woman. He departs satisfied and relieved.

A case recorded by Schrenck-Notzing very well represents both the nature of the impulse felt by the exhibitionist and the way in which it may originate. It is the case of a business man of 49, of neurotic

---

[1] Lasègue first drew attention to this sexual perversion and gave it its generally accepted name, "Les Exhibitionistes," *L'Union Médicale*, May, 1877. Magnan, on various occasions (for example, "Les Exhibitionistes," *Archives de l'Anthropologie Criminelle*, vol. v, 1890, p. 456), has given further development and precision to the clinical picture of the exhibitionist.

heredity, an affectionate husband and father of a family, who, to his own grief and shame, is compelled from time to time to exhibit his sexual organs to women in the street. As a boy of 10 a girl of 12 tried to induce him to coitus; both had their sexual parts exposed. From that time sexual contacts, as of his own naked nates against those of a girl, became attractive, as well as games in which the boys and girls in turn marched before each other with their sexual parts exposed, and also imitation of the copulation of animals. Coitus was first practiced about the age of 20, but sight and touch of the woman's sexual parts were always necessary to produce sexual excitement. It was also necessary—and this consideration is highly important as regards the development of the tendency to exhibition—that the woman should be excited by the sight of his organs. Even when he saw or touched a woman's parts orgasm often occurred. It was the naked sexual organs in an otherwise clothed body which chiefly excited him. He was not possessed of a high degree of potency. Girls between the ages of 10 and 17 chiefly excited him, and especially if he felt that they were quite ignorant of sexual matters. His self-exhibition was a sort of psychic defloration, and it was accompanied by the idea that other people felt as he did about the sexual effects of the naked organs, that he was shocking but at the same time sexually exciting a young girl. He was thus gratifying himself through the belief that he was causing sexual gratification to an innocent girl. This man was convicted several times, and was finally declared to be suffering from impulsive insanity. (Schrenck-Notzing, *Kriminal-psychologische und Psycho-pathologische Studien*, 1902, pp. 50-57.) In another case of Schrenck-Notzing's, an actor and portrait painter, aged 31, in youth masturbated and was fond of contemplating the images of the sexual organs of both sexes, finding little pleasure in coitus. At the age of 24, at a bathing establishment, he happened to occupy a compartment next to that occupied by a lady, and when naked he became aware that his neighbor was watching him through a chink in the partition. This caused him powerful excitement and he was obliged to masturbate. Ever since he has had an impulse to exhibit his organs and to masturbate in the presence of women. He believes that the sight of his organs excites the woman (*Ib.*, pp. 57-68). The presence of masturbation in this case renders it untypical as a case of exhibitionism. Moll at one time went so far as to assert that when masturbation takes place we are not entitled to admit exhibitionism, (*Untersuchungen über die Libido Sexualis*, bd. i, p. 661), but now accepts exhibitionism with masturbation ("Perverse Sexualempfindung," *Krankheiten und Ehe*). The act of exhibition itself gratifies the sexual impulse, and usually it suffices to replace both tumescence and detumescence.

A fairly typical case, recorded by Krafft-Ebing, is that of a German factory worker of 37, a good, sober and intelligent workman. His parents were healthy, but one of his mother's and also one of his father's sisters were insane; some of his relatives are eccentric in religion. He has a languishing expression and a smile of self-complacency. He never had any severe illness, but has always been eccentric and imaginative, much absorbed in romances (such as Dumas's novels) and fond of identifying himself with their heroes. No signs of epilepsy. In youth moderate masturbation, later moderate coitus. He lives a retired life, but is fond of elegant dress and of ornament. Though not a drinker, he sometimes makes himself a kind of punch which has a sexually exciting effect on him. The impulse to exhibitionism has only developed in recent years. When the impulse is upon him he becomes hot, his heart beats violently, the blood rushes to his head, and he is oblivious of everything around him that is not connected with his own act. Afterwards he regards himself as a fool and makes vain resolutions never to repeat the act. In exhibition the penis is only half erect and ejaculation never occurs. (He is only capable of coitus with a woman who shows great attraction to him.) He is satisfied with self-exhibition, and believes that he thus gives pleasure to the woman, since he himself receives pleasure in contemplating a woman's sexual parts. His erotic dreams are of self-exhibition to young and voluptuous women. He had been previously punished for an offense of this kind; medicolegal opinion now recognized the incriminated man's psychopathic condition. (Krafft-Ebing, *Op. cit.*, pp. 492-494.)

Trochon has reported the case of a married man of 33, a worker in a factory, who for several years had exhibited himself at intervals to shop-girls, etc., in a state of erection, but without speaking or making other advances. He was a hard-working, honest, sober man of quiet habits, a good father to his family and happy at home. He showed not the slightest sign of insanity. But he was taciturn, melancholic and nervous; a sister was an idiot. He was arrested, but on the report of the experts that he committed these acts from a morbid impulse he could not control he was released. (Trochon, *Archives de l'Anthropologie Criminelle*, 1888, p. 256.)

In a case of Freyer's (*Zeitschrift für Medizinalbeamte*, third year, No. 8) the occasional connection of exhibitionism with epilepsy is well illustrated by a barber's assistant, aged 35, whose father suffered from chronic alcoholism and was also said to have committed the same kind of offense as his son. The mother and a sister suffered nervously. From ages of 7 to 18 the subject had epileptic convulsions. From 16 to 21 he indulged in normal sexual intercourse. At about that time he had often to pass a playground and at times would urinate there; it happened that the children watched him with curiosity. He noticed that when thus watched sexual excitement was caused, inducing erection and even ejaculation. He gradually found pleasure in this kind of sexual gratification; finally he became indifferent to coitus. His erotic dreams, though still usually about normal coitus, were now sometimes concerned with exhibition before little girls. When overcome by the impulse he could see and hear nothing around him, though he did not lose consciousness. After the act was over he was troubled by his deed. In all other respects he was entirely reasonable. He was imprisoned many times for exhibiting himself to young schoolgirls, sometimes vaunting the beauty of his organs and inviting inspection. On one occasion he underwent mental examination, but was considered to be mentally sound. He was finally held to be a hereditarily tainted individual with neuropathic constitution. The head was abnormally broad, penis small, patellar reflex absent, and there were many signs of neurasthenia. (Krafft-Ebing, *Op. cit.*, pp. 490-492.)

The prevalence of epilepsy among exhibitionists is shown by the observations of Pelanda in Verona. He has recorded six cases of this perversion, all of which eventually reached the asylum and were either epileptics or with epileptic relations. One had a brother who was also an exhibitionist. In some cases the penis was abnormally large, in others abnormally small. Several had very weak sexual impulse; one, at the age of 62, had never effected coitus, and was proud of the fact that he was still a virgin, considering, he would say, the epoch of demoralization in which we live. (Pelanda, "Pornopatici," *Archivio di Psichiatria*, fasc. ii-iv, 1889.)

In a very typical case of exhibitionism which Garnier has recorded, a certain X., a gentleman engaged in business in Paris, had a predilection for exhibiting himself in churches, more especially in Saint-Roch. He was arrested several times for exposing his sexual organs here before ladies in prayer. In this way he finally ruined his commercial position in Paris and was obliged to establish himself in a small provincial town. Here again he soon exposed himself in a church and was again sent to prison, but on his liberation immediately performed the same act in the same church in what was described as a most imperturbable manner. Compelled to leave the town, he returned to Paris, and in a few weeks' time was again arrested for repeating his old offense in Saint Roch. When examined by Garnier, the information he supplied was vague and incomplete, and he was very embarrassed in the attempt to explain himself. He was unable to say why he chose a church, but he felt that it was to a church that he must go. He had, however, no thought of profanation and no wish to give offense. "Quite the contrary!" he declared. He had the sad and tired air of a man who is dominated by a force stronger than his will. "I know," he added, "what repulsion my conduct must inspire. Why am I made thus? Who will cure me?" (P. Garnier, "Perversions Sexuelles," *Comptes Rendus*, International Congress of Medicine at Paris in 1900, *Section de Psychiatrie*, pp. 433-435.)

In some cases, it would appear, the impulse to exhibitionism may be overcome or may pass away. This result is the more likely to come about in those cases in which exhibitionism has been largely conditioned by chronic alcoholism or other influences tending to destroy the inhibiting and restraining action of the higher centers, which may be overcome by hygiene and treatment. In this connection I may bring forward a case which has been communicated to me by a medical correspondent in London. It is that of an actor, of high standing in his profession and extremely intelligent, 49 years of age, married and father of a large family. He is sexually vigorous and of erotic temperament. His general health has always been good, but he is a high-strung, neurotic man, with quick mental reactions. His habits had for a long time been decidedly alcoholic, but two years ago, a small quantity of albumen being found in the urine, he was persuaded to leave off alcohol, and has since been a teetotaller. Though ordinarily very reticent about sexual matters, he began four or five years ago to commit acts of exhibitionism, exposing himself to servants in the house and occasionally to women in the country. This continued after the alcohol had been abandoned and lasted for several years, though the attention of the police was never attracted to the matter, and so far as possible he was quietly supervised by his friends. Nine months after, the acts of exhibitionism ceased, apparently in a spontaneous manner, and there has so far been no relapse.

Exhibitionism is an act which, on the face of it, seems nonsensical and meaningless, and as such, as an inexplicable act of madness, it has frequently been treated both by writers on insanity and on sexual perversion. "These acts are so lacking in common sense and intelligent reflection that no other reason than insanity can be offered for the patient," Ball concluded.[1] Moll, also, who defines exhibitionism somewhat too narrowly as a condition in which "the charm of the exhibition lies for the subject in the display itself," not sufficiently taking into consideration the imagined effect on the spectator, concludes that "the psychological basis of exhibitionism is at present by no means cleared up."[2]

We may probably best approach exhibitionism by regarding it as fundamentally a symbolic act based on a perversion of courtship. The exhibitionist displays the organ of sex to a

---

[1] B. Ball, *La Folie Erotique*, p 86.
[2] Moll, *Untersuchungen über die Libido Sexualis*, bd. i, p. 661.

feminine witness, and in the shock of modest sexual shame by which she reacts to that spectacle, he finds a gratifying similitude of the normal emotions of coitus.[1] He feels that he has effected a psychic defloration.

Exhibitionism is thus analogous, and, indeed, related, to the impulse felt by many persons to perform indecorous acts or tell indecent stories before young and innocent persons of the opposite sex. This is a kind of psychic exhibitionism, the gratification it causes lying exactly, as in physical exhibitionism, in the emotional confusion which it is felt to arouse. The two kinds of exhibitionism may be combined in the same person: Thus, in a case reported by Hoche (p. 97), the exhibitionist an intellectual and highly educated man, with a doctor's degree, also found pleasure in sending indecent poems and pictures to women, whom, however, he made no attempt to seduce; he was content with the thought of the emotions he aroused or believed that he aroused.

It is possible that within this group should come the agent in the following incident which was lately observed by a lady, a friend of my own. An elderly man in an overcoat was seen standing outside a large and well-known draper's shop in the outskirts of London; when able to attract the attention of any of the shop-girls or of any girl in the street he would fling back his coat and reveal that he was wearing over his own clothes a woman's chemise (or possibly bodice) and a woman's drawers; there was no exposure. The only intelligible explanation of this action would seem to be that pleasure was experienced in the mild shock of interested surprise and injured modesty which this vision was imagined to cause to a young girl. It would thus be a comparatively innocent form of psychic defloration.

It is of interest to point out that the sexual symbolism of active flagellation is very closely analogous to this symbolism of exhibitionism. The flagellant approaches a woman with the rod (itself a symbol of the penis and in some countries bearing names which are also applied to that organ) and inflicts on an

---

[1] "Exhibitionism in its most typical form is," Garnier truly says, "a *systematic act*, manifesting itself as the *strange equivalent of a sexual connection*, or its *substitution*." The brief account of exhibitionism (pp. 433-437) in Garnier's discussion of "Perversions Sexuelles" at the International Medical Congress at Paris in 1900 *(Section de Psychiatrie: Comptes-Rendus)* is the most satisfactory statement of the psychological aspects of this perversion with which I am acquainted. Garnier's unrivalled clinical knowledge of these manifestations, due to his position during many years as physician at the Depôt of the Prefecture of Police in Paris, adds great weight to his conclusions.

intimate part of her body the signs of blushing and the spasmodic movements which are associated with sexual excitement, while at the same time she feels, or the flagellant imagines that she feels, the corresponding emotions of delicious shame.[1] This is an even closer mimicry of the sexual act than the exhibitionist attains, for the latter fails to secure the consent of the woman nor does he enjoy any intimate contact with her naked body. The difference is connected with the fact that the active flagellant is usually a more virile and normal person than the exhibitionist. In the majority of cases the exhibitionist's sexual impulse is very feeble, and as a rule he is either to some degree a degenerate, or else a person who is suffering from an early stage of general paralysis, dementia, or some other highly enfeebling cause of mental disorganization, such as chronic alcoholism. Sexual feebleness is further indicated by the fact that the individuals selected as witnesses are frequently mere children.

It seems probable that a form of erotic symbolism somewhat similar to exhibitionism is to be found in the rare cases in which sexual gratification is derived from throwing ink, acid or other defiling liquids on women's dresses. Thoinet has recorded a case of this kind (*Attentats aux Moeurs*, 1898, pp. 484, *et seq.*). An instructive case has been presented by Moll. In this case a young man of somewhat neuropathic heredity had as a youth of 16 or 17, when romping with his young sister's playfellows, experienced sexual sensations on chancing to see their white underlinen. From that time white underlinen and white dresses became to him a fetich and he was only attracted to women so attired. One day, at the age of 25, when crossing the street in wet weather with a young lady in a white dress, a passing vehicle splashed the dress with mud. This incident caused him strong sexual excitement, and from that time he had the impulse to throw ink, perchloride of iron, etc., on to ladies' white dresses, and sometimes to cut and tear them, sexual excitement and ejaculation taking place every time he effected this. (Moll, "Gutachten über einem Sexual Perversen [Besudelungstrieb]," *Zeitschrift für Medizinalbeamte*, Heft XIII, 1900). Such a case is of considerable psychological interest. Thoinet considers that in these cases the fleck is a fetich. That is an incorrect account of the matter. In this case the

---

[1] The symbolism of coitus involved in flagellation has been touched on by Eulenburg (*Sexuale Neuropathie*, p. 121), and is more fully developed by Dühren (*Geschlechtsleben in England*, bd. ii, pp. 366, *et seq.*).

white garments constituted the primary fetich, but that fetich becomes more acutely realized, and at the same time both parties are thrown into an emotional state which to the fetichist becomes a mimicry of coitus, by the act of defilement. We may perhaps connect with this phenomenon the attraction which muddy shoes often exert over the shoe-fetichist, and the curious way in which, as we have seen (p. 18), Restif de la Bretonne associates his love of neatness in women with his attraction to the feet, the part, he remarks, least easy to keep clean.

Garnier applied the term *sadi-fetichism* to active flagellation and many similar manifestations such as we are here concerned with, on the grounds that they are hybrids which combine the morbid adoration for a definite object with the impulse to exercise a more or less degree of violence. From the standpoint of the conception of erotic symbolism I have adopted there is no need for this term. There is here no hybrid combination of two unlike mental states. We are simply concerned with states of erotic symbolism, more or less complete, more or less complex.

The conception of exhibitionism as a process of erotic symbolism, involves a conscious or unconscious attitude of attention in the exhibitionist's mind to the psychic reaction of the woman toward whom his display is directed. He seeks to cause an emotion which, probably in most cases, he desires should be pleasurable. But from one cause or another his finer sensibilities are always inhibited or in abeyance, and he is unable to estimate accurately either the impression he is likely to produce or the general results of his action, or else he is moved by a strong impulsive obsession which overpowers his judgment. In many cases he has good reason for believing that his act will be pleasurable, and frequently he finds complacent witnesses among the low-class servant girls, etc.

It may be pointed out here that we are quite justified in speaking of a penis-fetichism and also of a vulva-fetichism. This might be questioned. We are obviously justified in recognizing a fetichism which attaches itself to the pubic hair, or, as in a case with which I am acquainted, to the clitoris, but it may seem that we cannot regard the central sexual organs as symbols of sex, symbols, as it were, of themselves. Properly regarded, however, it is the sexual act rather than the sexual organ which is craved in normal sexual desire; the organ is regarded merely as the means and not as the end. Regarded as a means the organ is indeed an object of desire, but it only becomes a fetich when it arrests and fixes the attention. An attention thus pleasurably fixed, a vulva-fetichism or a penis-fetichism, is within the normal range of sexual emotion (this point has been mentioned in the previous volume when discussing the part played by the primary sexual organs in sexual selection), and in coarse-grained natures of either sex it is a normal allurement in its generalized shape, apart from any attraction to the person to whom the organs belong. In some morbid cases, however, this penis-fetichism may become a fully developed sexual perversion. A typical case of this kind has been recorded by Howard in the United States. Mrs. W., aged 39, was married at 20 to a strong, healthy man, but derived no pleasure from coitus, though she received great pleasure from masturbation practiced immediately after coitus, and nine years after marriage she ceased actual coitus, compelling her husband to adopt mutual masturbation. She would introduce men into the house at all times of the day or night, and after persuading them to expose their persons would retire to her room to masturbate. The same man never aroused desire more than once. This desire became so violent and persistent that she would seek out men in all sorts of public places and, having induced them to expose themselves, rapidly retreat to the nearest convenient spot for self-gratification. She once abstracted a pair of trousers she had seen a man wear and after fondling them experienced the orgasm. Her husband finally left her, after vainly attempting to have her confined in an asylum. She was often arrested for her actions, but through the intervention of friends set free again. She was a highly intelligent woman, and apart from this perversion entirely normal. (W. L. Howard, "Sexual Perversion," *Alienist and Neurologist*, January, 1896.) It is on the existence of a more or less developed penis-fetichism of this kind that the exhibitionist, mostly by an ignorant instinct, relies for the effects he desires to produce.

The exhibitionist is not usually content to produce a mere titillated amusement; he seeks to produce a more powerful effect which must be emotional whether or not it is pleasurable. A professional man in Strassburg (in a case reported by Hoche[1]) would walk about in the evening in a long cloak, and when he met ladies would suddenly throw his cloak back under a street lamp, or igniting a red-fire match, and thus exhibit his organs. There was an evident effort—on the part of a weak, vain, and effeminate man—to produce a maximum of emotional effect. The attempt to heighten the emotional shock is also seen in the fact that the exhibitionist frequently chooses a church as the scene of his exploits, not during service, for he

---

[1] A. Hoche, *Neurologische Centralblatt*, 1896, No. 2.

always avoids a concourse of people, but perhaps toward evening when there are only a few kneeling women scattered through
the edifice. The church is chosen, often instinctively rather than
deliberately, from no impulse to commit a sacrilegious outrage—
which, as a rule, the exhibitionist does not feel his act to be—but
because it really presents the conditions most favorable to the
act and the effects desired. The exhibitionist's attitude of mind
is well illustrated by one of Garnier's patients who declared that
he never wished to be seen by more than two women at once,
"just what is necessary," he added, "for an exchange of impressions." After each exhibition he would ask himself anxiously:
"Did they see me? What are they thinking? What do they
say to each other about me? Oh! how I should like to know!"
Another patient of Garnier's, who haunted churches for this purpose, made this very significant statement: "Why do I like going
to churches? I can scarcely say. *But I know that it is only there
that my act has its full importance.* The woman is in a devout
frame of mind, and she must see that such an act in such a place
is not a joke in bad taste or a disgusting obscenity; *that if I go
there it is not to amuse myself; it is more serious than that!*
I watch the effect produced on the faces of the ladies to whom
I show my organs. I wish to see them express a profound joy.
I wish, in fact, that they may be forced to say to themselves:
How impressive Nature is when thus seen!"

Here we trace the presence of a feeling which recalls the phenomena
of the ancient and world-wide phallic worship, still liable to reappear
sporadically. Women sometimes took part in these rites, and the
osculation of the male sexual organ or its emblematic representation by
women is easily traceable in the phallic rites of India and many other
lands, not excluding Europe even in comparatively recent times. (Dulaure in his *Divinités Génératices* brings together much bearing on these
points; *cf.*: Ploss and Bartels, *Das Weib*, vol. i, Chapter XVII, and
Bloch, *Beiträge zur Psychopathia Sexualis*, Teil I, pp. 115-117. Colin
Scott has some interesting remarks on phallic worship and the part it
has played in aiding human evolution, "Sex and Art," *American Journal
of Psychology*, vol. vii, No. 2, pp. 191-197. Irving Rosse describes some
modern phallic rites in which both men and women took part, similar
to those practiced in vaudonism, "Sexual Hypochondriasis," *Virginia
Medical Monthly*, October, 1892.)

Putting aside any question of phallic worship, a certain pride and more or less private feeling of ostentation in the new expansion and development of the organs of virility seems to be almost normal at adolescence. "We have much reason to assume," Stanley Hall remarks, "that in a state of nature there is a certain instinctive pride and ostentation that accompanies the new local development. I think it will be found that exhibitionists are usually those who have excessive growth here, and that much that modern society stigmatizes as obscene is at bottom more or less spontaneous and perhaps in some cases not abnormal. Dr. Seerley tells me he has never examined a young man largely developed who had the usual strong instinctive tendency of modesty to cover himself with his hands, but he finds this instinct general with those whose development is less than the average." (G. Stanley Hall, *Adolescence*, vol. ii, p. 97.) This instinct of ostentation, however, so far as it is normal, is held in check by other considerations, and is not, in the strict sense, exhibitionism. I have observed a full-grown telegraph boy walking across Hampstead Heath with his sexual organs exposed, but immediately he realized that he was seen he concealed them. The solemnity of exhibitionism at this age finds expression in the climax of the sonnet, "Oraison du Soir," written at 16 by Rimbaud, whose verse generally is a splendid and insolent manifestation of rank adolescence:—

"Doux comme le Seigneur du cèdre et des hysopes,
Je pisse vers les cieux bruns très haut et très loin,
Avec l'assentiment des grands héliotropes."

(J. A. Rimbaud, *Œuvres*, p. 68.)

In women, also, there would appear to be traceable a somewhat similar ostentation, though in them it is complicated and largely inhibited by modesty, and at the same time diffused over the body owing to the absence of external sexual organs. "Primitive woman," remarks Madame Renooz, "proud of her womanhood, for a long time defended her nakedness which ancient art has always represented. And in the actual life of the young girl to-day there is a moment when by a secret atavism she feels the pride of her sex, the intuition of her moral superiority, and cannot understand why she must hide its cause. At this moment, wavering between the laws of Nature and social conventions, she scarcely knows if nakedness should or should not affright her. A sort of confused atavistic memory recalls to her a period before clothing was known, and reveals to her as a paradisiacal ideal the customs of that human epoch." (Celine Renooz, *Psychologie Comparée de l'Homme et de la Femme*, p. 85.) It may be added that among primitive peoples, and even among some remote European populations to-day, the exhibition of feminine nudity has sometimes been regarded as a spectacle with religious or magic operation. Ploss, *Das Weib*, seventh edition, vol. ii,

pp. 663-680; Havelock Ellis, *Man and Woman*, fourth edition, p. 304.)
It is stated by Gopcevic that in the long struggle between the Albanians
and the Montenegrians the women of the former people would stand in
the front rank and expose themselves by raising their skirts, believing
that they would thus insure victory. As, however, they were shot down,
and as, moreover, victory usually fell to the Montenegrians, this custom
became discredited. (Quoted by Bloch, *Op. cit.*, Teil II, p. 307.)

With regard to the association, suggested by Stanley Hall, between
exhibitionism and an unusual degree of development of the sexual
organs, it must be remarked that both extremes—a very large and a
very small penis—are specially common in exhibitionists. The prevalence of the small organ is due to an association of exhibitionism with
sexual feebleness. The prevalence of the large organ may be due to the
cause suggested by Hall. Among Mahommedans the sexual organs are
sometimes habitually exposed by religious penitents, and I note that
Bernhard Stern, in his book on the medical and sexual aspects of life
in Turkey, referring to a penitent of this sort whom he saw on the
Stamboul bridge at Constantinople, remarks that the organ was very
largely developed. It may well be in such a case that the penitent's
religious attitude is reinforced by some lingering relic of a more fleshly
ostentation.

It is by a pseudo-atavism that this phallicism is evoked in
the exhibitionist. There is no true emergence of an ancestrally
inherited instinct, but by the paralysis or inhibition of the finer
and higher feelings current in civilization, the exhibitionist is
placed on the same mental level as the man of a more primitive
age, and he thus presents the basis on which the impulses belonging to a higher culture may naturally take root and develop.

Reference may here be made to a form of primitive exhibitionism,
almost confined to women, which, although certainly symbolic, is absolutely non-sexual, and must not, therefore, be confused with the phenomena we are here occupied with. I refer to the exhibition of the
buttocks as a mark of contempt. In its most primitive form, no doubt,
this exhibitionism is a kind of exorcism, a method of putting evil spirits,
primarily, and secondarily evil-disposed persons, to flight. It is the
most effective way for a woman to display sexual centers, and it shares
in the magical virtues which all unveiling of the sexual centers is believed by primitive peoples to possess. It is recorded that the women
of some peoples in the Balkan peninsula formerly used this gesture
against enemies in battle. In the sixteenth century so distinguished a
theologian as Luther when assailed by the Evil One at night was able
to put the adversary to flight by protruding his uncovered buttocks

from the bed. But the spiritual significance of this attitude is lost with the decay of primitive beliefs. It survives, but merely as a gesture of insult. The symbolism comes to have reference to the nates as the excretory focus, the seat of the anus. In any case it ignores any sexual attractiveness in this part of the body. Exhibitionism of this kind, therefore, can scarcely arise in persons of any sensitiveness or æsthetic perception, even putting aside the question of modesty, and there seems to be little trace of it in classic antiquity when the nates were regarded as objects of beauty. Among the Egyptians, however, we gather from Herodotus (Bk. II, Chapter LX) that at a certain popular religious festival men and women would go in boats on the Nile, singing and playing, and when they approached a town the women on the boats would insult the women of the town by injurious language and by exposing themselves. Among the Arabs, however, the specific gesture we are concerned with is noted, and a man to whom vengeance is forbidden would express his feelings by exposing his posterior and strewing earth on his head (Wellhausen, *Reste Arabischen Heidentums*, 1897, p. 195). It is in Europe and in mediæval and later times that this emphatic gesture seems to have flourished as a violent method of expressing contempt. It was by no means confined to the lower classes, and Kleinpaul, in discussing this form of "speech without words," quotes examples of various noble persons, even princesses, who are recorded thus to have expressed their feelings. (Kleinpaul, *Sprache ohne Worte*, pp. 271-273.) In more recent times the gesture has become merely a rare and extreme expression of unrestrained feeling in coarse-grained peasants. Zola, in the figure of Mouquette in *Germinal*, may be said to have given a kind of classic expression to the gesture. In the more remote parts of Europe it appears to be still not altogether uncommon. This seems to be notably the case among the South Slavs, and Krauss states that "when a South Slav woman wishes to express her deepest contempt for anyone she bends forward, with left hand raising her skirts, and with the right slapping her posterior, at the same time exclaiming: 'This for you!'" (Κρυπτάδια, vol. vi, p. 200.)

A verbal survival of this gesture, consisting in the contemptuous invitation to kiss this region, still exists among us in remote parts of the country, especially as an insult offered by an angry woman who forgets herself. It is said to be commonly used in Wales. ("Welsh Ædœology," Κρυπτάδια, vol. ii, pp. 358, *et seq.*) In Cornwall, when addressed by a woman to a man it is sometimes regarded as a deadly insult, even if the woman is young and attractive, and may cause a life-long enmity between related families. From this point of view the nates are a symbol of contempt, and any sexual significance is excluded. (The distinction is brought out by Diderot in *Le Neveu de Rameau: "Lui:—* Il y a d'autres jours où il ne m'en coûterait rien pour être vil tant qu'on voudrait; ces jours-là, pour un liard, je baiserais le cul à la petite Hus. *Moi:*—Eh! mais, l'ami, elle est blanche, jolie, douce, potelée, et c'est un acte d'humilité auquel un plus delicat que vous pourrait quelquefois s'abaisser. *Lui:*—Entendons-nous; c'est qu'il y a baiser le cul au simple, et baiser le cul au figuré.")

It must be added that a sexual form of exhibitionism of the nates must still be recognized. It occurs in masochism and expresses the desire for passive flagellation. Rousseau, whose emotional life was profoundly affected by the castigations which as a child he received from Mlle Lambercier, has in his *Confessions* told us how, when a youth, he would sometimes expose himself in this way in the presence of young women. Such masochistic exhibitionism seems, however, to be rare.

While the manifestations of exhibitionism are substantially the same in all cases, there are many degrees and varieties of the condition. We may find among exhibitionists, as Garnier remarks, dementia, states of unconsciousness, epilepsy, general paralysis, alcoholism, but the most typical cases, he adds, if not indeed the cases to which the term properly belongs, are those in which it is an impulsive obsession. Krafft-Ebing[1] divides exhibitionists into four clinical groups: (1) acquired states of mental weakness, with cerebral or spinal disease clouding consciousness and at the same time causing impotence; (2) epileptics, in whom the act is an abnormal organic impulse performed in a state of imperfect consciousness; (3) a somewhat allied group of neurasthenic cases; (4) periodical impulsive cases with deep hereditary taint. This classification is not altogether satisfactory. Garnier's classification, placing the group of obsessional cases in the foreground and leaving the other more vaguely defined groups in the background, is probably better. I am inclined to consider that most of the cases fall into one or other of two mixed groups. The first class includes cases in which there is more or less congenital abnormality, but otherwise a fair or even complete degree of mental integrity; they are usually young adults, they are more or less precisely conscious of the end they wish to attain, and it is often only with a severe struggle that they yield to their impulses. In the second class the

---

[1] *Op. cit.*, pp. 478, *et seq.*

beginnings of mental or nervous disease have diminished the sensibility of the higher centers; the subjects are usually old men whose lives have been absolutely correct; they are often only vaguely aware of the nature of the satisfaction they are seeking, and frequently no struggle precedes the manifestation; such was the case of the overworked clergyman described by Hughes,[1] who, after much study, became morose and absent-minded, and committed acts of exhibitionism which he could not explain but made no attempt to deny; with rest and restorative treatment his health improved and the acts ceased. It is in the first class of cases alone that there is a developed sexual perversion. In the cases of the second class there is a more or less definite sexual intention, but it is only just conscious, and the emergence of the impulse is due not to its strength but to the weakness, temporary or permanent, of the higher inhibiting centers.

Epileptic cases, with loss of consciousness during the act, can only be regarded as presenting a pseudo-exhibitionism. They should be excluded altogether. It is undoubtedly true that many cases of real or apparent exhibitionism occur in epileptics.[2] We must not, however, too hastily conclude that because these acts occur in epileptics they are necessarily unconscious acts. Epilepsy frequently occurs on a basis of hereditary degeneration, and the exhibitionism may be, and not infrequently is, a stigma of the degeneracy and not an indication of the occurrence of a minor epileptic fit. When the act of pseudo-exhibitionism is truly epileptic, it will usually have no psychic sexual content, and it will certainly be liable to occur under all sorts of circumstances, when the patient is alone or in a miscellaneous concourse of people. It will be on a level with the acts of the highly respectable young woman who, at the conclusion of an attack of *petit mal,* consisting chiefly of a sudden desire to pass urine, on

---

[1] C. H. Hughes, "Morbid Exhibitionism," *Alienist and Neurologist,* August, 1904. Another somewhat similar American case, also preceded by overwork, and eventually adjudged insane by the courts, is recorded by D. S. Booth, *Alienist and Neurologist,* February, 1905.

[2] Exhibitionism in epilepsy is briefly discussed by Féré, *L'Instinct Sexuel,* second edition, pp. 194-195.

one occasion lifted up her clothes and urinated at a public enter-
tainment, so that it was with difficulty her friends prevented her
from being handed over to the police.[1] Such an act is automatic, unconscious, and involuntary; the spectators are not even
perceived; it cannot be an act of exhibitionism. Whenever, on
the other hand, the place and the time are evidently chosen deliberately,—a quiet spot, the presence of only one or two young
women or children,—it is difficult to admit that we are in the
presence of a fit of epileptic unconsciousness, even when the subject is known to be epileptic.

Even, however, when we exclude those epileptic pseudo-
exhibitionists who, from the legal point of view, are clearly
irresponsible, it must still be remembered that in every case of
exhibitionism there is a high degree of either mental abnormality
on a neuropathic basis, or else of actual disease. This is true to
a greater extent in exhibitionism than in almost any other form
of sexual perversion. No subject of exhibitionism should be
sent to prison without expert medical examination.

---

[1] W. S. Colman, "Post-Epileptic Unconscious Automatic Actions,"
Lancet, July 5, 1890.

VI.

The Forms of Erotic Symbolism are Simulacra of Coitus—Wide Extension of Erotic Symbolism—Fetichism Not Covering the Whole Ground of Sexual Selection—It is Based on the Individual Factor in Selection—Crystallization—The Lover and the Artist—The Key to Erotic Symbolism to be Found in the Emotional Sphere—The Passage to Pathological Extremes.

WE have now examined several very various and yet very typical manifestations in all of which it is not difficult to see how, in some strange and eccentric form—on a basis of association through resemblance or contiguity or both combined—there arises a definite mimicry of the normal sexual act together with the normal emotions which accompany that act. It has become clear in what sense we are justified in recognizing erotic symbolism.

The symbolic and, as it were, abstracted nature of these manifestations is shown by the remarkable way in which they are sometimes capable of transference from the object to the subject. That is to say that the fetichist may show a tendency to cultivate his fetich in his own person. A foot-fetichist may like to go barefoot himself; a man who admired lame women liked to halt himself; a man who was attracted by small waists in women found sexual gratification in tight-lacing himself; a man who was fascinated by fine white skin and wished to cut it found satisfaction in cutting his own skin; Moll's coprolagnic fetichist found a voluptuous pleasure in his own acts of defecation. (See, *e.g.*, Krafft-Ebing, *Op. cit.*, p. 221, 224, 226; Hammond, *Sexual Impotence*, p. 74; *cf.* ante, p. 68.) Such symbolic transference seems to have a profoundly natural basis, for we may see a somewhat similar phenomenon in the well-known tendency of cows to mount a cow in heat. This would appear to be, not so much a homosexual impulse, as the dynamic psychic action of an olfactory sexual symbol in a transformed form.

We seem to have here a psychic process which is a curious reversal of that process of *Einfühlung*—the projection of one's own activities into the object contemplated—which Lipps has so fruitfully developed as the essence of every æsthetic condition. (T. Lipps, *Æsthetik*, Teil I, 1903.) By *Einfühlung* our own interior activity becomes the activity

(105)

of the object perceived, a thing being beautiful in proportion as it lends itself to our *Einfühlung*. But by this action of erotic symbolism, on the other hand, we transfer the activity of the object into ourselves.

When the idea of erotic symbolism as manifested in such definite and typical forms becomes realized, it further becomes clear that the vaguer manifestations of such symbolism are exceedingly widespread. When in a previous volume we were discussing and drawing together the various threads which unite "Love and Pain," it will now be understood that we were standing throughout on the threshold of erotic symbolism. Pain itself, in the sense in which we slowly learned to define it in this relationship—as a state of intense emotional excitement—may, under a great variety of special circumstances, become an erotic symbol and afford the same relief as the emotions normally accompanying the sexual act. Active algolagnia or sadism is thus a form of erotic symbolism; passive algolagnia or masochism is (in a man) an inverted form of erotic symbolism. Active flagellation or passive flagellation are, in exactly the same way, manifestations of erotic symbolism, the imaginative mimicry of coitus.

Binet and also Krafft-Ebing[1] have argued in effect that the whole of sexual selection is a matter of fetichism, that is to say, of erotic symbolism of object. "Normal love," Binet states, "appears as the result of a complicated fetichism." Tarde also seems to have regarded love as normally a kind of fetichism. "We are a long time before we fall in love with a woman," he remarks; "we must wait to see the detail which strikes and delights us, and causes us to overlook what displeases us. Only in normal love the details are many and always changing. Constancy in love is rarely anything else but a voyage around the beloved person, a voyage of exploration and ever new discoveries. The most faithful lover does not love the same woman in the same way for two days in succession."[2]

---

[1] Binet, *Etudes de Psychologie Expérimentale*, esp., p. 84; Krafft-Ebing, *Op. cit.*, p. 18.

[2] G. Tarde, "L'Amour Morbide," *Archives de l'Anthropologie Criminelle*, 1890, p. 585.

From that point of view normal sexual love is the sway of a fetich—more or less arbitrary, more or less (as Binet terms it) polytheistic—and it can have little objective basis. But, as we saw when considering "Sexual Selection in Man" in the previous volume, more especially when analyzing the notion of beauty, we are justified in believing that beauty has to a large extent an objective basis, and that love by no means depends simply on the capricious selection of some individual fetich. The individual factor, as we saw, is but one of many factors which constitute beauty. In the study of sexual selection that individual factor was passed over very lightly. We now see that it is often a factor of great importance, for in it are rooted all these outgrowths—normal in their germs, highly abnormal in their more extreme developments—which make up erotic symbolism.

Erotic symbolism is therefore concerned with all that is least generic, least specific, all that is most intimately personal and individual, in sexual selection. It is the final point in which the decreasing circle of sexual attractiveness is fixed. In the widest and most abstract form sexual selection in man is merely human, and we are atttracted to that which bears most fully the marks of humanity; in a less abstract form it is sexual, and we are attracted to that which most vigorously presents the secondary sexual characteristics; still narrowing, it is the type of our own nation and people that appeals most strongly to us in matters of love; and still further concentrating we are affected by the ideal—in civilization most often the somewhat exotic ideal—of our own day, the fashion of our own city. But the individual factor still remains, and amid the infinite possibilities of erotic symbolism the individual may evolve an ideal which is often, as far as he knows and perhaps in actuality, an absolutely unique event in the history of the human soul.

Erotic symbolism works in its finer manifestations by means of the idealizing aptitudes; it is the field of sexual psychology in which that faculty of crystallization, on which Stendhal loved to dwell, achieves its most brilliant results. In the solitary passage in which we seem to see a smile on the face of the austere poet of the *De Rerum Naturâ*, Lucretius tells us how every lover, however he may be amused by the amorous extravagances of other men, is himself blinded by passion: if his mistress is black she is a fascinating brunette, if she squints she is the rival of Pallas, if too tall she is majestic, if too short she is one of the Graces, *tota merum sal;* if too lean it is her delicate refinement, if too fat then a Ceres, dirty and she disdains adornment, a chatterer and brilliantly vivacious, silent and it is her exquisite modesty.[1]   Sixteen hundred years later Robert Burton, when describing the symptoms of love, made out a long and appalling list of the physical defects which the lover is prepared to admire.[2]

Yet we must not be too certain that the lover is wrong in this matter. We too hastily assume that the casual and hasty judgment of the world is necessarily more reliable, more conformed to what we call "truth," than the judgment of the lover which is founded on absorbed and patient study. In some cases where there is lack of intelligence in the lover and dissimulation in the object of his love, it may be so. But even a poem or a picture will often not reveal its beauty except by the expenditure of time and study. It is foolish to expect that the secret beauty of a human person will reveal itself more easily. The lover is an artist, an artist who constructs an image, it is true, but only by patient and concentrated attention to nature; he knows the defects of his image, probably better than anyone, but he knows also that art lies, not in the avoidance of defects, but in the realization of those traits which swallow up defects and so render them non-existent. A great artist, Rodin, after a life spent in the study of Nature, has declared that for art there is no ugliness in Nature. "I have arrived at this belief by the study of Nature," he said; "I can only grasp the beauty of the soul by the beauty of the body, but some day one will come who will explain what I only catch a glimpse of and will declare how the whole earth is beautiful, and all human beings beautiful. I have never been able to say this in sculpture so well as I wish

---

[1] Lucretius, Lib. IV, vv. 1150-1163.
[2] Burton, *Anatomy of Melancholy,* Part III, Section II, Mem. III, Subs. I.

and as I feel it affirmed within me. For poets Beauty has always been some particular landscape, some particular woman; but it should be all women, all landscapes. A negro or a Mongol has his beauty, however remote from ours, and it must be the same with their characters. There is no ugliness. When I was young I made that mistake, as others do; I could not undertake a woman's bust unless I thought her pretty, according to my particular idea of beauty; to-day I should do the bust of any woman, and it would be just as beautiful. And however ugly a woman may look, when she is with her lover she becomes beautiful; there is beauty in her character, in her passions, and beauty exists as soon as character or passion becomes visible, for the body is a casting on which passions are imprinted. And even without that, there is always the blood that flows in the veins and the air that fills the lungs."[1]

The saint, also, is here at one with the lover and the artist. The man who has so profoundly realized the worth of his fellow men that he is ready even to die in order to save them, feels that he has discovered a great secret. Cyples traces the "secret delights" that have thus risen in the hearts of holy men to the same source as the feelings generated between lovers, friends, parents, and children. "A few have at intervals walked in the world," he remarks, "who have, each in his own original way, found out this marvel. . . . Straightway man in general has become to them so sweet a thing that the infatuation has seemed to the rest of their fellows to be a celestial madness. Beggars' rags to their unhesitating lips grew fit for kissing, because humanity had touched the garb; there were no longer any menial acts, but only welcome services. . . . Remember by how much man is the subtlest circumstance in the world; at how many points he can attach relationships; how manifold and perennial he is in his results. All other things are dull, meager, tame beside him."[1]

---

[1] Judith Cladel, *Auguste Rodin Pris sur la Vie*, 1903, pp. 103-104. Some slight modifications have been made in the translation of this passage on account of the conversational form of the original.

[1] W. Cyples, *The Process of Human Experience*, p. 462. Even if (as we have already seen, *ante*, p. 58) the saint cannot always feel actual

It may be added that even if we still believe that lover and artist and saint are drawing the main elements of their conceptions from the depths of their own consciousness, there is a sense in which they are coming nearer to the truth of things than those for whom their conceptions are mere illusions. The aptitude for realizing beauty has involved an adjustment of the nerves and the associated brain centers through countless ages that began before man was. When the vision of supreme beauty is slowly or suddenly realized by anyone, with a reverberation that extends throughout his organism, he has attained to something which for his species, and for far more than his species, is truth, and can only be illusion to one who has artificially placed himself outside the stream of life.

In an essay on "The Gods as Apparitions of the Race-Life," Edward Carpenter, though in somewhat Platonic phraseology, thus well states the matter: "The youth sees the girl; it may be a chance face, a chance outline, amid the most banal surroundings. But it gives the cue. There is a memory, a confused reminiscence. The mortal figure without penetrates to the immortal figure within, and there rises into consciousness a shining form, glorious, not belonging to this world, but vibrating with the agelong life of humanity, and the memory of a thousand love-dreams. The waking of this vision intoxicates the man; it glows and burns within him; a goddess (it may be Venus herself) stands in the sacred place of his temple; a sense of awe-struck splendor fills him, and the world is changed." "He sees something" (the same writer continues in a subsequent essay, "Beauty and Duty") "which, in a sense, is more real than the figures in the street, for he sees something that has lived and moved for hundreds of years in the heart of the race; something which has been one of the great formative influences of his own life, and which has done as much to create those very figures in the street as qualities in the circulation of the blood may do to form a finger or other limb. He comes into touch with a very real Presence or Power—one of those organic centers of growth in the life of humanity—and feels this larger life within himself, subjective, if you like, and yet intensely objective. And more. For is it not also evident that the woman, the mortal woman who excites his Vision, *has* some closest relation to it, and is, indeed, far more than a mere mask or empty formula which reminds him of it? For she indeed has within her, just as much as the

---

physical pleasure in the intimate contact of humanity, the ardor of devoted service which his vision of humanity arouses remains unaffected.

man has, deep subconscious Powers working; and the ideal which has dawned so entrancingly on the man is in all probability closely related to that which has been working most powerfully in the heredity of the woman, and which has most contributed to mold *her* form and outline. No wonder, then, that her form should remind him of it. Indeed, when he looks into her eyes he sees *through* to a far deeper life even than she herself may be aware of, and yet which is truly hers—a life perennial and wonderful. The more than mortal in him beholds the more than mortal in her; and the gods descend to meet." (Edward Carpenter, *The Art of Creation*, pp. 137, 186.)

It is this mighty force which lies behind and beneath the aberrations we have been concerned with, a great reservoir from which they draw the life-blood that vivifies even their most fantastic shapes. Fetichism and the other forms of erotic symbolism are but the development and the isolation of the crystallizations which normally arise on the basis of sexual selection. Normal in their basis, in their extreme forms they present the utmost pathological aberrations of the sexual instinct which can be attained or conceived. In the intermediate space all degrees are possible. In the slightest degree the symbol is merely a specially fascinating and beloved feature in a person who is, in all other respects, felt to be lovable; as such its recognition is a legitimate part of courtship, an effective aid to tumescence. In a further degree the symbol is the one arresting and attracting character of a person who must, however, still be felt as a sexually attractive individual. In a still further degree of perversion the symbol is effective, even though the person with whom it is associated is altogether unattractive. In the final stage the person and even all association with a person disappear altogether from the field of sexual consciousness; the abstract symbol rules supreme.

Long, however, before the symbol has reached that final climax of morbid intensity we may be said to have passed beyond the sphere of sexual love. A person, not an abstracted quality, must be the goal of love. So long as the fetich is subordinated to the person it serves to heighten love. But love must be based on a complexus of attractive qualities, or it has no stability.[1] As soon as the fetich becomes isolated and omnipotent, so that the person sinks into the background as an unimportant appendage of the fetich, all stability is lost. The fetichist now follows an impersonal and abstract symbol withersoever it may lead him.

It has been seen that there are an extraordinary number of forms in which erotic symbolism may be felt. It must be remembered, and it cannot be too distinctly emphasized, that the links that bind together the forms of erotic symbolism are not to be found in objects or even in acts, but in the underlying emotion. A feeling is the first condition of the symbol, a feeling which recalls, by a subtle and unconscious automatic association of resemblance or of contiguity, some former feeling. It is the similarity of emotion, instinctively apprehended, which links on a symbol only partially sexual, or even apparently not sexual at all, to the great central focus of sexual emotion, the great dominating force which brings the symbol its life-blood.[2]

The cases of sexual hyperæsthesia, quoted at the beginning of this study, do but present in a morbidly comprehensive and sensitive form those possibilities of erotic symbolism which, in some degree, or at some period, are latent in most persons. They are genuinely instinctive and automatic, and have nothing in common with that fanciful and deliberate play of the intelligence around sexual imagery—not infrequently seen in abnormal and insane persons—which has no significance for sexual psychology.

It is to the extreme individualization involved by the developments of erotic symbolism that the fetichist owes his morbid and perilous isolation. The lover who is influenced by all the elements of sexual selection is always supported by the fellow-feeling of a larger body of other human beings; he has behind him his species, his sex, his nation, or at the very least a fashion. Even the inverted lover in most cases is soon able to create

---

[1] "To love," as Stendhal defined it (*De l'Amour*, Chapter II), "is to have pleasure in seeing, touching, and feeling by all the senses, and as near as possible, a beloved object by whom one is oneself loved."

[2] Pillon's study of "La Mémoire Affective" (*Revue Philosophique*, February, 1901) helps to explain the psychic mechanism of the process.

around him an atmosphere constituted by persons whose ideals resemble his own. But it is not so with the erotic symbolist. He is nearly always alone. He is predisposed to isolation from the outset, for it would seem to be on a basis of excessive shyness and timidity that the manifestations of erotic symbolism arc most likely to develop. When at length the symbolist realizes his own aspirations—which seem to him for the most part an altogether new phenomenon in the world—and at the same time realizes the wide degree in which they deviate from those of the rest of mankind, his natural secretiveness is still further reinforced. He stands alone. His most sacred ideals are for all those around him a childish absurdity, or a disgusting obscenity, possibly a matter calling for the intervention of the policeman. We have forgotten that all these impulses which to us seem so unnatural—this adoration of the foot and other despised parts of the body, this reverence for the excretory acts and products, the acceptance of congress with animals, the solemnity of self-exhibition—were all beliefs and practices which, to our remote forefathers, were bound up with the highest conceptions of life and the deepest ardors of religion.

A man cannot, however, deviate at once so widely and so spontaneously in his impulses from the rest of the world in which he himself lives without possessing an aboriginally abnormal temperament. At the very least he exhibits a neuropathic sensitiveness to abnormal impressions. Not infrequently there is more than this, the distinct stigmata of degeneration, sometimes a certain degree of congenital feeble-mindedness or a tendency to insanity.

Yet, regarded as a whole, and notwithstanding the frequency with which they witness to congenital morbidity, the phenomena of erotic symbolism can scarcely fail to be profoundly impressive to the patient and impartial student of the human soul. They often seem absurd, sometimes disgusting, occasionally criminal; they are always, when carried to an extreme degree, abnormal. But of all the manifestations of sexual psychology, normal and abnormal, they are the most specifically human. More than any others they involve the potently plastic force of the imagination. They bring before us the individual man, not only apart from his fellows, but in opposition, himself creating his own paradise. They constitute the supreme triumph of human idealism.

THE MECHANISM OF DETUMESCENCE.

I.

The Psychological Significance of Detumescence—The Testis and the Ovary—Sperm Cell and Germ Cell—Development of the Embryo—The External Sexual Organs—Their Wide Range of Variation—Their Nervous Supply—The Penis—Its Racial Variations—The Influence of Exercise—The Scrotum and Testicles—The Mons Veneris—The Vulva—The Labia Majora and their Varieties—The Pubic Hair and Its Characters—The Clitoris and Its Functions—The Anus as an Erogenous Zone—The Nymphæ and their Function—The Vagina—The Hymen—Virginity—The Biological Significance of the Hymen.

In analyzing the sexual impulse we have seen that the process whereby the conjunction of the sexes is achieved falls naturally into two phases: the first phase, of tumescence, during which force is generated in the organism, and the second phase, of detumescence, in which that force is discharged during conjugation.[1] Hitherto we have been occupied mainly with the first phase, that of tumescence, and with its associated psychic phenomena. It was inevitable that this should be so, for it is during the slow process of tumescence that sexual selection is decided, the crystallizations of love elaborated, and, to a large extent, the individual erotic symbols determined. But we can by no means altogether pass over the final phase of detumescence. Its consideration, it is true, brings us directly into the field of anatomy and physiology; while tumescence is largely under control of the will, when the moment of detumescence arrives the reins slip from the control of the will; the more fundamental and uncontrollable impulses of the organ-

---

[1] "Analysis of the Sexual Impulse," in vol. iii of these *Studies*.

ism gallop on unchecked; the chariot of Phaëthon dashes blindly down into a sea of emotion.

Yet detumescence is the end and climax of the whole drama; it is an anatomico-physiological process, certainly, but one that inevitably touches psychology at every point.[1] It is, indeed, the very key to the process of tumescence, and unless we understand and realize very precisely what it is that happens during detumescence, our psychological analysis of the sexual impulse must remain vague and inadequate.

From the point of view we now occupy, a man and a woman are no longer two highly sensitive organisms vibrating, voluptuously it may indeed be, but vaguely and indefinitely, to all kinds of influences and with fluctuating impulses capable of being directed into any channel, even in the highest degree divergent from the proper ends of procreation. They are now two genital organisms who exist to propagate the race, and whatever else they may be, they must be adequately constituted to effect the act by which the future of the race is ensured. We have to consider what are the material conditions which ensure the most satisfactory and complete fulfillment of this act, and how those conditions may be correlated with other circumstances in the organism. In thus approaching the subject we shall find that we have not really abandoned the study of the psychic aspects of sex.

The two most primary sexual organs are the testis and the ovary; it is the object of conjugation to bring into contact the sperm from the testis with the germ from the ovary. There is no reason to suppose that the germ-cell and the sperm-cell are essentially different from each other. Sexual conjugation thus remains a process which is radically the same as the non-sexual mode of propagation which preceded it. The fusion of the nuclei of the two cells was regarded by Van Beneden, who in 1875 first accurately described it, as a process of conjugation comparable to that of the protozoa and the protophyta. Boveri,

---

[1] "The accomplishment of no other function," Hyrtl remarks, "is so intimately connected with the mind and yet so independent of it."

who has further extended our knowledge of the process, considers that the spermatozoon removes an inhibitory influence preventing the commencement of development in the ovum; the spermatozoon replaces a portion of the ovum which has already undergone degeneration, so that the object of conjugation is chiefly to effect the union of the properties of two cells in one, sexual fertilization achieving a division of labor with reciprocal inhibition; the two cells have renounced their original faculty of separate development in order to attain a fusion of qualities and thus render possible that production of new forms and qualities which has involved the progress of the organized world.[1]

While in fishes this conjugation of the male and female elements is usually ensured by the female casting her spawn into an artificial nest outside the body, on to which the male sheds his milt, in all animals (and, to some extent, birds, who occupy an intermediate position) there is an organic nest, or incubation chamber as Bland Sutton terms it, the womb, in the female body, wherein the fertilized egg may develop to a high degree of maturity sheltered from those manifold risks of the external world which make it necessary for the spawn of fishes to be so enormous in amount. Since, however, men and women have descended from remote ancestors who, in the manner of aquatic creatures, exercised functions of sperm-extrusion and germ-extrusion that were exactly analogous in the two sexes, without any specialized female uterine organization, the early stages of human male and female fœtal development still display the comparatively undifferentiated sexual organization of those remote ancestors, and during the first months of fœtal life it is practically impossible to tell by the inspection of the genital regions whether the embryo would have developed into a man or into a woman. If we examine the embryo at an early stage of development we see that the hind end is the body stalk, this stalk in later stages becoming part of the umbilical cord.

---

[1] The process is still, however, but imperfectly understood; see Art. "Fécondation," by Ed. Retterer, in Richet's *Dictionnaire de Physiologie*, vol. vi, 1905.

The urogenital region, formed by the rapid extension of the hind end beyond its original limit, which corresponds to what is later the umbilicus, develops mainly by the gradual differentiation of structures (the Wolffian and Müllerian bodies) which originally exist identically in both sexes. This process of sexual differentiation is highly complex, so that it cannot yet be said that there is complete agreement among investigators as to its details. When some irregularity or arrest of development occurs in the process we have one or other of the numerous malformations which may affect this region. If the arrest occurs at a very early stage we may even find a condition of things which seems to approximate to that which normally exists in the adult reptilia.[1] Owing to the fact that both male and female organs develop from more primitive structures which were sexually undifferentiated, a fundamental analogy in the sexual organs of the sexes always remains; the developed organs of one sex exist as rudiments in the other sex; the testicles correspond to the ovaries; the female clitoris is the homologue of the male penis; the scrotum of one sex is the labia majora in the other sex, and so throughout, although it is not always possible at present to be quite certain in regard to these homologies.

Since the object to be attained by the sexual organs in the human species is identical with that which they subserve in their pre-human ancestors, it is not surprising to find that these structures have a clear resemblance to the corresponding structures in the apes, although on the whole there would appear to be in man a higher degree of sexual differentiation. Thus the uterus of various species of *semnopithecus* seems to show a noteworthy correspondence with the same organ in woman.[2] The somewhat less degree of sexual differentiation is well shown in the gorilla; in the male the external organs are in the passive state covered by the wrinkled skin of the abdomen, while in the

[1] Thus a male fœtus showing reptilian characters in sexual ducts was exhibited by Shattock at the Pathological Society of London, February 19, 1895.

[2] J. Kohlbrugge, "Die Umgestaltung des Uterus der Affen nach den Geburt," *Zeitschrift für Morphologie*, bd. iv, p. 1, 1901.

female, on the contrary, they are very apparent, and in sexual excitement the large clitoris and nymphæ become markedly prominent. The penis of the gorilla, however, more nearly resembles that of man, according to Hartmann, than does that of the other anthropoid apes, which diverge from the human type in this respect more than do the cynocephalic apes and some species of baboon.

From the psychological point of view we are less interested in the internal sexual organs, which are most fundamentally concerned with the production and reception of the sexual elements, than with the more external parts of the genital apparatus which serve as the instruments of sexual excitation, and the channels for the intromission and passage of the seminal fluid. It is these only which can play any part at all in sexual selection; they are the only part of the sexual apparatus which can enter into the formation of either normal or abnormal erotic conceptions; they are the organs most prominently concerned with detumescence; they alone enter normally into the conscious process of sex at any time. It seems desirable, therefore, to discuss them briefly at this point.

Our knowledge of the individual and racial variations of the external sexual organs is still extremely imperfect. A few monographs and collections of data on isolated points may be found in more or less inaccessible publications. As regards women, Ploss and Bartels have devoted a chapter to the sexual organs of women which extends to a hundred pages, but remains scanty and fragmentary. (*Das Weib*, vol. i, Chapter VI.) The most systematic series of observations have been made in the case of the various kinds of degenerates—idiots, the insane, criminals, etc.—but it would be obviously unsafe to rely too absolutely on such investigations for our knowledge of the sexual organs of the ordinary population.

There can be no doubt, however, that the external sexual organs in normal men and women exhibit a peculiarly wide range of variation. This is indicated not only by the unsystematic results attained by experienced observers, but also by more systematic studies. Thus Herman has shown by detailed measurements that there are great normal variations in the conformation of the parts that form the floor of the female pelvis. He found that the projection of the pelvic floor varied from nothing to as much as two inches, and that in healthy women who had borne no children the distance between the coccyx and anus, the length of the perineum, the distance between the fourchette and the symphysis pubis, and the length of the vagina are subject to wide variations. (*Lancet*, October 12, 1889.) Even the female urethral opening varies very greatly, as has been shown by Bergh, who investigated it in nearly 700 women and reproduces the various shapes found; while most usually (in about a third of the cases observed), a longtitudinal slit, it may be cross-shaped, star-shaped, crescentic, etc.; and while sometimes very small, in about 6 per cent. of the cases it admitted the tip of the little finger. (Bergh, *Monatsheft für Praktische Dermatologie*, 15 Sept., 1897.)

As regards both sexes, Stanley Hall states that "Dr. F. N. Seerley, who has examined over 2000 normal young men as well as many young women, tells me that in his opinion individual variations in these parts are much greater even than those of face and form, and that the range of adult and apparently normal size and proportion, as well as function, and of both the age and order of development, not only of each of the several parts themselves, but of all their immediate annexes, and in females as well as males, is far greater than has been recognized by any writer. This fact is the basis of the anxieties and fears of morphological abnormality so frequent during adolescence." (G. S. Hall, *Adolescence*, vol. i, p. 414).

In accordance with the supreme importance of the part they play, and the intimately psychic nature of that part, the sexual organs, both internal and external, are very richly supplied with nerves. While the internal organs are very abundantly furnished with sympathetic nerves and ganglia, the external organs show the highest possible degree of specialization of the various peripheral nervous devices which the organism has developed for receiving, accumulating, and transmitting stimuli to the brain.[1]

"The number of conducting cords which attach the genitals to the nervous centers is simply enormous," writes Bryan Robinson; "the pudic nerve is composed of nearly all the third sacral and branches from the second and fourth sacral. As one examines this nerve he is forced to the conclusion that it is an enormous supply for a small organ. The periphery of the pudic nerve spreads itself like a fan over the genitals." The lesser sciatic nerve supplies only one muscle—the gluteus maximus

---

[1] There are, however, no special nerve endings (Krause corpuscles), as was formerly supposed. The nerve endings in the genital region are the same as elsewhere. The difference lies in the abundance of superposed arboreal ramifications. See, *e.g.*, Ed. Retterer, Art. "Ejaculation," Richet's *Dictionnaire de Physiologie*, vol. v.

—and then sends the large pudendal branch to the side of the penis, and hence the friction of coitus induces active contraction of the gluteus maximus, "the main muscle of coition." The large pudic and the pudendal constitute the main supply of the external genitals. In women the pudic nerve is equally large, but the pudendal much smaller, possibly, Bryan Robinson suggests, because women take a less active part in coitus. The nerve supply of the clitoris, however, is three or four times as large as that of the penis in proportion to size. (F. B. Robinson, "The Intimate Nervous Connection of the Genito-Urinary Organs With the Cerebro-Spinal and Sympathetic Systems," *New York Medical Journal*, March 11, 1893; *id. The Abdominal Brain*, 1899.)

Of all the sexual organs the penis is without doubt that which has most powerfully impressed the human imagination. It is the very emblem of generation, and everywhere men have contemplated it with a mixture of reverence and shuddering awe that has sometimes, even among civilized peoples, amounted to horror and disgust. Its image is worn as an amulet to ward off evil and invoked as a charm to call forth blessing. The sexual organs were once the most sacred object on which a man could place his hands to swear an inviolate oath, just as now he takes up the Testament. Even in the traditions of the great classic civilization which we inherit the penis is *fascinus,* the symbol of all fascination. In the history of human culture it has had far more than a merely human significance; it has been the symbol of all the generative force of Nature, the embodiment of creative energy in the animal and vegetable worlds alike, an image to be held aloft for worship, the sign of all unconscious ecstasy. As a symbol, the sacred phallus, it has been woven in and out of all the highest and deepest human conceptions, so intimately that it is possible to see it everywhere, that it is possible to fail to see it anywhere.

In correspondence with the importance of the penis is the large number of names which men have everywhere bestowed upon it. In French literature many hundred synonyms may be found. They were also numerous in Latin. In English the literary terms for the penis seem to be comparatively few, but a large number of non-literary synonyms exist in colloquial and perhaps merely local usage. The Latin term penis, which has established itself among us as the most correct designation, is generally considered to be associated with *pendere* and to be connected therefore with the usually pendent position of the organ. In the middle ages the general literary term throughout Europe was *coles* (or *colis*) from *caulis*, a stalk, and *virga*, a rod. The only serious English literary term, yard (exactly equivalent to *virga*), as used by Chaucer—almost the last great English writer whose vocabulary was adequate to the central facts of life—has now fallen out of literary and even colloquial usage.

Pierer and Chaulant, in their anatomical and physiological *Real-Lexicon* (vol. vi, p. 134), give nearly a hundred synonyms for the penis. Hyrtl (*Topographisches Anatomie*, seventh edition, vol. ii, pp. 67-69), adds others. Schurig, in his *Spermatologia* (1720, pp. 89-91), also presents a number of names for the penis; in Chapter III (pp. 189-192) of the same book he discusses the penis generally with more fullness than most authors. Louis de Landes, in his *Glossaire Erotique* of the French language (pp. 239-242), enumerates several hundred literary synonyms for the penis, though many of them probably only occur once.

There is no thorough and comprehensive modern study of the penis on an anthropological basis (though I should mention a valuable and fully illustrated study of anthropological and pathological variations of the penis in a series of articles by Marandon de Montyel, "Des Anomalies des Organs Génitaux Externes Chez les Aliénées," etc., *Archives d'Anthropologie Criminelle*, 1895), and it would be out of place here to attempt to collect the scattered notices regarding racial and other variations. It may suffice to note some of the evidence showing that such variations seem to be numerous and important. The Arab penis (according to Kocher) is slender and long (a third longer than the average European penis) and with a club-shaped glans. It undergoes little change when it enters the erect state. The clothes leaves it quite free, and the Arab practices manual excitement at an early age to favor its development.

Among the Fuegians, also, according to Hyades and Deniker (*Cap Horn*, vol. vii, p. 153), the average length of the penis is 77 millimeters, which is longer than in Europeans.

In men of black race, also, the penis is decidedly large. Thus Sir H. H. Johnston (*British Central Africa*, p. 399) states this to be a universal rule. Among the Wankenda of Northern Nyassa, for instance, he remarks that, while the body is of medium size, the penis is generally large. He gives the usual length as about six inches, reaching nine or ten in erection. The prepuce, it is added, is often very long, and circumcision is practiced by many tribes.

Among the American negroes Hrdlicka has found, also (*Proceedings American Association for the Advancement of Science*, vol. xlvii, p. 475), that the penis in black boys is larger than in white boys.

The passages cited above suggest the question whether the penis becomes larger by exercise of its generative functions. Most old authors assert that frequent erection makes the penis large and long (Schurig, *Spermatologia*, p. 107). Galen noted that in singers and athletes, who were chaste in order to preserve their strength, the sexual parts were small and rugrose, like those of old men, and that exercise of the organs from youth develops them; Roubaud, quoting this observation (*Traité de l'Impuissance*, p. 373), agrees with the statement. It seems probable that there is an element of truth in this ancient belief. At the same time it must be remembered that the penis is only to small extent a muscular organ, and that the increase of size produced by frequent congestion of erectile tissues cannot be either rapid or pronounced. Variations in the size of the sexual organs are probably on the whole mainly inherited, though it is impossible to speak decisively on this point until more systematic observations become customary.

The scrotum has usually, in the human imagination, been regarded merely as an appendage of the penis, of secondary importance, although it is the garment of the primary and essential organs of sex, and the fact that it is not the seat of any voluptuous sensation has doubtless helped to confirm this position. Even the name is merely a mediæval perversion of *scortum,* skin or hide. In classic times it was usually called the pouch or purse. The importance of the testicles has not, however, been altogether ignored, as the very word *testis* itself shows, for the *testis* is simply the *witness* of virility.[1]

It is easy to understand why the penis should occupy this special place in man's thoughts as the supreme sexual organ. It is the one conspicuous and prominent portion of the sexual apparatus, while its aptitude for swelling and erecting itself involuntarily, under the influence of sexual emotion, gives it a peculiar and almost unique position in the body. At the same time it is the point at which, in the male body, all voluptuous sensation is concentrated, the only normal masculine center of sex.[2]

---

[1] Hyrtl, *Op. cit.*, vol. ii, p. 39.

[2] Sensations of pleasure without those of touch appear to be

It is not easy to find any correspondingly conspicuous symbol of sex in the sexual region of women. In the normal position nothing is visible but the peculiarly human cushion of fat picturesquely termed the Mons Veneris (because, as Palfyn said, all those who enroll themselves under the banner of Venus must necessarily scale it), and even that is veiled from view in the adult by the more or less bushy plantation of hair which grows upon it. A triangle of varyingly precise definition is thus formed at the lower apex of the trunk, and this would sometimes appear to have been regarded as a feminine symbol.[1] But the more usual and typical symbol of femininity is the idealized ring (by some savages drawn as a lozenge) of the vulvar opening—the *yoni* corresponding to the masculine *lingam*—which is normally closed from view by the larger lips arising from beneath the shadow of the *mons*. It is a symbol that, like the masculine phallus, has a double meaning among primitive peoples and is sometimes used to call down a blessing and sometimes to invoke a curse.[2]

This external opening of the feminine genital passage with its two enclosing lips is now generally called the vulva. It would appear that originally (as by Celsus and Pliny) this term included the womb, also, but when the term "uterus" came into use "vulva" was confined (as its sense of folding doors suggests that it should be) to the external entrance. The classic term *cunnus* for the external genitals was chiefly used by the poets; it has been the etymological source of various European names for this region, such as the old French *con,* which has now, however, disappeared from literature while even in popular usage it has given place to *lapin* and similar terms. But there is always a tendency, marked in most parts of the world, for the names of the external female parts to become indecorous. Even in classic antiquity this part was the *pudendum,* the part

---

normal at the tip of the penis, as pointed out by Scripture, quoted in *Alienist and Neurologist,* January, 1898.

[1] See the previous volume of these *Studies,* "Sexual Selection in Man," p 161.

[2] See, *e.g.,* Ploss and Bartels, *Das Weib,* vol. i, beginning of chapter VI.

to be ashamed of, and among ourselves the mass of the population, still preserving the traditions of primitive times, continue to cherish the same notion.

The anatomy, anthropology, folk-lore, and terminology of the external and to some extent the internal feminine sexual region may be studied in the following publications, among others: Ploss, *Das Weib*, vol. i, Chapter VI; Hyrtl, *Topographisches Anatomie*, vol. ii, and other publications by the same scholarly anatomist; W. J. Stewart Mackay, *History of Ancient Gynæcology*, especially pp. 244-250; R. Bergh, "Symbolæ ad Cognitionem Genitalium Externorum Fœminearum" (in Danish). *Hospitalstidende*, August, 1894; and also in *Monatshefte für Praktische Dermatologie*, 1897. D. S. Lamb, "The Female External Genital Organs," *New York Journal of Gynæcology*, August, 1894; R. L. Dickinson, "Hypertrophies of the Labia Minora and Their Significance," *American Gynecology*, September, 1902; Κρυπτάδια (in various languages), vol. viii, pp. 3-11, 11-13, and many other passages. Several of Schurig's works (especially *Gynæcologia, Muliebria*, and *Parthenologia*) contain full summaries of the statements of the early writers.

The external or larger lips, like the mons veneris, are specifically human in their full development, for in the anthropoid apes they are small as is the mons, and in the lower apes absent altogether; they are, moreover, larger in the white than in the other human races. Thus in the negro, and to a less degree in the Japanese (Wernich) and the Javanese (Scherzer) they are less developed than in women of white race. The greater lips develop in the fœtus later than the lesser lips, which are thus at first uncovered; this condition thus constitutes an infantile state which occasionally (in less than 2 per cent. of cases, according to Bergh) persists in the adult. Their generally accepted name, labia majora, is comparatively modern.[1]

The outer sides of the labia majora are covered with hair, and on the inner sides, which are smooth and moist, but are not true mucous membrane, there are a few sweat glands and numerous large sebaceous glands. Bergh considers that there is little or no hair on the inner sides of the labia majora, but Lamb states that careful examination shows that from one- to two-thirds of the inner surface in adult women

---

[1] Hyrtl states that the name *labia* was first used by Haller in the middle of the eighteenth century in his *Elements of Physiology*, being adopted by him from the Greek poet Erotion, who gave these structures the very obvious name χείλεα. lips. But this seems to be a mistake, for the seventeenth century anatomists certainly used the name "labia" for these parts.

show hairs like those of the external surface. In brunettes and women of dark races this surface is pigmented; in dark races it is usually a slate gray. From an examination of 2200 young Danish prostitutes Bergh has found that there are two main varieties in the shape of the labia majora, with transitional forms. In the first and most frequent form the labia tend to be less marked and more effaced and separated at the upper and anterior part, often being lost in the sides of the mons and presenting a fissure which is broader in its upper part and showing the inner lips more or less bare. In the second form the labia are thicker and more outstanding and the inner edges lie in contact throughout their whole length, showing the *rima pudendi* as a long narrow fissure. Whatever the form, the labia close more tightly together in virgins and in young individuals generally than in the deflowered and the elderly. In children, as Martineau pointed out, the vulva appears to look directly forward and the clitoris and urinary meatus easily appear, while in adult women, and especially after attempts at coitus have been made, the vulva appears directed more below and behind, and the clitoris and meatus more covered by the labia majora; so that the child urinates forward, while the adult woman is usually able to urinate almost directly downwards in the erect position, though in some cases (as may occasionally be observed in the street) she can only do so when bending slightly forwards. This difference in the direction of the stream formerly furnished one of the methods of diagnosing virginity, an uncertain one, since the difference is largely due to age and individual variation. The main factor in the position and aspect of the vulva is pelvic inclination. (See Havelock Ellis, *Man and Woman*, fourth edition, p. 64; Stratz, *Die Schönheit des Weiblichen Korpers*, Chapter XII.) In the European woman, according to Stratz, a considerable degree of pelvic inclination is essential to beauty, concealing all but the anterior third of the vulva. In negresses and other women of lower race the vulva, however, usually lies further back, being more conspicuous from behind than in European women; in this respect lower races resemble the apes. Those women of dark race, therefore, whose modesty is focussed behind rather than in front thus have sound anatomical considerations on their side.

As Ploss and Bartels remark, a very common variation among European women consists in an unusually posterior position of the vulva and vaginal entrance, so that unless a cushion is placed under the buttocks it is difficult for the man to effect coitus in the usual position without giving much pain to the woman. They add that another anomaly, less easy to remedy, consists in an abnormally anterior position of the vaginal entrance close beneath the pelvic bone, so that, although intromission is easy, the spasmodic contraction of the vagina at the culmination of orgasm presses the penis against the bone and causes intolerable pain to the man.

The mons veneris and the labia majora are, after the age of puberty, always normally covered by a more or less profuse growth of hair. It is notable that the apes, notwithstanding their general tendency to hairiness, show no such special development of hair in this region. We thus see that all the external and more conspicuous portions of the sexual sphere in woman —the mons veneris, the labia majora, and the hair—represent not so much an animal inheritance, such as we commonly misrepresent them to be, but a higher and genuinely human development. As none of these structures subserve any clear practical use, it would appear that they must have developed by sexual selection to satisfy the æsthetic demands of the eye.[1]

The character and arrangement of the pubic hair, investigated by Eschricht and Voigt more than half a century ago, have been more recently studied by Bergh. As these observers have pointed out, there are various converging hair streams from above and below, the clitoris seeming to be the center towards which they are directed. The hair-covering thus formed is usually ample and, as a rule, is more so in brunettes than in blondes. It is nearly always bent, curly and more or less spirally twisted.[1] There are frequently one or two curls at the commencement of the fissure, rolled outwards, and occasionally a well marked tuft in the middle line. In abundance the pubic hair corresponds with the axillary hair; when one region is defective in hair the other is usually so also. Strong eyebrows also usually indicate a strong development of pubic hair. But the hair of the head usually varies independently, and Bergh found that of 154 women with spare pubic hair 72 had good and often profuse hair on the head. Complete or almost

---

[1] Bergh tentatively suggests, as regards the pubic hair, that its appearance may be due to the upright walk in man and the human position during coitus, the hair preventing irritation of the genitals from the sweat pouring down from the body and protecting the skin from direct friction in coitus. (In both these suggestions he was, however, long previously anticipated by Fabricius ab Aquapendente.) The fanciful suggestion of Louis Robinson that the pubic hair has developed in order to enable the human infant to cling securely to his mother is very poorly supported by facts, and has not met with acceptance. It may be mentioned that (as stated by Ploss and Bartels) the women of the Bismarck Archipelago, whose pubic hair is very abundant, use it as a kind of handkerchief on which to clean their hands.

[2] Routh and Heywood Smith have noted that the pubic hair tends to lose its curliness and become straight in women who masturbate. (*British Gynæcological Journal*, February, 1887, p. 505.)

complete absence of pubic hair is in Bergh's experience only found in about 3 per cent. of women; these were all young and blonde.

Rothe, in his investigation of the pubic hair of 1000 Berlin women, found that no two women were really alike in this respect, but there was a tendency to two main types of arrangement, with minor subdivisions, according as the hair tended to grow chiefly in the middle line extending laterally from that line, or to grow equally over the whole extent of the pubic region; these two groups included half the cases investigated.

In men the pubic hair normally ascends anteriorly in a faint line up to the navel, with tendency to form a triangle with the apex above, and posteriorly extends backwards to the anus. In women these anterior and posterior extensions are comparatively rare, or at all events are only represented by a few stray hairs. Rothe found this variation in 4 per cent. of North German women, though a triangle of hair was only found in 2 per cent.; Lombroso found it in 5 per cent. of Italian women; Bergh found it in only 1.6 per cent. among 1000 Danish prostitutes, all sixteen of whom with three exceptions were brunettes. In Vienna, among 600 women, Coe found only 1 per cent. with this distribution of hair, and states that they were women of decidedly masculine type, though Ploss and Bartels, as well as Rothe, find, however, that heterogeny, as they term the masculine distribution, is more common in blondes. The anterior extension of hair is usually accompanied by the posterior extension around the anus, usually very slight, but occasionally as pronounced as in men. (According to Rothe, however, anterior heterogeny is comparatively rare.) These masculine variations in the extension of the pubic hair appear to be not uncommonly associated with other physical and psychic anomalies; it is on this account that they have sometimes been regarded as indications of a vicious or a criminal temperament; they are, however, found in quite normal women.

The pubic hair of women is usually shorter than that of men, but thick, and the individual hairs stronger and larger in diameter than those of men, as Pfaff first showed; dark hair is usually stronger than light. In both length and size the individual variations are considerable. The usual length is about 2 inches, or 3-5 centimeters, occasionally reaching about 4 inches, or 9-10 centimeters, in the larger curls. In a series of 100 women attended during confinement in London and the north of England I have only once (in a rather blonde Lancashire woman) found the hair on labia reaching a conspicuous length of several inches and forming an obstruction to the manipulations involved in delivery. But Jahn delivered a woman whose pubic hair was longer than that of her head, reaching below her knee; Paulini also knew a woman whose pubic hair nearly reached her knees and was sold to make wigs; Bartholin mentions a soldier's wife who plaited her pubic hair behind her back; while Brantôme has several references to abnormally long hair in ladies of the French court during the sixteenth century. In 8 cases out of 2200 Bergh found the pubic hair forming a large curly wig extending to the iliac spines. The individual hairs have occasionally been found so stiff and brush-like as to render coitus difficult.

In color the pubic hair, while generally approximating to that of the head, is sometimes (according to Rothe, in Germany, in one-third cases) lighter, and sometimes somewhat darker, as is found to be the case by Coe, especially in brunettes, and also by Bergh, in Denmark. Bergh remarks that it is generally intermediate in color between the eyebrows and the axillary hair, the latter being more or less decolorized by sweat, and that, owing to the influence of the urine and vaginal discharges, the labial hair is paler than that on the mons; blondes with dark eyebrows usually have dark hair on the mons. The hair on this spot, as Aristotle observed, is usually the last to turn gray.

The key to the genital apparatus in women from the psychic point of view, and, indeed, to some extent, its anatomical center, is to be found in the clitoris. Anatomically and developmentally the clitoris is the rudimentary analogue of the masculine penis. Functionally, however, its scope is very much smaller. While the penis both receives and imparts specific voluptuous sensations, and is at the same time both the intromittent organ for the semen and the conduit for the urine, the sole function of the clitoris is to enter into erection under the stress of sexual emotion and receive and transmit the stimulatory voluptuous sensations imparted to it by friction with the masculine genital apparatus. It is so insignificant an organ that it is only within recent times that its homology with the penis has been realized. In 1844 Kobelt wrote in his important book, *Die Mannlichen und Weiblichen Wollust-Organe,* that in his attempt to show that the female organs are exactly analogous to the male the reader will probably be unable to follow him, while even Johannes Müller, the father of scientific physiology, declared at about the same period that the clitoris is essentially different from the penis. It is indeed but three centuries since the clitoris was so little known that (in 1593) Realdus Columbus actually claimed the honor of discovering it.

Columbus was not its discoverer, for Fallopius speedily showed that Avicenna and Albucasis had referred to it.[1] The Arabs appear to have been very familiar with it, and, from the various names they gave it, clearly understood the important part it plays in generating voluptuous emotion.[2] But it was known in classic antiquity; the Greeks called it μύρτον, the myrtle-berry; Galen and Soranus callled it νύμφη because it is covered as a bride is veiled, while the old Latin name was *tentigo*, from its power of entering into erection, and *columella*, the little pillar, from its shape. The modern term, which is Greek and refers to the sensitiveness of the part to voluptuous titillation, is said to have originated with Suidas and Pollux.[3] It was mentioned, though not adopted, by Rufus.

"The clitoris," declared Haller, "is a part extremely sensible and wonderfully prurient." It is certainly the chief though by no means the only point through which the immediate call to detumescence is conveyed to the female organism. It is, indeed, as Bryan Robinson remarks, "a veritable electrical bell button which, being pressed or irritated, rings up the whole nervous system."

The nervous supply of this little organ is very large, and the dorsal nerve of the clitoris is relatively three or four times larger than that of the penis. Yet the sensitive point of this organ is only 5 to 7 millimeters in extent. The length of the clitoris is usually rather over 2 centimeters (or about an inch) and 3 centimeters when erect; a length of 4 centimeters or more was regarded by Martineau as within the normal range of variation. It is not usual to find the clitoris longer than this in Europe (for among some races like the negro the clitoris is generally large), but all degrees of magnitude may be found as rare exceptions. (See, *e.g.*, Sir J. Y. Simpson, "Hermaphrodites," *Obstetric Memoirs and Contributions*, vol. ii, pp. 217-226; also Dickinson, *loc. cit.*) It was formerly thought that the clitoris is easily enlarged by masturbation, and Martineau believed that in this way it might be doubled in length. It is probable that slight enlargement of the clitoris may be

---

[1] Schurig, *Muliebria*, p. 75. Plazzon in 1621 said that in Italian it had a popular name, *il besneegio*.

[2] Schurig brought together in his *Gynæcologia* (pp. 2-4) various early opinions concerning the clitoris as the seat of voluptuous feeling.

[3] Hyrtl, *Op. cit.*, vol. ii, p. 193.

caused by very frequent masturbation, but only to an insignificant extent, and it is impossible to diagnose masturbation from the size of the clitoris. Among the women of Lake Nyassa, as well as in the Caroline Islands, special methods are practiced for elongating the clitoris, but in Europe, at all events, it is probable that the variations in the size of the organ are mainly congenital. It may well be that a congenitally large clitoris is associated with an abnormally developed excitability of the sexual apparatus. Tilt stated (*On Uterine and Ovarian Inflammation*, p. 37) that in his experience there was a frequent though not invariable connection between a large clitoris and sexual proclivity. (Schurig referred to a case of intense and lifelong sexual obsession associated with an extremely large clitoris, *Gynæcologia*, pp. 16-17.) Of recent years considerable importance has been attached by some gynecologists (*e.g.*, R. T. Morris, "Is Evolution Trying to Do Away With the Clitoris?" *Transactions American Association of Obstetricians and Gynecologists*, vol. v, 1893) to preputial adhesions around the clitoris as a source of nervous disturbance and invalidism in young women.

While the clitoris is anatomically analogous to the penis, its actual mechanism under the stress of sexual excitement is somewhat different. As Liétaud long since pointed out, it cannot rise freely in erection as the penis can; it is apparently bound down by its prepuce and its frenulum. Waldeyer, in his book on the pelvis, states more precisely that, unlike the penis, when erect it retains its angle, only this becomes somewhat rounded so that the organ is to some slight extent lifted and protruded. Waldeyer considered that the clitoris was thus perfectly fitted to fulfill its part as the recipient of erotic stimulation from friction by the penis. Adler, however, has pointed out with considerable justice, that this is not altogether the case. The clitoris was developed in mammals who practiced the posterior mode of coitus; in this position the clitoris was beneath the penis, which was thus easily able in coitus to press it against the pubic bone close beneath which it is situated, and thus impart the compression and friction which the feminine organ craves. But in the human anterior mode of coitus it is not necessarily brought into close contact with the penis during the act of coitus, and thus fails to receive powerful stimulation. Its restricted position, which is an advantage in posterior coitus, is a disadvantage in anterior coitus. Adler observes that it thus comes about that the human method of coitus, while by bringing breast to breast and face to face it has added a new dignity and refinement, a fresh source of enjoyment, to the embrace of the sexes, has not been an unmixed advantage to woman, for while man has lost nothing by the change, woman has now to contend with an increased difficulty in attaining an adequate amount of pressure on that "electric button" which normally sets the whole mechanism in operation.[1]

We may well bring into connection with the changed conditions brought about by anterior coitus the interesting fact that while the clitoris remains the most exquisitely sensitive of the sexual centers in woman, voluptuous sensitivity is much more widely diffused in woman than in man. Over the whole body, indeed, it is apt to be more distinctly marked than is usually the case in man. But even if we confine ourselves to the genital region, while in man that portion of the penis which enters the vagina, and especially the glans, is normally the only portion which, even during turgescence, is sensitive to voluptuous contacts, in woman the whole of the region comprised within the larger lips, including even the anus and internally the vagina and the vaginal portion of the womb,[1] become sensitive to voluptuous contacts. Deprived of the penis the ability of a man to experience specifically sexual sensations becomes very limited indeed. But the loss of the clitoris or of any other structure involves no correspondingly serious disability on women. Ablation of the clitoris for sexual hyperæsthesia has for this reason been abandoned, except under special circumstances. The members of the Russian Skoptzy sect habitually amputate

---

[1] O. Adler, *Die Mangelhafte Geschlechtsempfindung des Weibes*, 1904, pp. 117-119.

[2] The voluptuous sensations caused by sexual contacts producing movements of the womb are probably normal and usual. They may even occur under circumstances unconnected with sexual emotion, and Mundé (*International Journal of Surgery*, March, 1893) mentions incidentally that in one case while titillating the cervix with a sound the woman very plainly showed voluptuous manifestations.

the clitoris, nymphæ, and breasts, yet many young Skoptzy women told the Russian physician, Guttceit, that they were perfectly well able to enjoy coitus.

Freud believes that in very young girls the clitoris is the exclusive seat of sexual sensation, masturbation at this age being directed to the clitoris alone, and spontaneous sexual excitement being confined to twitchings and erection of this organ, so that young girls are able, from their own experience, to recognize without instruction the signs of sexual excitement in boys. At a later age sexual excitability spreads from the clitoris to other regions—just as the easy inflammability of wood sets light to coal—though in the male the penis remains from first to last normally the almost exclusive seat of specific excitability. (S. Freud, *Drei Abhandlungen zur Sexualtheorie*, p. 62.)

The anus would, however, seem to be sometimes an erogenous zone even at an early age. Titillation of the anus appears to be frequently pleasurable in women; and this is not surprising considering the high degree of erotic sensitivity which is easily developed at the body orifices where skin meets mucous membrane. (Thus the meatus of the urethra is a highly erogenous zone, as is sufficiently shown by the frequency with which hair-pins and other articles used in masturbation find their way into the bladder.) It is in this germinal sensitivity, undoubtedly, that we find a chief key to the practice of *pedicatio*. Freud attaches great importance to the anus as a sexually erogenous zone at a very early age, and considers that it very frequently makes its influence felt in this respect. He believes that intestinal catarrhs in very early life and hæmorrhoids later tend to develop sensibility in the anus. He finds an indication that the anus has become a sexually erogenous zone when children wish to allow the contents of the rectum to accumulate so that defecation may by its increased difficulty involve voluptuous sensations, and adds that masturbatory excitation of the anus with the fingers is by no means rare in older children. (S. Freud, *Op. cit.*, pp. 40-42.) A medical correspondent in India tells me of a European lady who derived, she said, "quite as much, indeed more," pleasure from digitally titillating her rectum as from vulvo-vaginal titillation; she had several times submitted to *pedicatio* and enjoyed it, though it was painful during penetration. The anus may retain this erogenous irritability even in old age, and Routh mentions the case of a lady of over 70, the reverse of lustful, who was so excited by the act of defecation that she was invariably compelled to masturbate, although this state of things was a source of great mental misery to her. (C. H. F. Routh, *British Gynæcological Journal*, February, 1887, p. 48.)

Bölsche has sought the explanation of the erogenous nature of the anus, and the key to *pedicatio*, in an atavistic return to the very remote amphibian days when the anus was combined with the sexual parts in a common cloaca. But it is unnecessary to invoke any vestigial inheritance from a vastly remote past when we bear in mind that the innervation of these two adjoining regions is inevitably very closely related. The presence of a body exit with its marked and special sensitivity at a point where it can scarcely fail to receive the nervous overflow from an immensely active center of nervous energy quite adequately accounts for the phenomenon in question.

The inner lips, the nymphæ or labia minora, running parallel with the greater lips which enclose them, embrace the clitoris anteriorly and extend backward, enclosing the urethral exit between them as well as the vaginal entrance. They form little wings whence their old Latin name, *alæ,* and from their resemblance to the cock's comb were by Spigelius termed crista galli. The red and (especially in brunettes) dark appearance of the nymphæ suggests that they are mucous membrane and not integumentary; it is, however, now considered that even on the inner surface they are covered by skin and separated from the mucous membrane by a line.[1] In structure, as described by Waldeyer, they consist of fine connective tissue rich in elastic fibers as well as some muscular tissue, and full of large veins, so that they are capable of a considerable degree of turgescence resembling erection during sexual excitement, while Ballantyne finds that the nymphæ are supplied to a notable extent with nervous end-organs.

More than any other part of the sexual apparatus in either sex, the lesser lips, on account of their shape, their position, and their structure, are capable of acquired modifications, more especially hypertrophy and elongation. By stretching, it is stated, a labium can be doubled in its dimensions. The "Hottentot apron," or elongated nymphæ, commonly found among some peoples in South Africa, has long been a familiar phenomenon. In such cases a length or transverse diameter of 3 to 5 centimeters is commonly found. But such elongated

---

[1] Henle stated that fine hairs are frequently visible on the nymphæ; Stieda (*Zeitschrift für Morphologie*, 1902, p. 458) remarks that he has never been able to see them with the naked eye.

nymphæ are by no means confined to one part of the world or to one race; they are quite common among women of European race, and reach a size equal to most of the more reliably recorded Hottentot cases. Dickinson, who has very carefully studied this question in New York, finds that in 1000 consecutive gynæcological cases the labia showed some form of hypertrophy in 36 per cent., or more than 1 in 3; while among 150 of these cases who were neurasthenic, the proportion reached 56 per cent., even when minor or doubtful enlargements were disregarded. Bergh, in about 16 per cent. cases, found very enlarged nymphæ, the height reached in about 5 per cent. of the cases of enlargement being nearly six centimeters. Ploss and Bartels, in a full discussion of the "Hottentot apron," come to the conclusion that this condition is perhaps in most cases artificially produced. It is known that among the Basutos it is the custom for the elder girls to manipulate the nymphæ of younger children, when alone with them, almost from birth, and on account of the elastic nature of these structures such manipulation quite adequately accounts for the elongation. It is not necessary to suppose that the custom is practiced for the sake of producing sexual stimulation—though this may frequently occur—since there are numerous similar primitive customs involving deformation of the sexual organs without the production of sexual excitement. Dickinson has come to a similar conclusion as regards the corresponding elongation of the nymphæ in civilized European women. In 361 out of 1000 women of good social class he found elongation or thickening, often with a notable degree of wrinkling and pigmentation, and believes that this is always the result of frequently repeated masturbation practiced with the separation of the nymphæ; in 30 per cent. of the cases admission of masturbation was made.[1] While this conclusion is probably correct in the main, it requires some qualification. To assert

---

[1] R. L. Dickinson, "Hypertrophies of the Labia Minora and Their Significance," *American Gynæcologist*, September, 1902. It is perhaps noteworthy that Bergh found that in 302 cases in which the nymphæ were of unequal length, in all but 24 the left was longer.

that whenever in women who have not been pregnant the marked protrusion of the inner lips beyond the outer lips means that at some period manipulation has been practiced with or without the production of sexual excitement is to make too absolute a statement. It is highly probable that the nymphæ, like the clitoris, are congenitally more prominent in some of the lower human races, as they are also in the apes; among the Fuegians, for instance, according to Hyades and Deniker, the labia minora descend lower than in Europeans, although there is not the slightest reason to suppose that these women practice any manipulations. Among European women, again, the nymphæ sometimes protrude very prominently beyond the labia majora in women who are organically of somewhat infantile type; this occurs in cases in which we may be convinced that no manipulations have ever been practiced.[1]

It is difficult to speak very decisively as to the function of the labia minora. They doubtless exert some amount of protective influence over the entrance to the vagina, and in this way correspond to the lips of the mouth after which they are called. They fulfill, however, one very definite though not obviously important function which is indicated by the mythologic name they have received. There is, indeed, some obscurity in the origin of this term, nymphæ, which has not, I believe, been satisfactorily cleared up. It has been stated that the Greek name νύμφη has been transferred from the clitoris to the labia minora. Any such transfer could only have taken place when the meaning of the word had been forgotten, and νύμφη had become the totally different word nymphæ, the goddesses who presided over streams. The old anatomists were much exercised in their minds as to the meaning of the name, but on the whole were inclined to believe that it referred to the

---

[1] It may be remarked that Bergh believes that the nymphæ, and indeed the external genitals generally, are congenitally more strongly developed in libidinous persons, and at the same time in brunettes, while in public prostitutes this is not usually the case, which confirms the belief that exalted sexual sensibility does not usually lead to prostitution. He adds that prostitution, unless carried on for many years, has little effect on the shape of the external genitals.

action of the labia minora in directing the urinary stream. The term nymphæ was first applied in the modern sense, according to Bergh, in 1599, by Pinæus, mainly from the influence of these structures on the urinary stream, and he dilated in his *De Virginitate* on the suitability of the term to designate so poetic a spot.[1] In more modern times Luschka and Sir Charles Bell considered that it is one of the uses of the nymphæ to direct the stream of urine, and Lamb from his own observation thinks the same conclusion probable. In reality there cannot be the slightest doubt about the function of the nymphæ, as, in Hyrtl's phrase, "the naiads of the urinary source," and it can be demonstrated by the simplest experiment.[2]

The nymphæ form the intermediate portal of the vagina, as the canal which conducts to the womb was in anatomy first termed (according to Hyrtl) by De Graaf.[2] It is a secreting, erectile, more or less sensitive canal lined by what is usually considered mucous membrane, though some have regarded it as integument of the same character as that of the external genitals; it certainly resembles such integument more than, for instance, the mucous membrane of the rectum. In the woman who has never had sexual intercourse and has been subjected to no manipulations or accidents affecting this region, the vagina

---

[1] Schurig (*Muliebria*, 1729, Section II, cap. II) gives numerous quotations on this point; thus De Graaf wrote in his book on the sexual organs of women: "Tales protuberantiæ nymphæ appellantur ea propter quod aquis e vesica prosilientibus proxime adstare reperiantur, quandoquidem inter illas, tanquam duos parietes, urina magno impetu cum sibilo sæpe et absque labiorum irrigatione erumpit, vel quod sint castitatis præsides, aut sponsam primo intromittant."

[2] Havelock Ellis, "The Bladder as a Dynamometer," *American Journal of Dermatology*, May, 1902. If a woman who has never been pregnant, standing in the erect position before commencing the act of urination presses apart the labia minora with index and middle fingers the stream will be projected forward so as to fall usually at a considerable distance in front of a vertical line from the meatus; if when the act is half completed the fingers are removed, the labia close together and the stream, though maintained at a constant pressure, at once changes its character and direction.

[2] In poetry this term was employed by Plautus, *Pseudolus*, Act IV, Sc. 7. The Greek αιδοῖον sometimes meant vagina and sometimes the external sexual parts; κδλπος was used for the vagina alone.

is closed by a last and final gate of delicate membrane—scarcely admitting more than a slender finger—called the hymen.

The poets called the hymen "flos virginitatis," the flower of virginity, whence the medico-legal term *defloratio*. Notwithstanding the great significance which has long been attached to the phenomena connected with it, the hymen was not accurately known until Vesalius, Fallopius, and Spigelius described and named it. It was, however, recognized by the Arab authors, Avicenna and Averroes. The early literature concerning it is summarized by Schurig, *Muliebria*, 1729, Section II, cap. V. The same author's *Parthenologia* is devoted to the various ancient problems connected with the question of virginity.

To say that this delicate piece of membrane is from the non-physical point of view a more important structure than any other part of the body is to convey but a feeble idea of the immense importance of the hymen in the eyes of the men of many past ages and even of our own times and among our own people.[1] For the uses of the feminine body, or for its beauty, there is no part which is more absolutely insignificant. But in human estimation it has acquired a spiritual value which has made it far more than a part of the body. It has taken the place of the soul, that whose presence gives all her worth and dignity, even her name, to the unmarried woman, her purity, her sexual desirability, her market value. Without it—though in all physical and mental respects she might remain the same person—she has sometimes been a mark for contempt, a worthless outcast.[2]

So fragile a membrane scarcely possesses the reliability which should be possessed by a structure whose presence or absence has often meant so much. Its absence by no means necessarily signifies that a woman has had intercourse with a man. Its presence by no means signifies that she has never had such intercourse.

There are many ways in which the hymen may be destroyed apart from coitus. Among the Chinese (and also, it would appear, in India and some other parts of the East) the female parts are from infancy

[1] It is curious, however, that the European physicians of the seventeenth and even eighteenth centuries were doubtful of its value as a sign of virginity and considered it often absent.
[1] For a summary of the beliefs and practices of various peoples with regard to the hymen and virginity see Ploss and Bartels, *Das Weib*, vol. i, Chapter XVI.

kept so scrupulously clean by daily washing, the finger being introduced into the vagina, that the hymen rapidly disappears, and its existence is unknown even to Chinese doctors. Among some Brazilian Indians a similar practice exists among mothers as regards their young children, less, however, for the sake of cleanliness than in order to facilitate sexual intercourse in future years. (Ploss and Bartels, *Das Weib*, vol. i, Chapter VI.) The manipulations of vaginal masturbation will, of course, similarly destroy the hymen. It is also quite possible for the hymen to be ruptured by falls and other accidents. (See, *e.g.*, a lengthy study by Nina-Rodrigues, "Des Ruptures de l'Hymen dans les Chutes," *Annales d'Hygiène Publique*, September, 1903.)

On the other hand, integrity of the hymen is no proof of virginity, apart from the obvious fact that there may be intercourse without penetration. (The case has even been recorded of a prostitute with syphilitic condylomata, a somewhat masculine type of pubic arch, and vulva rather posteriorly placed, whose hymen had never been penetrated.) The hymen may be of a yielding or folding type, so that complete penetration may take place and yet the hymen be afterwards found unruptured. It occasionally happens that the hymen is found intact at the end of pregnancy. In some, though not all, of these cases there has been conception without intromission of the penis. This has occurred even when the entrance was very minute. The possibility of such conception has long been recognized, and Schurig (*Syllepsilogia*, 1731, Section I, cap. VIII, p. 2) quotes ancient authors who have recorded cases. For some typical modern cases see Guérard (*Centralblatt fur Gynäkologie*, No. 15, 1895), in one of whose cases the hymen of the pregnant woman scarcely admitted a hair; also Braun (*ib.*, No. 23, 1895).

The hymen has played a very definite and pronounced part in the social and moral life of humanity. Until recently it has been more difficult to decide what precise biological function it has exercised to ensure its development and preservation. Sexual selection, no doubt, has worked in its favor, but that influence has been very limited and comparatively very recent. Virginity is not usually of any value among peoples who are entirely primitive. Indeed, even in the classic civilization which we inherit, it is easy to show that the virgin and the admiration for virginity are of late growth; the virgin goddesses were not originally virgins in our modern sense. Diana was the many-breasted patroness of childbirth before she became the chaste and solitary huntress, for the earliest distinction would appear to have been simply between the woman who was attached to a man and the woman who followed an earlier rule of freedom and independence; it was a later notion to suppose that the latter woman was debarred from sexual intercourse. We certainly must not seek the origin of the hymen in sexual selection; we must find it in natural selection. And here it might seem at first sight that we come upon a contradiction in Nature, for Nature is always devising contrivances to secure the maximum amount of fertilization. "Increase and multiply" is so obviously the command of Nature that the Hebrews, with their usual insight, unhesitatingly dared to place it in the mouth of Jehovah. But the hymen is a barrier to fertilization. It has, however, always to be remembered that as we rise in the zoological scale, and as the period of gestation lengthens and the possible number of offspring is fewer, it becomes constantly more essential that fertilization shall be effective rather than easy; the fewer the progeny the more necessary it is that they shall be vigorous enough to survive. There can be little doubt that, as one or two writers have already suggested, the hymen owes its development to the fact that its influence is on the side of effective fertilization. It is an obstacle to the impregnation of the young female by immature, aged, or feeble males. The hymen is thus an anatomical expression of that admiration of force which marks the female in her choice of a mate. So regarded, it is an interesting example of the intimate manner in which sexual selection is really based on natural selection. Sexual selection is but the translation into psychic terms of a process which has already found expression in the physical texture of the body.

It may be added that this interpretation of the biological function of the hymen is supported by the facts of its evolution. It is unknown among the lower mammals, with whom fertilization is easy, gestation short and offspring numerous. It only begins to appear among the higher mammals in whom reproduction is already beginning to take on the characters which become fully developed in man. Various authors have found traces of a rudimentary hymen, not only in apes, but in elephants, horses, donkeys, bitches, bears, pigs, hyenas, and giraffes. (Hyrtl, *Op. cit.*, vol. ii, p. 189; G. Gellhoen, "Anatomy and Development of the Hymen," *American Journal Obstetrics*, August, 1904.)   It is in the human species that the tendency to limitation of offspring is most marked, combined at the same time with a greater aptitude for impregnation than exists among any lower mammals.   It is here, therefore, that a physical check is of most value, and accordingly we find that in woman alone, of all animals, is the hymen fully developed.

II.

The Object of Detumescence—Erogenous Zones—The Lips—The Vascular Characters of Detumescence—Erectile Tissue—Erection in Woman—Mucous Emission in Women—Sexual Connection—The Human Mode of Intercourse—Normal Variations—The Motor Characters of Detumescence—Ejaculation—The Virile Reflex—The General Phenomena of Detumescence—The Circulatory and Respiratory Phenomena—Blood Pressure—Cardiac Disturbance—Glandular Activity—Distillatio—The Essentially Motor Character of Detumescence—Involuntary Muscular Irradiation to Bladder, etc.—Erotic Intoxication—Analogy of Sexual Detumescence and Vesical Tension—The Specifically Sexual Movements of Detumescence in Man—In Woman—The Spontaneous Movements of the Genital Canal in Woman—Their Function in Conception—Part Played by Active Movement of the Spermatozoa—The Artificial Injection of Semen—The Facial Expression During Detumescence—The Expression of Joy—The Occasional Serious Effects of Coitus.

WE have seen what the object of detumescence is, and we have briefly considered the organs and structures which are chiefly concerned in the process. We have now to inquire what are the actual phenomena which take place during the act of detumescence.

Detumescence is normally linked closely to tumescence. Tumescence is the piling on of the fuel; detumescence is the leaping out of the devouring flame whence is lighted the torch of life to be handed on from generation to generation. The whole process is double and yet single; it is exactly analogous to that by which a pile is driven into the earth by the raising and then the letting go of a heavy weight which falls on to the head of the pile. In tumescence the organism is slowly wound up and force accumlated; in the act of detumescence the accumulated force is let go and by its liberation the sperm-bearing instrument is driven home. Courtship, as we commonly term the process of tumescence which takes place when a woman is first sexually approached by a man, is usually a highly pro-

(142)

longed process. But it is always necessary to remember that every repetition of the act of coitus, to be normally and effectively carried out on both sides, demands a similar double process; detumescence must be preceded by an abbreviated courtship.

This abbreviated courtship by which tumescence is secured or heightened in the repetition of acts of coitus which have become familiar, is mainly tactile.[1] Since the part of the man in coitus is more active and that of the woman more passive, the sexual sensitivity of the skin seems to be more pronounced in women. There are, moreover, regions of the surface of a woman's body where contact, when sympathetic, seems specially liable to arouse erotic excitement. Such erogenous zones are often specially marked in the breasts, occasionally in the palm of the hand, the nape of the neck, the lobule of the ear, the little finger; there is, indeed, perhaps no part of the surface of the body which may not, in some individuals at some time, become normally an erogenous zone. In hysteria the erotic excitability of these zones is sometimes very intense. The lips are, however, without doubt, the most persistently and poignantly sensitive region of the whole body outside the sphere of the sexual organs themselves. Hence the significance of the kiss as a preliminary of detumescence.[2]

The importance of the lips as a normal erogenous zone is shown by the experiments of Gualino. He applied a thread, folded on itself several times, to the lips, thus stimulating them in a simple mechanical manner. Of 20 women, between the ages of 18 and 31, only 8 felt this as a merely mechanical operation, 4 felt a vaguely erotic element in the proceeding, 3 experienced a desire for coitus and in 5 there was actual sexual excitement with emission of mucus. Of 25 men, between the ages of 20 and 30, in 15 all sexual feeling was absent, in 7 erotic ideas were suggested with congestion of the sexual organs without erection, and in 3 there was the beginning of erection. It should be added that both the women and the men in whom this sexual reflex was more especially

----

[1] The elements furnished by the sense of touch in sexual selection have been discussed in the first section of the previous volume of these *Studies*.

[2] See Appendix A. "The Origins of the Kiss," in the previous volume.

marked were of somewhat nervous temperament; in such persons erotic reactions of all kinds generally occur most easily. (Gualino, "Il Rifflesso Sessuale nell' eccitamento alle labbre," *Archivio di Psichiatria*, 1904, p. 341.)

As tumescence, under the influence of sensory stimulation, proceeds toward the climax when it gives place to detumescence, the physical phenomena become more and more acutely localized in the sexual organs. The process which was at first predominantly nervous and psychic now becomes more prominently vascular. The ancient sexual relationship of the skin asserts itself; there is marked surface congestion showing itself in various ways. The face tends to become red, and exactly the same phenomenon is taking place in the genital organs; "an erection," it has been said, "is a blushing of the penis." The difference is that in the genital organs this heightened vascularity has a definite and specific function to accomplish—the erection of the male organ which fits it to enter the female parts—and that consequently there has been developed in the penis that special kind of vascular mechanism, consisting of veins in connective tissue with unstriped muscular fibers, termed erectile tissue.[1]

It is not only the man who is supplied with erectile tissue which in the process of tumescence becomes congested and swollen. The woman also, in the corresponding external genital region, is likewise supplied with erectile tissue now also charged with blood, and exhibits the same changes as have taken place in her partner, though less conspicuously visible. In the anthropoid apes, as the gorilla, the large clitoris and the nymphæ become prominent in sexual excitement, but the less development of the clitoris in women, together with the specifically human evolution of the mons veneris and larger lips, renders this sexual turgescence practically invisible, though it is perceptible to touch in an increased degree of spongy and elastic tension. The whole feminine genital canal, including the uterus, indeed, is richly supplied with blood-vessels, and is ca-

---

[1] See, *e.g.*, Art. "Erection," by Retterer, in Richet's *Dictionnaire de Physiologie*, vol. v.

pable during sexual excitement of a very high degree of turgescence, a kind of erection.

The process of erection in woman is accompanied by the pouring out of fluid which copiously bathes all parts of the vulva around the entrance to the vagina. This is a bland, more or less odorless mucus which, under ordinary circumstances, slowly and imperceptibly suffuses the parts. When, however, the entrance to the vagina is exposed and extended, as during a gynæcological examination which occasionally produces sexual excitement, there may be seen a real ejaculation of the fluid which, as usually described, comes largely from the glands of Bartholin, situated at the mouth of the vagina. Under these circumstances it is sometimes described as being emitted in a jet which is thrown to a distance.[1] This mucous ejaculation was in former days regarded as analogous to the seminal ejaculation in man, and hence essential to conception. Although this belief was erroneous the fluid poured out in this manner whenever a high degree of tumescence is attained, and before the onset of detumescence, certainly performs an important function in lubricating the entrance to the genital canal and so facilitating the intromission of the male organ.[2] Menstruation has a similar influence in facilitating coitus, as Schurig long since pointed out.[3] A like process takes place during parturition when the same parts are being lubricated and stretched in preparation for the protrusion of the fœtal head. The occurrence of the mucous flow in tumescence always indicates that that process is actively affecting the central sexual organs, and that voluptuous emotions are present.[4]

---

[1] Guibaut, *Traité Clinique des Maladies des Femmes*, p. 242. Adler discusses the sexual secretions in women and their significance, *Die Mangelhafte Geschlechtsempfindung des Weibes*, pp. 19-26.

[2] In some parts of the world this is further aided by artificial means. Thus it is stated by Riedel (as quoted by Ploss and Bartels) that in the Gorong Archipelago the bridegroom, before the first coitus, anoints the bride's pudenda with an ointment containing opium, musk, etc. I have been told of an English bride who was instructed by her mother to use a candle for the same purpose.

[3] *Parthenologia*, pp. 302, *et seq.*

[4] The connection of this mucous flow with sexual emotion was dis-

The secretions of the genital canal and outlet in women are somewhat numerous. We have the odoriferous glands of sebaceous origin,
and with them the prepuce of the clitoris which has been described as
a kind of gigantic sebaceous follicle with the clitoris occupying its
interior. (Hyrtl.) There is the secretion from the glands of Bartholin.
There is again the vaginal secretion, opaque and albuminous, which
appears to be alkaline when secreted, but becomes acid under the de-
composing influence of bacteria, which are, however, harmless and not
pathogenic. (Gow, *Obstetrical Society of London*, January 3, 1894.)
There is, finally, the mucous uterine secretion, which is alkaline, and,
being poured out during orgasm, is believed to protect the spermatozoa
from destruction by the acid vaginal secretion.

The belief that the mucus poured out in women during sexual
excitement is feminine semen and therefore essential to conception had
many remarkable consequences and was widespread until the seventeenth century. Thus, in the chapter "De Modo coeundi et de regimine
eorum qui coeunt" of *De Secretis Mulicrum*, there is insistence on the
importance of the proper mixture of the male semen with the female
semen and of arranging that it shall not escape from the vagina. The
woman must lie quiet for several hours at least, not rising even to
urinate, and when she gets up, be very temperate in eating and drinking,
and not run or jump, pretending that she has a headache. It was the
belief in feminine semen which led some theologians to lay down that
a woman might masturbate if she had not experienced orgasm in coitus.
Schurig in his *Muliebria* (1729, pp. 159, *et seq.*) discusses the opinions
of old authors regarding the nature, source, and uses of the female
genital secretions, and quotes authorities against the old view that it
was female semen. In a subsequent work (*Syllepsilogia*, 1731, pp. 3,
et seq.) he returns to the same question, quotes authors who accept a
feminine semen, shows that Harvey denied it any significance, and himself decides against it. It has not seriously been brought forward since.

When erection is completed in both the man and the woman
the conditions necessary for conjugation have at last been ful-
filled. In all animals, even those most nearly allied to man,
coitus is effected by the male approaching the female posteriorly.
In man the normal method of male approach is anteriorly, face
to face. Leonardo da Vinci, in a well-known drawing representing a sagittal section of a man and a woman connected in
this position of so-called Venus obversa, has shown how well

cussed early in the eighteenth century by Schurig in his *Gynœcologia*,
pp. 8-11; it is frequently passed over by more modern writers.

adapted the position is to the normal position of the organs in the human species.[1]

Among monkeys, it is stated, congress is sometimes performed when the female is on all fours; at other times the male brings the female between his thighs when he is sitting, holding her with his fore-paws. Froriep informed Lawrence that the male sometimes supported his feet on the female's calves. (Sir W. Lawrence, *Lectures on Physiology*, 1823, p. 186.) A summary of the methods of congress practiced by the various animals below mammals will be found in the article "Copulation" by H. de Varigny in Richet's *Dictionnaire de Physiologie*, vol. iv.

The anterior position in coitus, with the female partner lying supine, is so widespread throughout the world that it may fairly be termed the most typically human attitude in sexual congress. It is found represented in Egyptian graves at Benihassan, belonging to the Twelfth Dynasty; it is regarded by Mohammedans as the normal position, although other positions are permitted by the Prophet: "Your wives are your tillage: go in unto your tillage in what manner soever you will;" it is that adopted in Malacca; it appears, from Peruvian antiquities, to have been the position generally, though not exclusively, adopted in ancient Peru; it is found in many parts of Africa, and seems also to have been the most usual position among the American aborigines.

Various modifications of this position are, however, found. Thus, in some parts of the world, as among the Suahelis in Zanzibar, the male partner adopts the supine position. In Loango, according to Pechuel-Loesche, coitus is performed lying on the side. Sometimes, as on the west coast of Africa, the woman is supine and the man more or less erect; or, as among the Queenslanders (as described by Roth) the woman is supine and the man squats on his heels with her thighs clasping his flanks, while he raises her buttocks with his hands.

The position of coitus in which the man is supine is without doubt a natural and frequent variation of the specifically human obverse method of coitus. It was evidently familiar to the Romans. Ovid mentions it (*Ars Amatoria*, III, 777-8), recommending it to little women, and saying that Andromache was too tall to practice it with Hector. Aristophanes refers to it, and there are Greek epigrams in which women boast of their skill in riding their lovers. It has sometimes been viewed with a certain disfavor because it seems to confer a superiority on the woman. "Cursed be he," according to a Mohammedan saying, "who maketh woman heaven and man earth."

---

[1] The drawing is reproduced by Ploss and Bartels, *Das Weib*, vol. i, Chapter XVII; many facts bearing on the ethnography of coitus are brought together in this chapter.

Of special interest is the wide prevalence of an attitude in coitus recalling that which prevails among quadrupeds. The frequency with which on the walls of Pompeii coitus is represented with the woman bending forward and her partner approaching her posteriorly has led to the belief that this attitude was formerly very common in Southern Italy. However that may be, it is certainly normal at the present day among various more or less primitive peoples in whom the vulva is often placed somewhat posteriorly. It is thus among the Soudanese, as also, in an altogether different part of the world, among the Eskimo Innuit and Koniags. The New Caledonians, according to Foley, cohabit in the quadrupedal manner, and so also the Papuans of New Guinea (Bongu), according to Vahness. The same custom is also found in Australia, where, however other postures are also adopted. In Europe the quadrupedal posture would seem to prevail among some of the South Slavs, notably the Dalmatians. (The different methods of coitus practiced by the South Slavs are described in Κρυπτάδια vol. vi, pp. 220, et scq.)

This method of coitus was recommended by Lucretius (lib. iv) and also advised by Paulus Æginetus as favorable to conception. (The opinions of various early physicians are quoted by Schurig, *Spermatologia*, 1720, pp. 232, *et seq*.). It seems to be a position that is not infrequently agreeable to women, a fact which may be brought into connection with the remarks of Adler already quoted (p. 131) concerning the comparative lack of adjustment of the feminine organs to the obverse position. It is noteworthy that in the days of witchcraft hysterical women constantly believed that they had had intercourse with the Devil in this manner. This circumstance, indeed, probably aided in the very marked disfavor in which coitus *a posteriori* fell after the decay of classic influences. The mediæval physicians described it as *mos diabolicus* and mistakenly supposed that it produced abortion (Hyrtl, *op. cit.*, vol. ii, p. 87). The theologians, needless to say, were opposed to the *mos diabolicus*, and already in the Anglo-Saxon Penitential of Theodore, at the end of the seventh century, 40 days' penance is prescribed for this method of coitus.

From the frequency with which they have been adopted by various peoples as national customs, most of the postures in coitus here referred to must be said to come within the normal range of variation. It is a mistake to regard them as vicious perversions.

Up to the point to which we have so far considered it, the process of detumescence has been mainly nervous and vascular in character; it has, in fact, been but the more acute stage of a process which has been going on throughout tumescence. But now we reach the point at which a new element comes in : muscular action. With the onset of muscular action, which is mainly involuntary, even when it affects the voluntary muscles, detumescence proper begins to take place. Henceforward purposeful psychic action, except by an effort, is virtually abolished. The individual, as a separate person, tends to disappear. He has become one with another person, as nearly one as the conditions of existence ever permit; he and she are now merely an instrument in the hands of a higher power—by whatever name we may choose to call that Power—which is using them for an end not themselves.

The decisive moment in the production of the instinctive and involuntary orgasm occurs when, under the influence of the stimulus applied to the penis by friction with the vagina, the tension of the seminal fluid poured into the urethra arouses the ejaculatory center in the spinal cord and the bulbo-cavernosus muscle surrounding the urethra responsively contracts in rhythmic spasms. Then it is that ejaculation occurs.[1]

"The circulation quickens, the arteries beat strongly," wrote Roubaud in a description of the physical state during coitus which may almost be termed classic; "the venous blood, arrested by muscular contraction, increases the general heat, and this stagnation, more pronounced in the brain by the contraction of the muscles of the neck and the throwing of the head backward, causes a momentary cerebral congestion, during which intelligence is lost and the faculties abolished. The eyes, violently injected, become haggard, and the look uncertain, or, in the majority of cases, the eyes are closed spasmodically to

---

[1] Onanoff (Paris Société de Biologie, May 3, 1890) proposed the name of bulbo-cavernous reflex for the smart contraction of the ischio- and bulbo-cavernosus muscles (erector penis and accelerator urinæ) produced by mechanical excitation of the glans. This reflex is clinically elicited by placing the index-finger of the left hand on the region of the bulb while the right hand rapidly rubs the dorsal surface of the glands with the edge of a piece of paper or lightly pinches the mucous membrane; a twitching of the region of the bulb is then perceived. This reflex is always present in healthy adult subjects and indicates the integrity of the physical mechanism of detumescence. It has been described by Hughes. (C. H. Hughes, "The Virile or Bulbo-cavernous Reflex," *Alienist and Neurologist*, January, 1898.)

avoid the contact of the light. The respiration is hurried, sometimes interrupted, and may be suspended by the spasmodic contraction of the larynx, and the air, for a time compressed, is at
last emitted in broken and meaningless words. The congested
nervous centers only communicate confused sensations and voli-
tions; mobility and sensation show extreme disorder; the limbs
are seized by convulsions and sometimes by cramps, or are
thrown wildly about or become stiff like iron bars. The jaws,
tightly pressed, grind the teeth, and in some persons the delir-
ium is carried so far that they bite to bleeding the shoulders
their companions have imprudently abandoned to them. This
frantic state of epilepsy lasts but a short time, but it suffices to
exhaust the forces of the organism, especially in man. It is,
I believe, Galen, who said: 'Omne animal post coitum triste
præter mulierem gallumque.' "[1] Most of the elements that
make up this typical picture of the state of coitus are not absolutely essential to that state, but they all come within the normal range of variation. There can be no doubt that this range
is considerable. There would appear to be not only individual,
but also racial, differences; there is a remarkable passage in
Vatsyayana's *Kama Sutra* describing the varying behavior of
the women of different races in India under the stress of sexual
excitement—Dravidian women with difficulty attaining erethism, women of the Punjaub fond of being caressed with the
tongue, women of Oude with impetuous desire and profuse flow
of mucus, etc.—and it is highly probable, Ploss and Bartels
remark, that these characterizations are founded on exact observations.[2]

The various phenomena included in Roubaud's description
of the condition during coitus may all be directly or indirectly
reduced to two groups: the first circulatory and respiratory,
the second motor. It is necessary to consider both these aspects
of the process of detumescence in somewhat greater detail, although while it is most convenient to discuss them separately,

---

[1] Roubaud, *Traité de l'Impuissance*, 1855, p. 39.
[2] *Das Weib*, seventh edition, vol. i, p. 510.

it must be borne in mind that they are not really separable; the circulatory phenomena are in large measure a by-product of the involuntary motor process.

With the approach of detumescence the respiration becomes shallow, rapid, and to some extent arrested. This characteristic of the breathing during sexual excitement is well recognized; so that in, for instance, the *Arabian Nights,* it is commonly noted of women when gazing at beautiful youths whose love they desired, that they ceased breathing.[1] It may be added that exactly the same tendency to superficial and arrested respiration takes place whenever there is any intense mental concentration, as in severe intellectual work.[2]

The arrest of respiration tends to render the blood venous, and thus aids in stimulating the vasomotor centers, raising the blood-pressure in the body generally, and especially in the erectile tissues. High blood-pressure is one of the most marked features of the state of detumescence. The heart beats are stronger and quicker, the surface arteries are more visible, the conjunctivæ become red. The precise degree of blood-pressure attained during coitus has been most accurately ascertained in the dog. In Bechterew's laboratory in St. Petersburg a manometer was introduced into the central end of the carotid artery of a bitch; a male dog was then introduced, and during coitus observations were made on the blood-pressure at the peripheral and central ends of the artery. It was found that there was a great general elevation of blood-pressure, intense hyperæmia of the brain, rapid alternations, during the act, of vasoconstriction and vasodilatation of the brain, with increase and diminution of the general arterial tension in relation with the various phases of the act, the greatest cerebral vasodilatation and hyperæmia coinciding with the moment following the intromission of the penis; the end of the act is followed by a considerable

---

[1] The influence of impeded respiration in exciting more or less perverted forms of sexual gratification has been discussed in a section of "Love and Pain" in the third volume of these *Studies.*

[2] See, *e.g.,* the experiments of Obici on this point, *Revista Sperimentale di Freniatria,* 1903, pp. 689, *et seq.*

fall in the blood-pressure.[1] I am not acquainted with any precise observations on the blood-pressure in human subjects during detumescence, and there are obvious difficulties in the way of such observations. It is probable, however, that the conditions found would be substantially the same. This is indicated, so far as the very marked increase of blood-pressure is concerned, by some observations made by Vaschide and Vurpas with the sphygmanometer on a lady under the influence of sexual excitement. In this case there was a relationship of sympathy and friendly tenderness between the experimenter and the subject, Madame X, aged 25. Experimenter and subject talked sympathetically, and finally, we are told, while the latter still had her hands in the sphygmanometer, the former almost made a declaration of love. Madame X was greatly impressed, and afterward admitted that her emotions had been genuine and strong. The blood-pressure, which was in this subject habitually 65 millimeters, rose to 150 and even 160, indicating a very high pressure, which rarely occurs; at the same time Madame X looked very emotional and troubled.[2]

Some authorities are of opinion that irregularities in the accomplishment of the sexual act are specially liable to cause disturbances in the circulation. Thus Kisch, of Prague, refers to the case of a couple practising coitus interruptus—the husband withdrawing before ejaculation—in which the wife, a vigorous woman, became liable after some years to attacks termed by Kisch *neurasthenia cordis vasomotoria*, in which there was at daily or longer intervals palpitation, with feelings of anxiety, headache, dizziness, muscular weakness and tendency to faint. He regards coitus as a cause of various heart troubles in women: (1) Attacks of tachycardia in very excitable and sexually inclined women; (2) attacks of tachycardia with dyspnœa in young women, with vaginismus; (3) cardiac symptoms with lowered vascular tone in women who for a long time have practised coitus interruptus without complete sexual gratification (Kisch, "Herzbeschwerden der Frauen verursacht

---

[1] Summarized in *Archives d'Anthropologie Criminelle*, March, 1903, p. 188. The tendency to closure of the eyes noted by Roubaud, to avoid contact of the light, indicates dilatation of the pupils, for which we need not seek other explanation than the general tendency of all peripheral stimulation, according to Schiff's law, to produce such dilatation.

[2] Vaschide and Vurpas, "Du Coefficient Sexuel de l'Impulsion Musicale," *Archives de Neurologie*, May, 1904.

durch den Cohabitationsact," *Münchener Medizinisches Wochenschrift,* 1897, p. 617). In this connection, also, reference may probably be made to those attacks of anxiety which Freud associates with psychic sexual lesions of an emotional character.

Associated with this vascular activity in detumescence we find a general tendency to glandular activity. Various secretions are formed abundantly. Perspiration is copious, and the ancient relationship between the cutaneous and sexual systems seems to evoke a general activity of the skin and its odoriferous secretions. Salivation, which also occurs, is very conspicuous in many lower animals, as for instance in the donkey, notably the female, who just before coitus stands with mouth open, jaws moving, and saliva dribbling. In men, corresponding to the more copious secretion in women, there is, during the latter stages of tumescence, a slight secretion of mucus—Fürbringer's *urethrorrhœa ex libidine*—which appears in drops at the urethral orifice. It comes from the small glands of Littré and Cowper which open into the urethra. This phenomenon was well known to the old theologians, who called it *distillatio,* and realized its significance as at once distinct from semen and an indication that the mind was dwelling on voluptuous images; it was also known in classic times[1]; more recently it has often been confused with semen and has thus sometimes caused needless anxiety to nervous persons. There is also an increased secretion of urine, and it is probable that if the viscera were more accessible to observation we might be able to demonstrate that the glands throughout the body share in this increased activity.

The phenomena of detumescence culminate, however, and have their most obvious manifestation in motor activity. The genital act, as Vaschide and Vurpas remark, consists essentially

---

[1] In the *Priapeia* is an inscription which has thus been translated:—

"You see this organ, after which I'm called
And which is my certificate, is humid;
This moisture is not dew nor drops of rain,
It is the outcome of sweet memory,
Recalling thoughts of a complacent maid."

The translator supposes that semen is referred to, but without doubt the allusion is to the theologians' *distillatio.*

in "a more and more marked tension of the motor state which, reaching its maximum, presents a short tonic phase, followed by a clonic phase, and terminates in a period of adynamia and repose." This motor activity is of the essence of the impulse of detumescence, because without it the sperm cells could not be brought into the neighborhood of the germ cell and be propelled into the organic nest which is assigned for their conjunction and incubation.

The motor activity is general as well as specifically sexual. There is a general tendency to more or less involuntary movement, without any increase of voluntary muscular power, which is, indeed, decreased, and Vaschide and Vurpas state that dynamometric results are somewhat lower than normal during sexual excitement, and the variations greater.[1] The tendency to diffused activity of involuntary muscle is well illustrated by the contraction of the bladder associated with detumescence. While this occurs in both sexes, in men erection produces a mechanical impediment to any evacuation of the bladder. In women there is not only a desire to urinate but, occasionally, actual urination. Many quite healthy and normal women have, as a rare accident supervening on the coincidence of an unusually full bladder with an unusual degree of sexual excitement, experienced a powerful and quite involuntary evacuation of the bladder at the moment of orgasm. In women with less normal nervous systems this has, more rarely, been almost habitual. Brantôme has perhaps recorded the earliest case of this kind in referring to a lady he knew who "quand on lui faisait cela

---

[1] A woman of 30, normal and intelligent, after conversing on love and passion, and then listening to the music of Grieg and Schumann, felt real and strong sexual excitement, increased by memories recalled by the presence of a sympathetic person. When then tested by the dynamometer the average of ten efforts with the right hand was found to be 28.2 (her normal average being 31.1) and with the left hand 28.0 (the normal being 30.0). There was, however, great variability in the individual pressures which sometimes equaled and even exceeded the subject's normal efforts. The voluntary muscles are thus in harmony with the approaching general sexual avalanche. (Vaschide and Vurpas, "Quelques Données Expérimentales sur l'Influence de l'Excitation Sexuelle," *Archivio di Psichiatria*, 1903, fasc. v-vi.)

elle se compissait à bon escient."[1] The tendency to trembling, constriction of throat, sneezing, emission of internal gas, and the other similar phenomena occasionally associated with detumescence, are likewise due to diffusion of the motor disturbance. Even in infancy the motor signs of sexual excitement are the most obvious indications of orgasm; thus West, describing masturbation in a child of six or nine months who practiced thigh-rubbing, states that when sitting in her high chair she would grasp the handles, stiffen herself, and stare, rubbing her thighs quickly together several times, and then come to herself with a sigh, tired, relaxed, and sweating, these seizures, which lasted one or two minutes, being mistaken by the relations for epileptic fits.[2]

The essentially motor character of detumescence is well shown by the extreme forms of erotic intoxication which sometimes appear as the result of sexual excitement. Féré, who has especially called attention to the various manifestations of this condition, presents an instructive case of a man of neurotic heredity and antecedents, in whom it occasionally happened that sexual excitement, instead of culminating in the normal orgasm, attained its climax in a fit of uncontrollable muscular excitement. He would then sing, dance, gesticulate, roughly treat his partner, break the objects around him, and finally sink down exhausted and stupefied. (Féré, *L'Instinct Sexuel*, Chapter X.) In such a case a diffused and general detumescence has taken the place of the normal detumescence which has its main focus in the sexual sphere.

The same relationship is shown in a case of impotence accompanied by cramps in the calves and elsewhere, which has been recorded by Brügelmann ("Zur Lehre vom Perversen Sexualismus,' *Zeitschrift für Hypnotismus*, 1900, Heft I). These muscular conditions ceased for several days whenever coitus was effected.

An instructive analogy to the motor irradiations preceding the moment of sexual detumescence may be found in the somewhat similar motor irradiations which follow the delayed expulsion of a highly distended bladder. These sometimes become very marked in a child or

[1] *Cf.* MacGillicuddy, *Functional Disorders of the Nervous System in Women.* p. 110; Féré, *L'Instinct Sexuel*, second edition, p. 238; *id,* "Note sur une Anomalie de l'instinct Sexuel," *Belgique Médicale*, 1905; also "Analysis of the Sexual Impulse," in an earlier volume of these *Studies.*

[2] J. P. West, "Masturbation in Early Childhood," *Medical Standard*, November, 1895.

young woman unable to control the motor system absolutely. The legs are crossed, the foot swung, the thighs tightly pressed together, the toes curled. The fingers are flexed in rhythmic succession. The whole body slowly twists as though the seat had become uncomfortable. It is difficult to concentrate the mind; the same remark may be automatically repeated; the eyes search restlessly, and there is a tendency to count surrounding objects or patterns. When the extreme degree of tension is reached it is only by executing a kind of dance that the explosive contraction of the bladder is restrained.

The picture of muscular irradiation presented under these circumstances differs but slightly from that of the onset of detumescence. In one case the explosion is sought, in the other case it is dreaded; but in both cases there is a retarded muscular tension,—in the one case involuntary, in the other case voluntary—maintained at a point of acute intensity, and in both cases the muscular irradiations of this tension spread over the whole body.

The increased motor irritability of the state of detumescence somewhat resembles the conditions produced by a weak anæsthetic and there is some interest in noting the sexual excitement liable to occur in anæsthesia. I am indebted to Dr. J. F. W. Silk for some remarks on this point:—

"I. Sexual emotions may apparently be aroused during the stage of excitement preceding or following the administration of any anæsthetic; these emotions may take the form of mere delirious utterances, or may be associated with what is apparently a sexual orgasm. Or reflex phenomena connected with the sexual organs may occasionally be observed under special circumstances; or, to put it in another way, such reflex possibilities are not always abolished by the condition of narcosis or anæsthesia.

"II. Of the particular anæsthetics employed I am inclined to think that the possibility of such conditions arising is inversely proportionate to their strength, e.g., they are more frequently observed with a weak anæsthetic like nitrous oxide than with chloroform.

"III. Sexual emotions I believe to be rarely observable in men, and this is remarkable, or, I should say, particularly noticeable, for the presence of nurses, female students, etc., might almost have led one to expect that the contrary would have been the case. On the other hand, it is among men that I have frequently observed a reflex phenomenon which has usually taken the shape of an erection of the penis when the structures in the neighborhood of the spermatic cord have been handled.

"IV. Among females the emotional sexual phenomena most frequently obtrude themselves, and I believe that if it were possible to induce people to relate their dreams they would very often be found to be of a sexual character."

Much more important than the general motor phenomena, more purposive though involuntary, are the specifically sexual muscular movements. From the very beginning of detumescence, indeed, muscular activity makes itself felt, and the peripheral muscles of sex act, according to Kobelt's expression, as a peripheral sexual heart. In the male these movements are fairly obvious and fairly simple. It is required that the semen should be expressed from the vesiculæ seminales, propelled along the urethra, in combination with the prostatic fluid which is equally essential, and finally ejected with a certain amount of force from the urethral orifice. Under the influence of the stimulation furnished by the contact and friction of the vagina, this process is effectively caried out, mainly by the rhythmic contractions of the bulbo-cavernosus muscle, and the semen is emitted in a jet which may be ejaculated to a distance varying from a few centimeters to a meter or more.

With regard to the details of the psychic sides of this process a correspondent, a psychologist, writes as follows:—

"I have never noticed in my reading any attempt to analyze the sensations which accompany the orgasm, and, as I have made a good many attempts to make such an analysis myself, I will append the results on the chance that they may be of some value. I have checked my results so far as possible by comparing them with the experience of such of my friends as had coitus frequently and were willing to tell me as much as they could of the psychology of the process.

"The first fact that I hit upon was the importance of pressure. As one of my informants picturesquely phrases it—'the tighter the fit the greater the pleasure.' This agrees, too, with their unanimous testimony that the pleasurable sensations were much greater when the orgasm occurred simultaneously in the man and woman. Their analysis seldom went further than this, but a few remarked that the distinctive sensations accompanying the orgasm seem to begin near the root of the penis or in the testes, and that they are qualitatively different from the tickling sensations which precede them.

"These tickling sensations are caused, I think, by the friction of the glands against the vaginal walls, and are supplemented by other sensations from the urethra, whose nerves are stimulated by pressure of the vaginal walls and sphincter. The specific sensation of the orgasm begins, I believe, with a strong contraction of the muscles of the urethral walls along the entire length of the canal, and is felt as a peculiar ache starting from the base of the penis and quickly becoming diffused through the whole organ. This sensation reaches its climax with the expulsion of the semen into the urethra and the consequent feeling of distention, which is instantly followed by the rhythmic peristaltic contractions of the urethral muscles which mark the climax of the orgasm.

"The most careful introspection possible under the circumstances seems to show that these sensations arise almost wholly from the urethra and in a far less degree from the corona. During periods of great sexual excitement the nerves of the urethra and corona seem to possess a peculiar sensitivity and are powerfully stimulated by the violent peristaltic contractions of the muscles in the urethral walls during ejaculation. It seems possible that the intensity and volume of sensation felt at the glans may be due in part to the greater area of sensitive surface presented in the fossa as well as to the sensitivity of the corona, and in part to the fact that during the orgasm the glans is more highly congested than at any other time, and the nerve endings thus subjected to additional pressure.

"If the foregoing statements are true, it is easy to see why the pleasure of the man is much increased when the orgasm occurs at the same time in his partner and himself, for the contractions of the vagina upon the penis would increase the stimulation of all the nerve endings in that organ for which a mechanical stimulus is adequate, and the prominence of the corpus spongiosum and corona would ensure them the greatest stimulation. It seems not improbable that the specific sensation of orgasm rises from the stimulation of the peculiar form of nerve end-bulbs which Krause found in the corpus spongiosum and in the glans.

"The characteristic massiveness of the experience is probably due largely to the great number of sensations of strain and pressure caused by the powerful reflex contraction of so many of the voluntary muscles.

"Of course, the foregoing analysis is purely tentative, and I offer it only on the chance that it may suggest some line of inquiry which may lead to results of value to the student of sexual psychology."

In man the whole process of detumescence, when it has once really begun, only occupies a few moments. It is so likewise in many animals; in the genera Bos, Ovis, etc., it is very short, almost instantaneous, and rather short also in the Equidæ (in a vigorous stallion, according to Colin, ten to twelve seconds). As Disselhorst has pointed out, this is dependent on the fact that these animals, like man, possess a vas deferens which broadens into an ampulla serving as a receptacle which holds the semen ready for instant emission when required. On the other hand, in the dog, cat, boar, and the Canidæ, Felidæ, and Suidæ generally, there is no receptacle of this kind, and coitus is slow, since a longer time is required for the peristaltic action of the vas to bring the semen to the urogenital sinus. (R. Disselhorst, *Die Accessorischen Geschlechts-drusen der Wirbelthiere*, 1897, p. 212.)

In man there can be little doubt that detumescence is more rapidly accomplished in the European than in the East, in India, among the yellow races, or in Polynesia. This is probably in part due to a deliberate attempt to prolong the act in the East, and in part to a greater nervous erethism among Westerns.

In the woman the specifically sexual muscular process is less visible, more obscure, more complex, and uncertain. Before detumescence actually begins there are at intervals involuntary rhythmic contractions of the walls of the vagina, seeming to have the object of at once stimulating and harmonizing with those that are about to begin in the male organ. It would appear that these rhythmic contractions are the exaggeration of a phenomenon which is normal, just as slight contraction is normal and constant in the bladder. Jastreboff has shown, in the rabbit, that the vagina is in constant spontaneous rhythmic contraction from above downward, not peristaltic, but in segments, the intensity of the contractions increasing with age and especially with sexual development. This vaginal contraction which in women only becomes well marked just before detumescence, and is due mainly to the action of the sphincter cunni (analogous to the bulbo-cavernosus in the male), is only a part of the localized muscular process. At first there would appear to be a reflex peristaltic movement of the Fallopian tubes and uterus. Dembo observed that in animals stimulation of the upper anterior wall of the vagina caused gradual contraction of the uterus, which is erected by powerful contraction of its muscular fiber and round ligaments while at the same time it descends toward the vagina, its cavity becoming more and more diminished and mucus being forced out. In relaxing, Aristotle long ago remarked, it aspirates the seminal fluid.

Although the active participation of the sexual organs in woman, to the end of directing the semen into the womb at the moment of detumescence, is thus a very ancient belief, and harmonizes with the Greek view of the womb as an animal in the body endowed with a considerable amount of activity,[1] precise observation in modern times has offered but little confirmation of the reality of this participation. Such observations as have been made have usually been the accidental result of sexual excitement and orgasm occurring during a gynæcological examination. As, however, such a result is liable to occur in erotic subjects, a certain number of precise observations have accumulated during the past century. So far as the evidence goes, it would seem that in women, as in mares, bitches, and other animals, the uterus becomes shorter, broader, and softer during the orgasm, at the same time descending lower into the pelvis, with its mouth open intermittently, so that, as one writer remarks, spontaneously recurring to the simile which commended itself to the Greeks, "the uterus might be likened to an animal gasping for breath."[2] This sensitive, responsive mobility of the uterus is, indeed, not confined to the moment of detumescence, but may occur at other times under the influence of sexual emotion.

It would seem probable that in this erection, contraction, and descent of the uterus, and its simultaneous expulsion of mucus, we have the decisive moment in the completion of detumescence in woman, and it is probable that the thick mucus, unlike the earlier more limpid secretion, which women are sometimes aware of after orgasm, is emitted from the womb at this time. This is, however, not absolutely certain. Some authorities regard detumescence in women as accomplished in the pouring out of secretions, others in the rhythmic genital contractions; the sexual parts may, however, be copiously bathed in mucus for an indefinitely long period before the final stage of detumescence is achieved, and the rhythmic contractions are also taking place at a somewhat early period; in neither respect is there any obvious increase at the final moment of orgasm. In women this would seem to be more conspicuously a nervous manifestation than in men. On the subjective side it is very

---

[1] *Cf.* the discussion of hysteria in "Auto-Erotism," vol. i of these *Studies.*

[2] Hirst, *Text-Book of Obstetrics*, 1899, p. 67.

pronounced, with its feeling of relieved tension and agreeable repose—a moment when, as one woman expresses it, together with intense pleasure, there is, as it were, a floating up into a higher sphere, like the beginning of chloroform narcosis—but on the objective side this culminating moment is less easy to define.

Various observations and remarks made during the past two or three centuries by Bond, Valisneri, Dionis, Haller, Günther, and Bischoff, tending to show a sucking action of the uterus in both women and other female animals, have been brought together by Litzmann in R. Wagner's *Handwörterbuch der Physiologie* (1846, vol. iii, p. 53). Litzmann added an experience of his own: "I had an opportunity lately, while examining a young and very erethic woman, to observe how suddenly the uterus assumed a more erect position, and descended deeper in the pelvis; the lips of the womb became equal in length, the cervix rounded, softer, and more easily reached by the finger, and at the same time a high state of sexual excitement was revealed by the respiration and voice."

The general belief still remained, however, that the woman's part in conjugation is passive, and that it is entirely by the energy of the male organ and of the male sexual elements, the spermatozoa, that conjunction with the germ cell is attained. According to this theory, it was believed that the spermatozoa were, as Wilkinson expresses it, in a history of opinion on this question, "endowed with some sort of intuition or instinct; that they would turn in the direction of the os uteri, wading through the acid mucus of the vagina; travel patiently upward and around the vaginal portion of the uterus; enter the uterus and proceed onward in search of the waiting ovum." (A. D. Wilkinson, "Sterility in the Female," *Transactions of the Lincoln Medical Society*, Nebraska, 1896.)

About the year 1859 Fichstedt seems to have done something to overthrow this theory by declaring his belief that the uterus was not, as commonly supposed, a passive organ in coitus, but was capable of sucking in the semen during the brief period of detumescence. Various authorities then began to bring forward arguments and observations in the same sense. Wernich, especially, directed attention to this point in 1872 in a paper on the erectile properties of the lower segment of the uterus ("Die Erectionsfahigkeit des untern Uterus-Abschnitts," *Beiträge zur Geburtshülfe und Gynækologie*, vol. i, p. 296). He made precise observations and came to the conclusion that owing to erectile properties in the neck of the uterus, this part of the womb elongates during congress and reaches down into the pelvis with an aspiratory movement, as if to meet the glans of the male. A little later, in a case of partial prolapse, Beck, in ignorance of Wernich's theory, was enabled to make a very precise observation of the action of the uterus during excitement. In this case the woman was sexually very excitable even under ordinary examination, and Beck carefully noted the phenomena that took place during the orgasm. "The os and cervix uteri," he states, "had been about as firm as usual, moderately hard and, generally speaking, in a natural and normal condition, with the external os closed to such an extent as to admit of the uterine probe with difficulty; but the instant that the height of excitement was at hand, the os opened itself to the extent of fully an inch, as nearly as my eye can judge, made five or six successive gasps as if it were drawing the external os into the cervix, each time powerfully, and, it seemed to me, with a regular rhythmical action, at the same time losing its former density and hardness and becoming quite soft to the touch. Upon the cessation of the action, as related, the os suddenly closed, the cervix again hardened itself, and the intense congestion was dissipated." (J. R. Beck, "How do the Spermatozoa Enter the Uterus?" *American Journal of Obstetrics*, 1874.) It would appear that in the early part of this final process of detumescence the action of the uterus is mainly one of contraction and ejaculation of any mucus that may be contained; Dr. Paul Mundé has described "the gushing, almost in jets," of this mucus which he has observed in an erotic woman under a rather long digital and specular examination. (*American Journal of Obstetrics*, 1893.) It is during the latter part of detumescence, it would seem, and perhaps for a short time after the orgasm is over, that the action of the uterus is mainly aspiratory.

While the active part played by the womb in detumescence can no longer be questioned, it need not too hastily be assumed that the belief in the active movements of the spermatozoa must therefore be denied. The vigorous motility of the tadpole-like organisms is obvious to anyone who has ever seen fresh semen under the microscope; and if it is correct, as Clifton Edgar states, that the spermatozoa may retain their full activity in the female organs for at least seventeen days, they have ample time to exert their energies. The fact that impregnation sometimes occurs without rupture of the hymen is not decisive evidence that there has been no penetration, as the hymen may dilate without rupturing; but there seems no reason to doubt that conception has sometimes taken place when ejaculation has occurred without penetration; this is indicated in a fairly objective manner when, as has been occasionally observed, conception has occurred in women whose vaginas were so narrow as scarcely to admit the entrance of a goose-quill; such was the condition in the case of a pregnant woman brought forward by Roubaud. The stories, repeated in various books, of women who have conceived after homosexual relations with partners who had just left their husbands' beds are not therefore inherently impossible.[1] Janke quotes numerous cases in which there has been impregnation in virgins who have merely allowed the penis to be placed in contact with the vulva, the hymen remaining unruptured until delivery.[2]

It must be added, however, that even if the semen is effused merely at the mouth of the vagina, without actual penetration, the spermatozoa are still not entirely without any resource save their own motility in the task of reaching the ovum. As we have seen, it is not only the uterus which takes an active part in detumescence; the vagina also is in active movement, and it seems highly probable that, at all events in some women and under some circumstances, such movement favoring aspiration toward the womb may be communicated to the external mouth of the vagina.

Riolan (*Anthropographia*, 1626, p. 294) referred to the constriction and dilation of the vulva under the influence of sexual excitement. It is said that in Abyssinia women can, when adopting the straddling posture of coitus, by the movements of their own vaginal muscles alone, grasp the male organ and cause ejaculation, although the man remains passive. According to Lorion the Annamites, adopting the normal posture of coitus, introduce the penis when flaccid or only half erect, the contraction of the vaginal walls completing the process; the penis is very small in this people. It is recognized by gynæcologists that the condition of vaginismus, in which there is spasmodic contraction of the vagina, making intercourse painful or impossible, is but a morbid exaggeration of the normal contraction which occurs in sexual excitement. Even in the absence of sexual excitement there is a vague affection, occurring in both married and unmarried women, and not, it would seem,

---

[1] The earliest story of the kind with which I am acquainted, that of a widow who was thus impregnated by a married friend, is quoted in Schurig's *Spermatologia* (p. 224) from Amatus Lusitanus, *Curationum Centuriæ Septem*, 1620.

[2] Janke, *Die Willkürliche Hervorbringen des Geschlechts*, p. 238.

necessarily hysterical, characterized by quivering or twitching of the vulva; I am told that this is popularly termed "flackering of the shape" in Yorkshire and "taittering of the lips" in Ireland. It may be added that quivering of the gluteal muscles also takes place during detumescence, and that in Indian medicine this is likewise regarded as a sign of sexual desire in women, apart from coitus.

A non-medical correspondent in Australia, W. J. Chidley, from whom I have received many communications on this subject, is strongly of opinion from his own observations that not only does the uterus take an active part in coitus, but that under natural conditions the vagina also plays an active part in the process. He was led to suspect such an action many years ago, as well by an experience of his own, as also by hearing from a young woman who met her lover after a long absence that by the excitement thus aroused a tape attached to the underclothes had been drawn into the vagina. Since then the confidences of various friends, together with observations of animals, have confirmed him in the view that the general belief that coitus must be effected by forcible entry of the male organ into a passive vagina is incorrect. He considers that under normal circumstances coitus should take place but rarely, and then only under the most favorable circumstances, perhaps exclusively in spring, and, most especially, only when the woman is ready for it. Then, when in the arms of the man she loves, the vagina, in sympathy with the active movements of the womb, becomes distended at the touch of the turgescent, but not fully erect, penis, "flashes open and draws in the male organ." "All animals," he adds, "have sexual intercourse by the male organ being *drawn*, not forced, into the female. I have been borne out in this by friends who have seen horses, camels, mules and other large animals in the coupling season. What is more absurd, for instance, than to say that an entire *penetrates* the mare? His penis is a sensitive, beautiful piece of mechanism, which brings its light head here and there till it touches the right spot, when the mare, *if ready*, takes it in. An entire's penis could not penetrate anything; it is a curve, a beautiful curve which would easily bend. A bull's, again, is turned down at the end and, more palpably still, would fold on itself if pressed with force. The womb and vagina of a beautiful and healthy woman constitute a living, vital, moving organ, sensitive to a look, a word, a thought, a hand on the waist."

A well-known American author thus writes in confirmation of the foregoing view: "In nature the woman wooes. When impassioned her vagina becomes erect and dilated, and so lubricated with abundant mucus to the lips that entrance is easy. This dilatation and erectile expansion of vagina withdraws the hymen so close to the walls that penetration need not tear it or cause pain. The more muscular, primitive and healthy the woman the tougher and less sensitive the hymen, and the less likely to break or bleed. I think one great function of the foreskin also is to moisten the glans, so that it can be lubricated for entrance, and then to retract, moist side out, to make entrance still easier. I think that in nature the glans penetrates within the labia, is withstood a moment, vibrating, and then all resistance is withdrawn by a sudden 'flashing open' of the gates, permitting easy entrance, and that the sudden giving up of resistance, and substitution of welcome, with its instantaneous deep entrance, causes an almost immediate male orgasm (the thrill being irresistibly exciting). Certainly this is the process as observed in horses, cattle, goats, etc., and it seems likely something analogous is natural in man."

While it is easily possible to carry to excess a view which would make the woman rather than the man the active agent in coitus (and it may be recalled that in the Cebidæ the penis, as also the clitoris, is furnished with a bone), there is probably an element of truth in the belief that the vagina shares in the active part which, there can now be little doubt, is played by the uterus in detumescence. Such a view certainly enables us to understand how it is that semen effused on the exterior sexual organs can be conveyed to the uterus.

It was indeed the failure to understand the vital activity of the semen and the feminine genital canal, co-operating together towards the junction of sperm cell and germ cell, which for so long stood in the way of the proper understanding of conception. Even the genius of Harvey, which had grappled successfully with the problem of the circulation, failed in the attempt to comprehend the problem of generation. Mainly on account of this difficulty, he was unable to see how the male element could possibly enter the uterus, although he devoted much observation and study to the question. Writing of the uterus of the doe after copulation, he says: "I began to doubt, to ask myself whether the semen of the male could by any possibility make its way by attraction or injection to the seat of conception, and repeated examination led me to the conclusion that none of the semen reached this seat." (*De-Generatione Animalium*, Exercise lxvii.) "The woman," he finally concluded, "after contact with the spermatic fluid *in coitu*, seems to receive an influence and become fecundated without the co-operation of any sensible corporeal agent, in the same way as iron touched by the magnet is endowed with its powers."

Although the specifically sexual muscular process of detumescence in women—as distinguished from the general muscular phenomena of sexual excitement which may be fairly obvious—is thus seen to be somewhat complex and obscure, in women as well as in men detumescence is a convulsion which discharges a slowly accumulated store of nervous force. In women also, as in men, the motor discharge is directed to a specific end—the intromission of the semen in the one sex, its reception in the other. In both sexes the sexual orgasm and the pleasure and satisfaction associated with it, involve, as their most essential element, the motor activity of the sexual sphere.[1]

The active co-operation of the female organs in detumescence is probably indicated by the difficulty which is experienced in achieving conception by the artificial injection of semen. Marion Sims stated in 1866, in *Clinical Notes on Uterine Surgery*, that in 55 injections in six women he had only once been successful; he believed that that was the only case at that time on record. Jacobi had, however, practiced artificial fecundation in animals (in 1700) and John Hunter in man. See Gould and Pyle, *Anomalies and Curiosities of Medicine*, p. 43; also Janke *(Die Willkurliche Hervorbringen des Geschlechts, pp. 230 et seq.)* who discusses the question of artificial fecundation and brings together a mass of data.

The facial expression when tumescence is completed is marked by a high degree of energy in men and of loveliness in women. At this moment, when the culminating act of life is about to be accomplished, the individual thus reaches his supreme state of radiant beauty. The color is heightened, the eyes are larger and brighter, the facial muscles are more tense, so that in mature individuals any wrinkles disappear and youthfulness returns.

At the beginning of detumescence the features are frequently more discomposed. There is a general expression of eager receptivity to sensory impressions. The dilatation of the pupils, the expansion of the nostrils, the tendency to salivation and to movements of the tongue, all go to make up a picture which indicates an approaching gratification of sensory desires; it is significant that in some animals there is at this moment erection of the ears.[2] There is sometimes a tendency to utter broken and meaningless words, and it is noted that sometimes

---

[1] *Cf.* Adler, *Die Mangelhafte Geschlechtsempfindung des Weibes*, pp. 29-38.

[2] Féré, *Pathologie des Emotions*, p. 51.

women have called out on their mothers.[1] The dilatation of
the pupils produces photophobia, and in the course of detumescence the eyes are frequently closed from this cause. At the
beginning of sexual excitement, Vaschide and Vurpas have observed, tonicity of the eye-muscles seems to increase; the ele-
vators of the upper lids contract, so that the eyes look larger
and their mobility and brightness are heightened; with the increase of muscular tonicity strabismus occurs, owing to the
greater strength of the muscles that carry the eyes inward.[2]

The facial expression which marks the culmination of tumescence,
and the approach of detumescence is that which is generally expressive
of joy. In an interesting psycho-physical study of the emotion of joy,
Dearborn thus summarizes its characteristics: "The eyes are brighter
and the upper eyelid elevated, as also are the brows, the skin over the
glabella, the upper lip and the corners of the mouth, while the skin at
the outer canthi of the eye is puckered. The nostrils are moderately
dilated, the tongue slightly extended and the cheeks somewhat expanded,
while in persons with largely developed pinnal muscles the ears tend
somewhat to incline forwards. The whole arterial system is dilated, with
consequent blushing from this effect on the dermal capillaries of the face,
neck, scalp and hands, and sometimes more extensively even; from the
same cause the eyes slightly bulge. The whole glandular system likewise is stimulated, causing the secretions,—gastric, salivary, lachrymal,
sudoral, mammary, genital, etc.—to be increased, with the resulting rise
of temperature and increase in the katobolism generally. Volubility is
almost regularly increased, and is, indeed, one of the most sensitive and
constant of the correlations in emotional delight. . . . Pleasantness
is correlated in living organisms by vascular, muscular and glandular
extension or expansion, both literal and figurative." (G. Dearborn, "The
Emotion of Joy," *Psychological Review Monograph Supplements*, vol. ii,
No. 5, p. 62.) All these signs of joy appear to occur at some stage of
the process of sexual excitement.

In some monkeys it would seem that the muscular movement which
in man has become the smile is the characteristic facial expression of
sexual tumescence or courtship. Discussing the facial expression of
pleasure in children, S. S. Buckman has the following remarks: "There

---

[1] This is an instinctive impulse under all strong emotion in primitive persons. "The Australian Dieri," says A. W. Howitt (*Journal
Anthropological Institute*, August, 1890), "when in pain or grief cry out
for their father or mother."

[2] Vaschide and Vurpas, *Archives de Neurologie*, May, 1904.

is one point in such expression which has not received due consideration, namely, the raising of lumps of flesh each side of the nose as an indication of pleasure. Accompanying this may be seen small furrows, both in children and adults, running from the eyes somewhat obliquely towards the nose. What these characters indicate may be learned from the male mandril, whose face, particularly in the breeding season, shows colored fleshy prominences each side of the nose, with conspicuous furrows and ridges. In the male mandril these characters have been developed because, being an unmistakable sign of sexual ardor, they gave the female particular evidence of sexual feelings. Thus such characters would come to be recognized as habitually symptomatic of pleasurable feelings. Finding similar features in human beings, and particularly in children, though not developed in the same degree, we may assume that in our monkey-like ancestors facial characters similar to those of the mandril were developed, though to a less extent, and that they were symptomatic of pleasure, because connected with the period of courtship. Then they became conventionalized as pleasurable symptoms." (S. S. Buckmann, "Human Babies: What They Teach," *Nature*, July 5, 1900.) If this view is accepted, it may be said that the smile, having in man become a generalized sign of amiability, has no longer any special sexual significance. It is true that a faint and involuntary smile is often associated with the later stages of tumescence, but this is usually lost during detumescence, and may even give place to an expression of ferocity.

When we have realized how profound is the organic convulsion involved by the process of detumescence, and how great the general motor excitement involved, we can understand how it is that very serious effects may follow coitus. Even in animals this is sometimes the case. Young bulls and stallions have fallen in a faint after the first congress; boars may be seriously affected in a similar way; mares have been known even to fall dead.[1] In the human species, and especially in men—probably, as Bryan Robinson remarks, because women are protected by the greater slowness with which detumescence occurs in them— not only death itself, but innumerable disorders and accidents have been known to follow immediately after coitus, these results being mainly due to the vascular and muscular excitement involved by the processes of detumescence. Fainting, vomiting,

---

[1] F. B. Robinson, *New York Medical Journal*, March 11, 1893.

urination, defæcation have been noted as occurring in young men after a first coitus. Epilepsy has been not infrequently recorded. Lesions of various organs, even rupture of the spleen, have sometimes taken place. In men of mature age the arteries have at times been unable to resist the high blood-pressure, and cerebral hæmorrhage with paralysis has occurred. In elderly men the excitement of intercourse with strange women has sometimes caused death, and various cases are known of eminent persons who have thus died in the arms of young wives or of prostitutes.[1]

These morbid results, are, however, very exceptional. They usually occur in persons who are abnormally sensitive, or who have imprudently transgressed the obvious rules of sexual hygiene. Detumscence is so profoundly natural a process; it is so deeply and intimately a function of the organism, that it is frequently harmless even when the bodily condition is far from absolutely sound. Its usual results, under favorable circumstances, are entirely beneficial. In men there normally supervenes, together with the relief from the prolonged tension of tumescence, with the muscular repose and falling blood-pressure,[2] a sense of profound satisfaction, a glow of diffused well-being,[3] perhaps an agreeable lassitude, occasionally also a sense of mental liberation from an overmastering obsession. Under reasonably

---

[1] Féré deals fully with the various morbid results which may follow coitus, *L'Instinct Sexuel*, Chapter X; *id. Pathologie des Emotions,* p. 99.

[2] With regard to the relationship of detumescence to the blood-pressure Haig remarks: "I think that as the sexual act produces low and falling blood-pressure, it will of necessity relieve conditions which are due to high and rising blood-pressure, such, for instance, as mental depression and bad temper; and, unless my observation deceives me, we have here a connection between conditions of high blood-pressure, with mental and bodily depression, and the act of masturbation, for this act will relieve those conditions, and will tend to be practiced for this purpose." (A. Haig, *Uric Acid*, sixth edition, p. 154.)

[3] A medical correspondent speaks of subjective feelings of temperature coming over the body from 20 to 24 hours after congress, and marked by sensations of cooling of body and glow of cheeks. In another case, though lassitude appears on the second day after congress, the first day after is marked by a notable increase in mental and physical activity.

happy circumstances there is no pain, or exhaustion, or sadness, or emotional revulsion. The happy lover's attitude toward his partner is not expressed by the well-known Sonnet (CXXIX) of Shakespeare:—

> "Past reason hunted, and no sooner had
> Past reason hated."

He feels rather with Boccaccio that the kissed mouth loses not its charm,

> "Bocca baciata non perde ventura."

In women the results of detumescence are the same, except that the tendency to lassitude is not marked unless the act has been several times repeated; there is a sensation of repose and self-assurance, and often an accession of free and joyous energy. After completely satisfactory detumescence she may experience a feeling as of intoxication, lasting for several hours, an intoxication that is followed by no evil reaction.

Such, so far as our present vague and imperfect knowledge extends, are the main features in the process of detumescence. In the future, without doubt, we shall learn to know more precisely a process which has been so supremely important in the life of man and of his ancestors.

III.

The Constituents of Semen—Function of the Prostate—The Properties of Semen—Aphrodisiacs—Alcohol, Opium, etc.—Anaphrodisiacs—The Stimulant Influence of Semen in Coitus—The Internal Effects of Testicular Secretions—The Influence of Ovarian Secretion.

THE germ cell never comes into the sphere of consciousness and cannot therefore concern us in the psychological study of the phenomena of the sexual instinct. But it is otherwise with the sperm cell, and the seminal fluid has a relationship, both direct and indirect, to psychic phenomena which it is now necessary to discuss.

While the spermatozoa are formed in the glandular tissue of the testes, the seminal fluid as finally emitted in detumescence is not a purely testicular product, but is formed by mixture with the fluids poured out at or before detumescence by various glands which open into the urethra, and notably the prostate.[1] This is a purely sexual gland, which in animals only becomes large and active during the breeding season, and may even be hardly distinguishable at other times; moreover, if the testes are removed in infancy, the prostate remains rudimentary, so that during recent years removal of the testes has been widely advocated and practiced for that hypertrophy of the prostate which is sometimes a distressing ailment of old age. It is the prostatic fluid, according to Fürbringer, which imparts its characteristic odor to semen. It appears, however, to be the main function of the prostatic fluid to arouse and maintain the motility of the spermatozoa; before meeting the prostatic fluid the spermatozoa are motionless; that fluid seems to fur-

---

[1] The composite character of the semen was recognized by various old authors, some of whom said, (*e.g.*, Wharton) that it had three constituents, which they usually considered to be: (1) The noblest and most essential part, from the testicles; (2) a watery element from the vesiculæ; (3) an oily element from the prostate. Schurig, *Spermatologia*, 1720, p. 17.

nish a thinner medium in which they for the first time gain their full vitality.[1]

When at length the semen is ejaculated, it contains various substances which may be separated from it,[2] and possesses various qualities, some of which have only lately been investigated, while others have evidently been known to mankind from a very early period. "When held for some time in the mouth," remarked John Hunter, "it produces a warmth similar to spices, which lasts some time."[3] Possibly this fact first suggested that semen might, when ingested, possess valuable stimulant qualities, a discovery which has been made by various savages, notably by the Australian aborigines, who, in many parts of Australia, administer a potion of semen to dying or feeble members of the tribe.[4] It is perhaps noteworthy that in Central Africa the testes of the goat are consumed as an aphrodisiac.[5] In eighteenth century Europe, Schurig, in his *Spermatologia,* still found it necessary to discuss at considerable length the possible medical properties of human semen, giving many prescriptions which contained it.[6] The stimulation produced by the ingestion of semen would appear to form in some cases a part of the attraction exerted by *fellatio;* De Sade emphasized this point; and in a case recorded by Howard semen appears to have acted as a stimulant for which the craving was as irresistible as is that for alcohol in dipsomania.[7]

It must be remembered that the early history of this subject is more or less inextricably commingled with folk-lore practices of magical

---

[1] See, *e.g.,* C. Mansell Moulin, "A Contribution to the Morphology of the Prostate," *Journal of Anatomy and Physiology,* January, 1895; G. Walker, " A Contribution to the Anatomy and Physiology of the Prostate Gland, and a Few Observations on Ejaculation," *Johns Hopkins Hospital Bulletin,* October, 1900.

[2] For a study of the semen and its constituents, see Florence, "Du Sperme," *Archives d'Anthropologie Criminelle,* 1895.

[3] J. Hunter, *Essays and Observations,* vol. i, p. 189.

[4] As regards one part of Australia, Walter Roth, *Ethnological Studies Among the Queensland Aborigines,* p. 174.

[5] Sir H. H. Johnston, *British Central Africa,* p. 438.

[6] Cap. VII, pp. 327-357, "De Spermaticis virilis usu Medico."

[7] W. L. Howard, "Sexual Perversion," *Alienist and Neurologist,* January, 1896.

origin, not necessarily founded on actual observation of the physiological effects of consuming the semen or testes. Thus, according to W. H. Pearse (*Scalpel*, December, 1897), it is the custom in Cornwall for country maids to eat the testicles of the young male lambs when they are castrated in the spring, the survival, probably, of a very ancient religious cult. (I have not myself been able to hear of this custom in Cornwall.) In Burchard's Penitential (Cap. CLIV, Wasserschleben, *op. cit.*, p. 660) seven years' penance is assigned to the woman who swallows her husband's semen to make him love her more. In the seventeenth century (as shown in William Salmon's *London Dispensatory*, 1678) semen was still considered to be good against witchcraft and also valuable as a love-philter, in which latter capacity its use still survives. (Bourke, *Scatalogic Rites*, pp. 343, 355.) In an earlier age (Picart, quoted by Crawley, *The Mystic Rose*, p. 109) the Manichæans, it is said, sprinkled their eucharistic bread with human semen, a custom followed by the Albigenses.

The belief, perhaps founded in experience, that semen possesses medical and stimulant virtues was doubtless fortified by the ancient opinion that the spinal cord is the source of this fluid. This was not only held by the highest medical authorities in Greece, but also in India and Persia.

The semen is thus a natural stimulant, a physiological aphrodisiac, the type of a class of drugs which have been known and cultivated in all parts of the world from time immemorial. (Dufour has discussed the aphrodisiacs used in ancient Rome, *Histoire de la Prostitution*, vol. II, ch. 21.) It would be vain to attempt to enumerate all the foods and medicaments to which has been ascribed an influence in heightening the sexual impulse. (Thus, in the sixteenth century, aphrodisiacal virtues were attributed to an immense variety of foods by Liébault in his *Thresor des Remèdes Secrets pour les Maladies des Femmes*, 1585, pp. 104, *et seq.*) A large number of them certainly have no such effect at all, but have obtained this credit either on some magical ground or from a mistaken association. Thus the potato, when first introduced from America, had the reputation of being a powerful aphrodisiac, and the Elizabethan dramatists contain many references to this supposed virtue. As we know, potatoes, even when taken in the largest doses, have not the slightest aphrodisiac effect, and the Irish peasantry, whose diet consists very largely of potatoes, are even regarded as possessing an unusually small measure of sexual feeling. It is probable that the mistake arose from the fact that potatoes were originally a luxury, and luxuries frequently tend to be regarded as aphrodisiacs, since they are consumed under circumstances which tend to arouse the sexual desires. It is possible also that, as has been plausibly suggested, the misunderstanding may have been due to sailors—the first to be familiar with the potato—

who attributed to this particular element of their diet ashore the generally stimulating qualities of their life in port. The eryngo (*Eryngium maritimum*), or sea holly, which also had an erotic reputation in Elizabethan times, may well have acquired it in the same way. Many other vegetables have a similar reputation, which they still retain. Thus onions are regarded as aphrodisiacal, and were so regarded by the Greeks, as we learn from Aristophanes. It is notewhorthy that Marro, a reliable observer, has found that in Italy, both in prisons and asylums, lascivious people are fond of onions (*La Pubertà*, p. 297), and it may perhaps be worth while to recall the observation of Sérieux that in a woman in whom the sexual instinct only awoke in middle age there was a horror of leeks. In some countries, and especially in Belgium, celery is popularly looked upon as a sexual stimulant. Various condiments, again, have the same reputation, perhaps because they are hot and because sexual desire is regarded, rightly enough, as a kind of heat. Fish—skate, for instance, and notably oysters and other shellfish—are very widely regarded as aphrodisiacs, and Kisch attributes this property to caviar. It is probable that all these and other foods which have obtained this reputation, in so far as they have any action whatever on the sexual appetite, only possess it by virtue of their generally nutritious and stimulating qualities, and not by the presence of any special principle having a selective action on the sexual sphere. A beefsteak is probably as powerful a sexual stimulant as any food; a nutritious food, however, which is at the same time easily digestible, and thus requiring less expenditure of energy for its absorption, may well exert a specially rapid and conspicuous stimulant effect. But it is not possible to draw a line, and, as Aquinas long since said, if we wish to maintain ourselves in a state of purity we shall fear even an immoderate use of bread and water.

More definitely aphrodisiacal effects are produced by drugs, and especially by drugs which in large doses are poisons. The aphrodisiac with the widest popular reputation is cantharides, but its sexually exciting effects are merely an accidental result of its action in causing inflammation of the genito-urinary passage, and it is both an uncertain and a dangerous result, except in skillful hands and when administered in small doses. Nux vomica (with its alkaloid strychnia), by virtue of its special action on the spinal cord, has a notably pronounced effect in heightening the irritability of the spinal ejaculatory center, though it by no means necessarily exerts any strengthening influence. Alcohol exerts a sexually exciting effect, but in a different manner; it produces little stimulation of the cord and, indeed, even paralyzes the lumbar sexual center in large doses, but it has an influence on the peripheral nerve-endings and on the skin, and also on the cerebral centers, tending to arouse desire and to diminish inhibition. In this latter way, as Adler remarks, it may, in small doses, under some circumstances, be beneficial in men with an excessive nervousness or dread of coitus, and women, in whom orgasm has been difficult to reach, have frequently found this facilitated by some previous indulgence in alcohol. The aphrodisiac effect of alcohol seems specially marked on women. But against the use of alcohol as an aphrodisiac it must be remembered that it is far from being a tonic to detumescence, at all events in men, and that there is much evidence tending to show that not only chronic alcoholism, but even procreation during intoxication is perilous to the offspring (see, *e.g.*, Andriezen, *Journal of Mental Science*, January, 1905, and *cf.* W. C. Sullivan, "Alcoholism and Suicidal Impulses," *ib.*, April, 1898, p. 268); it may be added that Bunge has found a very high proportion of cases of immoderate use of alcohol in the fathers of women unable to suckle their infants (G. von Bunge, *Die Zunehmende Unfähigkeit der Frauen ihre Kinder zu Stillen*, 1903) while even an approximation to the drunken state is far from being a desirable prelude to the creation of a new human being. It is obvious that those who wish, for any reason, to cultivate a strict chastity of thought and feeling would do well to avoid alcohol altogether, or only in its lightest forms and in moderation. The aphrodisiacal effects of wine have long been known; Ovid refers to them (*e.g.*, *Ars Am.*, Bk. III, 765). Clement of Alexandria, who was something of a man of science as well as a Christian moralist, points out the influence of wine in producing lasciviousness and sexual precocity. (*Pædagogus*, Bk. II, Chapter II). Chaucer makes the Wife of Bath say in the Wife of Bath's Prologue:—

"And, after wyn, on Venus moste [needs] I thinke:
For al so siken as cold engendreth hayl,
A likerous mouth moste have a likerous tayl,
In womman vinolent is no defense,
This knowen lechours by experience."

Alcohol, as Chaucer pointed out, comes to the aid of the man, who is unscrupulous in his efforts to overcome a woman, and this not merely by virtue of its aphrodisiacal effects, and the apparently special influence which it seems to exert on women, but also because it lulls the mental and emotional characteristics which are the guardians of personality. A correspondent who has questioned on this point a number of prostitutes he has known, writes: "Their accounts of the first fall were nearly always the same. They got to know a 'gentleman,' and on one occasion they drank too much; before they quite realized what was happening they were no longer virgins." "In the mental areas, under the influence of alcohol," Schmiedeberg remarks (in his *Elements of Pharmacology*), "the finer degrees of observation, judgment, and reflection are the first to disappear, while the remaining mental functions remain in a normal condition. The soldier acts more boldly because he notices dangers less and reflects over them less; the orator does not allow himself to be influenced by any disturbing side-considerations as to his audience, hence he speaks more freely and spiritedly; self-consciousness is lost to a very great extent, and many are astounded at the ease with which they can express their thoughts, and at the acuteness of their judgment in matters which, when they are perfectly sober, with difficulty reach their minds; and then afterwards they are ashamed at their mistakes."

The action of opium in small doses is also to some extent aphrodisiacal; it slightly stimulates both the brain and the spinal cord, and has sensory effects on the skin like alcohol; these effects are favored by the state of agreeable dreaminess it produces. In the seventeenth century Venette (*La Génération de l'Homme*, Part II, Chapter V) strongly recommended small doses of opium, then little known, for this purpose; he had himself, he says, in illness experienced its joys, "a shadow of those of heaven." In India opium (as well as cannabis indica) has long been a not uncommon aphrodisiac; it is specially used to diminish local sensibility, delaying the orgasm and thus prolonging the sexual act. (W. D. Sutherland, "De Impotentia," *Indian Medical Gazette*, January, 1900). Its more direct and stimulating influence on the sexual emotions seems indicated by the statement that prostitutes are found standing outside the opium-smoking dens of Bombay, but not outside the neighboring liquor shops. (G. C. Lucas, *Lancet*, February 2, 1884.) Like alcohol, opium seems to have a marked aphrodisiacal effect on women. The case is recorded of a mentally deranged girl, with no nymphomania though she masturbated, who on taking small doses of opium at once showed signs of nymphomania, following men about, etc. (*American Journal Obstetrics*, May, 1901, p 74.) It may well be believed that opium acts beneficially in men when the ejaculatory centers are weak but irritable; but its actions are too widespread over the organism to make it in any degree a valuable aphrodisiac. Various other drugs have more or less reputation as aphrodisiacs; thus bromide of gold, a nervous and glandular stimulant, is said to have as one of its effects a heightening of sexual feeling. Yohimbin, an alkaloid derived from the West African Yohimbehe tree, has obtained considerable repute during recent years in the treatment of impotence; in some cases (see, *e.g*, Toff's results, summarized in *British Medical Journal*, February 18, 1905) it has produced good results, apparently by increasing the blood supply to the sexual organs, but has not been successful in all cases or in all hands. It must always be remembered that in cases of psychical impotence suggestion necessarily exerts a beneficial influence, and this may work through any drug or merely with the aid of bread pills. All exercise, often even walking, may be a sexual stimulant, and it is scarcely necessary to add that powerful stimulation of the skin in the sexual sphere, and more especially of the nates, is often a more effective aphrodisiac than any drug, whether the irritation is purely mechanical, as by flogging, or mechanico-chemical, as by urtication or the application of nettles. Among the Malays (with whom both men and women often use a variety of plants as aphrodisiacs, according to Vaughan Stevens) Breitenstein states (*21 Jahre in India*, Theil I, p. 228) that both massage and gymnastics are used to increase sexual powers. The local application of electricity is one of the most powerful of aphrodisiacs, and McMordie found on applying one pole to a uterine sound in the uterus and the other to the abdominal wall that in the majority of healthy women the orgasm occurred.

Among anaphrodisiacs, or sexual sedatives, bromide of potassium, by virtue of its antidotal relationship to strychnia, is one of the drugs whose action is most definite, though, while it dulls sexual desire, it also dulls all the nervous and cerebral activities. Camphor has an ancient reputation as an anaphrodisiac, and its use in this respect was known to the Arabs (as may be seen by a reference to it in the *Perfumed Garden*); while, as Hyrtl mentions (*loc. cit.* ii, p 94), rue (*Ruta graveolens*) was considered a sexual sedative by the monks of old, who on this account assiduously cultivated it in their cloister gardens to make *vinum rutæ*. Recently heroin in large doses (see, *e.g*, Becker, *Berliner Klinische Wochenschrift*, November 23, 1903) has been found to have a useful effect in this direction. It may be doubted, however, whether there is any satisfactory and reliable anaphrodisiac. Charcot, indeed, it is said, used to declare that the only anaphrodisiac in which he had any confidence was that used by the uncle of Heloïse in the case of Abelard. "*Cela* (he would add with a grim smile) *tranche la difficulte.*"

If semen is a stimulant when ingested, it is easy to suppose that it may exert a similar action on the woman who receives it into the vagina in normal sexual congress. It is by no means improbable that, as Mattei argued in 1878, this is actually the case. It is known that the vagina possesses considerable absorptive power. Thus Coen and Levi, among others, have shown that if a tampon soaked in a solution of iodine is introduced into the vagina, iodine will be found in the urine within an hour. And the same is true of various other substances.[1] If the vagina absorbs drugs it probably absorbs semen. Toff, of Braila (Roumania), who attaches much importance to such absorption, considers that it must be analogous to the ingestion of organic extractives. It is due to this influence, he believes,

[1] *Zentralblatt für Gynäkologie*, 1894, No. 49.

that weak and anæmic girls so often become full-blooded and robust after marriage, and lose their nervous tendencies and shyness.[1]

It is, however, most certainly a mistake to suppose that the beneficial influence of coitus on women is exclusively, or even mainly, dependent upon the absorption of semen. This is conclusively demonstrated by the fact that such beneficial influence is exerted, and in full measure, even when all precautions have been taken to avoid any contact with the semen. In so far as *coitus reservatus* or *interruptus* may lead to haste or discomfort which prevents satisfactory orgasm on the part of the woman, it is without doubt a cause of defective detumescence and incomplete satisfaction. But if orgasm is complete the beneficial effects of coitus follow even if there has been no possibility of the absorption of semen. Even after *coitus interruptus,* if it can be prolonged for a period long enough for the woman to attain full and complete satisfaction, she is enabled to experience what she may describe as a feeling of intoxication, lasting for several hours. It is in the action of the orgasm itself, and the vascular, secretory, and metabolic activities set up by the psychic and nervous influence of coitus with a beloved person, that we must seek the chief key to the effects produced by coitus on women, however these effects may possibly be still further heightened by the actual absorption of semen.[1]

The positive action of semen, or rather of the testicular products, has been much investigated during recent years, and appears on the whole to be demonstrated. The notable dis-

---

[1] E. Toff, "Uber Imprägnierung," *Zentralblatt für Gynäkologie,* April, 1903. In a similar but somewhat more precise manner Dufougère has argued ("La Chlorose, ses rapports avec le marriage, son traitement par le liquide orchitique," Thèse de Bordeaux, 1902) that semen when absorbed by the vagina stimulates the secretion of the ovaries and thus exerts an influence over the blood in anæmia; in this way he seeks to explain why it is that coitus is the best treatment for chlorosis.

[1] In this connection I may refer to an interesting and suggestive paper by Harry Campbell on "The Craving for Stimulants" (*Lancet,* October 21, 1899). No reference is made to coitus, but the author discusses stimulants as normal and beneficial products of the organism, and deals with the nature of the "physiological intoxication" they produce.

covery by Brown-Séquard, a quarter of a century ago, that the
ingestion of the testicular juices in states of debility and senility acted as a beneficial stimulant and tonic, opened the way
to a new field of therapeutics. Many investigators in various
countries have found that testicular extracts, and more especially the spermin as studied by Poehl,[1] and by him
regarded as a positive katalysator or accelerator of metabolic
processes, exert a real influence in giving tone to the heart and
other muscles, and in improving the metabolism of the tissues
even when all influences of mental suggestion have been excluded.[2]

As the ovaries are strictly analogous to the testes, it was surmised that ovarian extract might prove a drug equally valuable with
testicular products. As a matter of fact, ovarian extract, in the form
of ovarin, etc., would seem to have proved beneficial in various disorders,
more especially in anæmia and in troubles due to the artificial menopause. In most conditions, however, in which it has been employed the
results are doubtful or uncertain, and some authorities believe that the
influence of suggestion plays a considerable part here.

There is, however, another use which is subserved by the
testicular products, a use which may indeed be said to be implied
in those uses to which reference has already been made, but is
yet historically the latest to be realized and studied. It was
not until 1869 that Brown-Séquard first suggested that an important secretion was elaborated by the ductless glands and
received into the circulation, but that suggestion proved to be
epoch-making. If these glandular secretions are so valuable
when administered as drugs to other persons, must they not be
of far greater value when naturally secreted and poured out
into the circulation in the living body? It is now generally

---

[1] Spermin was first discovered in the sperm by Schreiner in 1878;
it has also been found in the thyroid, ovaries and various other glands.
"The spermin secreting and elaborating organs," Howard Kelly remarks
(*British Medical Journal*, January 29, 1898), "may be called the 'apothe-
caries' of the body, secreting many important medicaments, much more
active and more accurately representing its true wants than artificially
administered drugs."

[2] See, *e.g.*, a summary of Buschan's comprehensive discussion of the
subject of organotherapy (Eulenburg's *Real-Encyclopædie der Gesammten
Heilkunde*) in *Journal of Mental Science*, April, 1899, p. 355.

believed, on the basis of a large and various body of evidence, that this is undoubtedly so. In a very crude form, indeed, this belief is by no means modern. In opposition to the old writers who were inclined to regard the semen as an excretion which it was beneficial to expel, there were other ancient authorities who argued that it was beneficial to retain it as being a vital fluid which, if reabsorbed, served to invigorate the body. The great physiologist, Haller, in the middle of the eighteenth century, came very near to the modern doctrine when he stated in his *Elements of Physiology* that the sperm accumulated in the seminical vesicles is pumped back into the blood, and thus produces the beard and the hair together with the other surprising changes of puberty which are absent in the eunuch. The reabsorption of semen can scarcely be said to be a part of the modern physiological doctrine, but it is at least now generally held that the testes secrete substances which pass into the circulation and are of immense importance in the development of the organism.

The experiments of Shattock and Seligmann indicate that the semen and its reabsorption in the seminal vesicles, or the nervous reactions produced by its presence, can have no part in the formation of secondary sexual characters. These investigators occluded the vas deferens in sheep by ligature, at an early age, rendering them later sterile though not impotent. The secondary sexual characters appeared as in ordinary sheep. Spermatogenesis, these inquirers conclude, may be the initial factor, but the results must be attributed to the elaboration by the testicles of an internal secretion and its absorption into the general circulation.[1]

When animals are castrated there is enlargement of the ductless glands in the body, notably the thyroid and the suprarenal capsules.[2] It is evident, therefore, that the secretions of

---

[1] "Observations Upon the Acquirement of Secondary Sexual Characters, Indicating the Formation of an Internal Secretion by the Testicles," *Proceedings Royal Society*, vol. lxxiii, p. 49.

[2] See, *e.g.*, the experiments of Cecca and Zappi, summarized in *British Medical Journal*, July 2, 1904.

these ductless glands are in some degree compensatory to those of the testes. But this compensatory action is inadequate to produce any sexual development in the absence of the testes.

We see, therefore, how extremely important is the function of the testis. Its significance is not alone for the race, it is not simply concerned with the formation of the spermatozoa which share equally with the ova the honor of making the mankind of the future. It also has a separate and distinct function which has reference to the individual. It elaborates those internal secretions which stimulate and maintain the physical and mental characters, constituting all that is most masculine in the male animal, all that makes the man in distinction from the eunuch. Among various primitive peoples, including those of the European race whence we ourselves spring, the most solemn form of oath was sworn by placing the hand on the testes, dimly recognized as the most sacred part of the body. A crude and passing phase of civilization has ignorantly cast ignominy upon the sexual organs; the more primitive belief is now justified by our advancing knowledge.

In these as in other respects the ovaries are precisely analogous to the testes. They not only form the ova, but they elaborate for internal use a secretion which develops and maintains the special physical and mental qualities of womanhood, as the testicular secretion those of manhood. Moreover, as Cecca and Zappi found, removal of the ovaries has exactly the same effect on the abnormal development of the other ductless glands as has removal of the testes. It is of interest to point out that the internal secretion of the ovaries and its important functions seem to have been suggested before any other secretion than the sperm was attributed to the testes. Early in the nineteenth century Cabanis argued ("De l'Influence des Sexes sur le Caractère des Idées et des Affections Morales," *Rapport du Physique et du Moral de l'Homme*, 1824, vol. ii, p. 18) that the ovaries are secreting glands, forming a "particular humor" which is reabsorbed into the blood and imparts excitations which are felt by the whole system and all its organs.

IV.

The Aptitude for Detumescence—Is There an Erotic Temperament?
—The Available Standards of Comparison—Characteristics of the Cas-
trated—Characteristics of Puberty—Characteristics of the State of De-
tumescence—Shortness of Stature—Development of the Secondary
Sexual Characters—Deep Voice—Bright Eyes—Glandular Activity—
Everted Lips—Pigmentation—Profuse Hair—Dubious Significance of
Many of These Characters.

WHAT, if any, are the indications which the body generally
may furnish as to the individual's aptitude and vigor for the
orgasm of detumescence? Is there an erotic temperament out-
wardly and visibly displayed? That is a question which has
often occupied those who have sought to penetrate the more
intimate mysteries of human nature, and since we are here concerned with human beings in their relationship to the process
of detumescence, we cannot altogether pass over this question,
difficult as it is to discuss it with precision.

The old physiognomists showed much confidence in dealing with
the matter. Possibly they had more opportunities for observation than
we have, since they often wrote in days when life was lived more nakedly
than among ourselves, but their descriptions, while sometimes showing
much insight, are inextricably mixed up with false science and superstition.

In the *De Secretis Mulierum*, wrongly attributed to Albertus
Magnus, we find a chapter entitled "Signa mulieris calidæ naturæ et
quæ coit libenter," which may be summarized here. "The signs," we are
told, "of a woman of warm temperament, and one who willingly cohabits
are these: youth, an age of over 12, or younger, if she has been
seduced, small, high breasts, full and hard, hair in the usual positions;
she is bold of speech, with a delicate and high voice, haughty and
even cruel of disposition, of good complexion, lean rather than
stout, inclined to like drinking. Such a woman always desires coitus,
and receives satisfaction in the act. The menstrual flow is not abundant
nor always regular. If she becomes pregnant the milk is not abundant.
Her perspiration is less odorous than that of the woman of opposite

(182)

temperament; she is fond of singing, and of moving about, and delights in adornments if she has any."

Polemon, in his *Sulla Physionomia*, has given among the signs of libidinous impulse: knees turned inwards, abundance of hairs on the legs, squint, bright eyes, a high and strident voice, and in women length of leg below the knee. Aristotle had mentioned among the signs of wantonness: paleness, abundance of hair on the body, thick and black hair, hairs covering the temples, and thick eyelids.

In the seventeenth century Bouchet, in his *Serées* (Troisième Serée), gave as the signs of virility which indicated that a man could have children: a great voice, a thick rough black beard, a large thick nose.

G. Tourdes (Art. "Aphrodisie," *Dictionnaire Encyclopédique des Sciences Médicales*) thus summarized the ancient beliefs on this subject: "The erotic temperament has been described as marked by a lean figure, white and well-ranged teeth, a developed hairy system, a characteristic voice, air, and expression, and even a special odor."

In approaching the question of the general physical indications of a special aptitude to the manifestation of vigorous detumescence, the most obvious preliminary would seem to be a study of the castrated. If we know the special peculiarities of those who by removal of the sexual glands at a very early age have been deprived of all ability to present the manifestations of detumescence, we shall probably be in possession of a type which is the reverse of that which we may expect in persons of a vigorously erotic temperament.

The most general characteristics of eunuchs would appear to be an unusual tendency to put on fat, a notably greater length of the legs, absence of hair in the sexual and secondary sexual regions, a less degree of pigmentation, as noted both in the castrated negro and the white man, a puerile larynx and puerile voice. In character they are usually described as gentle, conciliatory, and charitable.

There can be little doubt that castration in man tends to lead to lengthening of the legs (tibia and fibula) at puberty, from delayed ossification of the epiphyses. The hands and feet are also frequently longer and sometimes the forearms. At the same time the bones are more slender. The pelvis also is narrower. The eunuchs of Cairo are said to be easily seen in a crowd from their tall stature. (Collineau, quoting Lortet, *Revue Mensuelle de l'Ecole d'Anthropologie*, May, 1896.) The

castrated Skoptzy show increased stature, and, it seems, large ears, with
decreased chest and head (L. Pittard, *Revue Scientifique*, June 20, 1903.)
Féré shows that in most of these respects the eunuch resembles beardless and infantile subjects. ("Les Proportions des Membres et les
Caractères Sexuels," *Journal de l'Anatomie et de la Physiologie*, Novem-
ber-December, 1897.) Similar phenomena are found in animals generally.
Sellheim, carefully investigating castrated horses, swine, oxen and fowls,
found retardation of ossification, long and slender extremities, long,
broad, but low skull, relatively smaller pelvis and small thorax. ("Zur
Lehre von den Sekundären Geschlechtscharakteren," *Beiträge zur
Geburtshulfe und Gynäcologie*, 1898, summarized in *Centralblatt für
Anthropologie*, 1900, Heft IV.)

As regards the mental qualities and moral character of the castrated, Griffiths considers that there is an undue prejudice against
euunchs, and refers to Narses, who was not only one of the first generals
of the Roman Empire, but a man of highly estimable character. (*Lancet*,
March 30, 1895.) Matignon, who has carefully studied Chinese eunuchs,
points out that they occupy positions of much responsibility, and,
though regarded in many respects as social outcasts, possess very excellent and amiable moral qualities (*Archives Cliniques de Bordeaux*, May,
1896.) In America Everett Flood finds that epileptics and feeble-minded
boys are mentally and morally benefited by castration. ("Notes on the
Castration of Idiot Children," *American Journal of Psychology*, January,
1899.) It is often forgotten that the physical and psychic qualities
associated with and largely dependent on the ability to experience the
impulse of detumescence, while essential to the perfect man, involve
many egoistic, aggressive and acquisitive characteristics which are of
little intellectual value, and at the same time inimical to many moral
virtues.

We have a further standard—positive this time rather than
negative—to aid us in determining the erotic temperament:
the phenomena of puberty. The efflorescence of puberty is essentially the manifestation of the ability to experience detumescence. It is therefore reasonable to suppose that the individuals
in whom the special phenomena of puberty develop most markedly are those in whom detumescence is likely to be most
vigorous. If such is the case we should expect to find the erotic
temperament marked by developed larynx and deep voice, a considerable degree of pigmentary development in hair and skin,

and a marked tendency to hairiness; while in women there should be a pronounced growth of the breasts and pelvis.[1]

There is yet another standard by which we may measure the individual's aptitude for detumescence: the presence of those activities which are most prominently brought into play during the process of detumescence. The individual, that is to say, who is organically most apt to manifest the physiological activities which mainly make up the process of detumescence, is most likely to be of pronounced erotic temperament.

"Erotic persons are of motor type," remark Vaschide and Vurpas, "and we may say generally that nearly all persons of motor type are erotic." The state of detumescence is one of motor and muscular energy and of great vascular activity, so that habitual energy of motor response and an active circulation may reasonably be taken to indicate an aptitude for the manifestation of detumescence.

These three types may be said, therefore, to furnish us valuable though somewhat general indications. The individual who is farthest removed from the castrated type, who presents in fullest degree the characters which begin to emerge at the period of puberty, and who reveals a physiological aptitude for the vigorous manifestation of those activities which are called into action during detumescence, is most likely to be of erotic temperament. The most cautious description of the characteristics of this temperament given by modern scientific writers, unlike the more detailed and hazardous descriptions of the early physiognomists, will be found to be fairly true to the standards thus presented to us.

The man of sexual type, according to Biérent (*LaPuberté*, p. 148), is hairy, dark and deep-voiced.

"The men most liable to satyriasis," Bouchereau states (art. "Satyriasis," *Dictionnaire Encyclopédique des Sciénces Médicales*), "are those with vigorous nervous system, developed muscles, abundant hair on body, dark complexion, and white teeth."

---

[1] See Biérent, *La Puberté;* Marro, *La Pubertà* (and enlarged French translation, *La Puberté*), and portions of G. S. Hall's *Adolescence;* also Havelock Ellis, *Man and Woman* (fourth edition, revised and enlarged).

Mantegazza, in his *Fisiologia del Piacere,* thus describes the sexual temperament: "Individuals of nervous temperament, those with fine and brown skins, rounded forms, large lips and very prominent larynx enjoy in general much more than those with opposite characteristics. A universal tradition," he adds, "describes as lascivious humpbacks, dwarfs, and in general persons of short stature and with long noses."

In a case of nymphomania in a young woman, described by Alibert (and quoted by Laycock, *Nervous Diseases of Women,* p. 28) the hips, thighs and legs were remarkably plump, while the chest and arms were completely emaciated. In a somewhat similar case described by Marc in his *De la Folie* a peasant woman, who from an early age had experienced sexual hyperæsthesia, so that she felt spasmodic voluptuous feelings at the sight of a man, and was thus the victim of solitary excesses and of spasmodic movements which she could not repress, the upper part of the body was very thin, the hips, legs and thighs highly developed.

In his work on *Uterine and Ovarian Inflammation* (1862, p. 37) Tilt observes: "The restless, bashful eye, and changing complexion, in presence of a person of the opposite sex, and a nervous restlessness of body, ever on the move, turning and twisting on sofa or chair, are the best indications of sexual temperament."

An extremely sensual little girl of 8, who was constantly masturbating when not watched, although brought up by nuns, was described by Busdraghi (*Archivio di Psichiatria,* fas. i, 1888, p. 53) as having chestnut hair, bright black eyes, an elevated nose, small mouth, pleasant round face, full colored cheeks, and plump and healthy aspect.

A highly intelligent young Italian woman with strong and somewhat perverted sexual impulses is described as of attractive appearance, with olive complexion, small black almond-shaped eyes, dilated pupils, oblique thin eyebrows, very thick black hair, rather prominent cheekbones, largely developed jaw, and with abundant down on lower part of cheeks and on upper lip. (*Archivio di Psichiatria,* 1899, fasc. v-vi.)

As the type of the sensual woman in word and act, led by her passions to commit various sexual offenses, Ottolenghi describes (*Archivio di Psichiatria,* vol. xii, fasc. v-vi, p. 496) a woman of 32 who attempted to kill her lover. The daughter of parents who were neurotic and themselves very erotic, she was a highly intelligent and vivacious woman, with a pleasing and open face, very thick dark chestnut hair, large cheek-bones, adipose buttocks almost resembling those of a Hottentot, and very thick pubic hair. She was very fond of salt things. Sexual inclination began at the age of 7.

Adler and Moll remark, very truly, that, so far at least as women are concerned, sexual anæsthesia or sexual proclivity cannot be unfailingly read on the features. Every woman desires to please, and coquetry is the sign of a cold, rather than of an erotic temperament.[1] It may be added that a considerable degree of congenital sexual anæsthesia by no means prevents a woman from being beautiful and attractive, though it must probably still always be said that, as Roubaud points out,[2] the woman of cold and intellectual temperament, the "femme de tête," however beautiful and skillful she may be, cannot compete in the struggle for love with the woman whose qualities are of the heart and of the emotions. But it seems sufficiently clear that the practical observations of skilled and experienced observers agree in attributing to persons of erotic type certain general characteristics which accord with those negative and positive standards we may frame on the basis of castration, of puberty, and of detumescence. It may be worth while to note a few of these characteristics briefly.

The abnormal lengthening of the long bones at the age of puberty in the castrated is, as we have seen, very pronounced. There is little tendency to associate length of limb with an erotic temperament, and a certain amount of data as well as of more vague opinion points in the opposite direction. The Arabs would appear to believe that it is short rather than tall people in whom the sexual instinct is strongly developed, and we read in the *Perfumed Garden*. "Under all circumstances little women love coitus more and evince a stronger affection for the virile member than women of a large size." In his elaborate investigation of criminals Marro found that prostitutes and women guilty of sexual offenses, as also male sexual offenders, tend to be short and thick set.[3] In European folk-lore the thick, bull neck is regarded as a sign of strong sexuality.[2] Mantegazza refers to a strong sexual temperament as being associated with arrest or disorder of bony development, and Marro suggests that

---

[1] Adler, *Die Mangelhafte Geschlechtsempfindung des Weibes*, p. 174; Moll, "Perverse Sexualempfindung, Psychische Impotenz und Ehe" (Section II), in Senator and Kaminer, *Krankheiten und Ehe*.

[2] Roubaud, *Traité de l'Impuissance*, p. 524.

[3] Marro, *Caratteri dei Delinquenti*, p. 374.

[2] Κρυπτάδια, vol. ii, p. 258.

the proverbial salacity of rachitic individuals may be due to an increased activity of the sexual organs.[1] It may be added that acromegaly, with its excessive bony growths, tends to be associated with premature sexual involution.

A further point which is frequently mentioned in the case of women is the development of the chief secondary sexual regions: the pelvis and the breasts. It is, indeed, almost inevitable that there should be some degree of correlation between the aptitude for bearing children and the aptitude for experiencing detumescence. The reality of such a connection is not only evidenced by medical observations, but receives further testimony in popular beliefs. In Italy women with large buttocks are considered wanton, and among the South Slavs they are regarded as especially fruitful.[2] Blumenbach asserted that precocious venery will enlarge the breasts, and believed that he had found evidence of this among young London prostitutes.[3]

The association of the aptitude for detumescence with a tendency to a deep rather than to a high voice, both in men and women, has frequently been noted and has seldom been denied. The onset of puberty always affects the voice; in general, Biérent states, the more bass the voice is the more marked is the development of the sexual apparatus; "a very robust man, with very developed sexual organs, and very dark and abundant hairy system, a man of strong puberty in a word, is nearly always a bass."[4] The influence of sexual excitement in deepening the voice is shown by the rules of sexual hygiene prescribed to tenors, while a bass has less need to observe similar precautions. In women every phase of sexual life—puberty, menstruation, coitus, pregnancy—tends to affect the voice and always by giving it a deeper character. The deepening of the voice by sexual intercourse was an ancient Greek observation, and Martial refers to a woman's good or bad singing as an index to her recent

---

[1] Marro, *La Pubertà*, p. 196. In Italy, the sensuality of the lame is the subject of proverbs.

[2] *Archivio di Psichiatria*, 1896, p. 515; Κρυπτάδια, vol. vi, p. 212.

[3] Blumenbach, *Anthropological Treatises*, p. 248.

[4] Biérent, *La Puberté*, p. 148.

sexual habits. Prostitutes tend to have a deep voice. Venturi points out that married women preserve a fresh voice to a more advanced age than spinsters, this being due to the precocious senility in the latter of an unused function. Such a phenomenon indicates that the relationship of detumescence to the deepening of the voice is not quite simple. This is further indicated by the fact that in robust men abstinence still further deepens the voice (the monk of melodrama always has a bass voice), while excessive or precocious sexual indulgence tends to be associated with the same kind of puerile voice as is found in those persons in whom pubertal development has not been carried very far, or who are of what Griffiths terms eunuchoid type. Idiot boys, who are often sexually undeveloped, tend to have a high voice, while idiot girls (who often manifest marked sexual proclivities) not infrequently have a deep voice.[1]

Bright dilated eyes are among the phenomena of detumescence, and are very frequently noted in persons of a pronounced erotic temperament. This is, indeed, an ancient observation, and Burton says of people with a black, lively, and sparkling eye, "without question they are most amorous," drawing his illustrations mostly from classic literature.[2] Tardieu described the erotic woman as having bright eyes, and Heywood Smith states that the eyes of lascivious women resemble, though in a less degree, those of the insane.[3] Sexual excitement is one among many causes—intellectual excitement, pain, a loud noise, even any sensory irritation—which produce dilatation of the pupils and enlargement of the palpebral fissure, with some protrusion of the eyeball. The influence of the sexual system upon the eye appears to be far less potent in men than in women.[4] Sexual desire is, however, by no means the only irritant within the sexual sphere which may thus influence the eye; morbid irritations may produce the same effect. Milner Fothergill, in his book on *Indigestion,* vividly describes the appearance of the

---

[1] Venturi, *Degenerazioni Psico-sessuali,* pp. 408-410.
[2] *Anatomy of Melancholy,* Part III, Section II, Mem. II, Sub. II.
[3] *British Gynæcological Journal,* Febuary, 1887, p. 505.
[4] Power, *Lancet,* November 26, 1887.

eyes sometimes seen in ovarian disorder: "The glittering flash which glances out from some female irides is the external indication of ovarian irritation, and 'the ovarian gleam' has features quite its own. The most marked instance which ever came under my notice was due to irritation in the ovaries, which had been forced down in front of the uterus and been fixed there by adhesions. Here there was little sexual proclivity, but the eyes were very remarkable. They flashed and glittered unceasingly, and at times perfect lightning bolts shot from them. Usually there is a bright glittering sheen in them which contrasts with the dead look in the irides of sexual excess or profuse uterine discharges."

The activity of the glandular secretions, and especially those of the skin, during detumescence, would lead us to expect that such secretory activity is an index to an aptitude for detumescence. As a matter of fact it is occasionally, though not frequently, noted by medical observers. It is stated that the erotic temperament is characterized by a special odor.[1] The activity of the sweat-glands is seldom referred to by medical observers in describing persons of erotic temperament, although the descriptions of novelists not infrequently contain allusions to this point, and the literature of an earlier age shows that the tendency to perspiration, especially the moist hand, was regarded as a sure sign of a sensual temperament. "The moist-handed Madonna Imperia, a most rare and divine creature," remarks Lazarillo in Middleton's comedy *Blurt, Master-Constable,* to quote one of many allusions to this point in the Elizabethan drama.

The lips are sometimes noted as red and everted, perhaps thick[1]; Tardieu remarked that the typically erotic woman has thick red lips. This corresponds with the characteristic type of the satyr in classic statues as in later paintings; his lips are

---

[1] With regard to the sexual relationships of personal odor, see the previous volume of these *Studies,* "Sexual Selection in Man," section on Smell.

[1] In European folk-lore thick lips in a woman are sometimes regarded as a sign of sensuality, Κρυπτάδια, vol. ii, p. 258.

always thick and everted. Fullness, redness, and eversion of the lips are correlated with good breathing, the absence of anæmia, laughter, a well-fleshed face.

This kind of mouth indicates, perhaps, not so much a congenitally erotic temperament, as an abandonment to impulse. The opposite type of mouth—with inverted, thin, and retracted lips—would appear to be found with especial frequency in persons who habitually repress their impulses on moral grounds. Any kind of effort to restrain involuntary muscular action may lead to retraction of the lips: the effort to overcome anger or fear, or even the resistance to a strong desire to urinate or defecate. In religious young men, however, it becomes habitual and fixed. I recall a small band of medical students, gathered together from a large medical school, who were accustomed to meet together for prayer and Bible-reading; the majority showed this type of mouth to a very marked degree: pale faces, with drawn, retracted lips. It may be termed the Christian or pious *facies*. It is much less frequently seen in religious women (unless of masculine type), doubtless because religion for women is in a much less degree than for men a moral discipline.

It may be added that an interesting form of this contraction of the lips, and one that is not purely repressive, is that which indicates the state of muscular tension associated with the impulse to guard and protect. In this form the contracted mouth is the index of tenderness, and is characteristic of the mother who is watching over the infant she is suckling at her breast. I have observed precisely the same expression in the face of a boy of 14 with a large congenital scrotal hernia; when the tumor was being examined his lower lip became retracted, well marked lines appearing from the angles downwards, though the upper lip retained its normal expression It was precisely the tender look we may see in the faces of mothers who are watching anxiously over their offspring, and the emotion is evidently the same in both cases: solicitude for a sensitive and tenderly guarded object.

The degree of pigmentation is clearly correlated with sexual vigor. "In general," Heusinger laid down, in 1823, "the quantity of pigment is proportional to the functional effectiveness of the genital organs." This connection is so profound that it may be traced very widely throughout the organic world.

The connection between pigmentation and sexual activity is very ancient. Even leaving out of account the wedding apparel of animals, nearly always gorgeous in scales and plumage and hair, the sexual orifice shows a more or less marked tendency to pigmentation during the breeding season from fishes upward, while in mammals the darker pigmentation of this region is a constant phenomenon in sexually mature individuals.[1]

In the human species both the negative standard of castration and the positive standard of puberty alike indicate a correlation of this kind. Those individuals in whom puberty never fully develops and who are consequently said to be affected by infantilism, reveal a relative absence of pigment in the sexual centers which are normally pigmented to a high degree.[2] Among those Asiatic races who extirpate the ovaries in young girls the skin remains white in the perineum, round the anus, and in the armpits.[3] Even in mature women who undergo ovariotomy, as Kepler found, the pigmentation of the nipples and areola disappears, as well as of the perineum and anus, the skin taking on a remarkable whiteness.

Normally the sexual centers, and in a high degree the genital orifice, represent the maximum of pigmentation, and under some circumstances this is clearly visible even in infancy. Thus babies of mixed black and white blood may show no traces of negro ancestry at birth, but there will always be increased pigmentation about the external genitalia.[4] The linea fusca, which reaches from the pubes to the navel and occasionally to the ensiform cartilage, is a line of sexual pigmentation sometimes regarded as characteristic of pregnancy, but as Andersen, of Copenhagen, has found by the examination of several hundred children of both sexes, it exists in a slight form in about 75 per cent. of young girls, and in almost as large a proportion of boys. But there is no doubt that it tends to increase with age as well as to become marked at pregnancy. At puberty there is a general tendency to changes in pigmentation; thus Godin found

---

[1] The direct dependence of sexual pigmentation on the primary sexual glands is well illustrated by a true hermaphroditic adult finch exhibited at the Academy of Sciences of Amsterdam (May 31, 1890); this bird had a testis on the right side and an ovary on the left, and on the right side its plumage was of the male's colors, on the left of the female's color.

[2] See, e.g., Papillault, *Bulletin Société d'Anthropologie*, 1899, p. 446.

[3] Guinard, Art. "Castration," Richet's *Dictionnaire de Physiologie*.

[4] J. Whitridge Williams, *Obstetrics*, 1903, p. 132.

that in 28 per cent. adolescent changes occurred in the eyes and hair at this period, the hair becoming darker, though the eyes sometimes become lighter. Ammon, in his investigation of conscripts at the age of 20 (*post,* p. 196), discovered the significant fact that the eyes and hair darken *pari passu* with sexual development. In women, during menstruation, there is a general tendency to pigmentation; this is especially obvious around the eyes, and in some cases black rings of true pigment form in this position. Even the skin of the negro women of Loango sometimes becomes a few shades darker during menstruation.[1] During pregnancy this tendency to pigmentation reaches its climax. Pregnancy constantly gives rise to pigmentation of the face, the neck, the nipples, the abdomen, and this is especially marked in brunettes.

This association of pigmentation and sexual aptitudes has been recognized in the popular lore of some peoples. Thus the Sicilians, who admire brown skin and have no liking either for a fair skin or light hair, believe that a white woman is incapable of responding to love. It is the brown woman who feels love; as it is said in Sicilian dialect: "Fimmina scura, fimmina amurusa."[2]

The dependence of pigmentation upon the sexual system is shown by the fact that irritation of the genital organs by disease will frequently suffice to produce a high degree of pigmentation. This may appear on the face, the neck, the trunk, the hands. Simpson long since noted that uterine irritation apart from pregnancy may produce pigmentation of the areolæ of the nipples (*Obstetric Works,* vol. i, p. 345). Engelmann discussed the subject and gave cases, "The Hystero-Neuroses," pp. 124-139, in *Gynecological Transactions,* vol. xii, 1887; and a summary of a memoir by Fouquet on this subject in *La Gynécologie,* February, 1903, will be found in *British Medical Journal,* March 28, 1903,

---

[1] *Zeitschrift für Ethnologie,* 1878, p. 19.

[2] C. Pitre, *Medicina Populare Siciliana,* p. 47. In England, from notes sent to me by one correspondent, it would appear that the proportion of dark and sexually apt women to fair and sexually apt women is as 3 to 1. The experience of others would doubtless give varying results, and in any case the fallacies are numerous. See, in the previous volume of these *Studies,* "Sexual Selection in Man," Section IV.

Of all physical traits vigor of the hairy system has most frequently perhaps been regarded as the index of vigorous sexuality. In this matter modern medical observations are at one with popular belief and ancient physiognomical assertions.[1] The negative test of castration and the positive test of puberty point in the same direction.

It is at puberty that all the hair on the body, except that on the head, begins to develop; indeed, the very word "puberty" has reference to this growth as the most obvious sign of the whole process. When castration takes place at an early age all this development of pubescent hair is arrested. When the primary sexual organs are undeveloped the sexual hair is also undeveloped, as in a case, recorded by Plant,[2] of a girl with rudimentary uterus and ovaries who had little or no axilliary and pubic hair, although the hair of the head was long and strong.[3]

The pseudo-Michael Scot among the *Signa mulieris calidæ naturæ et quæ coit libenter* stated that her hair, both on the head and body, is thick and coarse and crisp, and Della Porta, the greatest of the physiognomists, said that thickness of hair in women meant wantonness. Venette, in his *Génération de l'Homme*, remarked that men who have much hair on the body are most amorous. At a more recent period Roubaud has said that pubic hair in its quantity, color and curliness is an index of genital energy. A poor pilous system, on the other hand, Roubaud regarded as a probable though not an irrefragable proof of sexual frigidity in women. "In the cold woman the pilous system is remarkable for the languor of its vitality; the hairs are fair, delicate, scarce and smooth, while in ardent natures there are little curly tufts about the temples." (*Traité de l'Impuissance*, pp. 124, 523.) Martineau declared (*Leçons sur les Déformations Vulvaires*, p. 40) that "the more developed the genital organs the more abundant the hair covering them;

---

[1] In Japan the same belief would appear to be held. In a nude figure representing the typical voluptuous woman by the Japanese painter Marugama Okio (reproduced in Ploss's *Das Weib*) the pubic and axillary hair is profuse, though usually sparse in Japan.

[2] *Centralblatt für Gynäkologie*, No. 9, 1896.

[3] It is important to remember that there is little correlation in this matter between the hair of the head and the sexual hair, if not a certain opposition. (See *ante*, p. 127.) According to one of the aphorisms of Hippocrates, repeated by Buffon, eunuchs do not become bald, and Aristotle seems to have believed that sexual intercourse is a cause of baldness in men. (Laycock, *Nervous Diseases of Women*, p. 23.)

abundance of hair appears to be in relation to the perfect development of the organs." Tardieu described the typically erotic woman as very hairy.

Bergh found that among 2200 young Danish prostitutes those who showed an unusual extension and amount of pubic hair included several women who were believed to be libidinous in a very high degree. (Bergh, "Symbolæ," etc., *Hospitalstidende*, August, 1894.) Moraglia, again, in Italy, in describing various women, mostly prostitutes, of unusually strong sexual proclivities, repeatedly notes very thick hair, with down on the face. (*Archivio di Psichiatria*, vol. xvi, fasc. iv-v.)

Marro, also, in Italy found that abundance of hair and down is especially marked in women who are guilty of infanticide (as also Pasini has found), though criminal women generally, in his experience, tend to have abnormally abundant hair. (*Caratteri dei Delinquenti*, cap. XXII.) Lombroso finds that prostitutes generally tend to be hairy (*Donna Delinquente*, p. 320.)

A lad of 14, guilty of numerous crimes of violence having a sexual source, is described by Arthur Macdonald in America as having hair on the chest as well as all over the pubes. (A. Macdonald, *Archives de L'Anthropologie Criminelle*, January, 1893, p. 55.) The association of hairiness with abnormal sexuality in the weak-minded has been noted at Bicêtre (*Recherches Cliniques sur l'Epilepsie*, vol. xix, pp. 69, 77.)

Hypertrichosis universalis, a general hairiness of body, has been described by Cascella in a woman with very strong sexual desires, who eventually became insane. (*Revista Mensile di Psichiatria*, 1903, p. 408.) Bucknill and Tuke give the case of a religiously minded girl, with very strong and repressed sexual desires, who became insane; the only abnormal feature in her physical development was the marked growth of hair over the body.

Brantôme refers to a great lady known to him whose body was very hairy, and quotes a saying to the effect that hairy people are either rich or wanton; the lady in question, he adds, was both. (Brantôme, *Vie des Dames Galantes*, Discours II.)

De Sade, whose writings are now regarded as a treasure house of true observations in the domain of sexual psychology, makes the Rodin of *Justine* dark, with much hair and thick eyebrows, while his very sexual sister is described as dark, thin and very hairy. (Dühren, *Der Marquis de Sade*, third edition, p. 440.)

A correspondent who has always taken a special interest in the condition as regards hairiness of the women to whom he has been attracted, has sent me notes concerning a series of 12 women. It may be gathered from these notes that 5 women were neither markedly sexual nor markedly hairy (either as regards head or pubes), 6 cases both hairy and sexual, 1 was sexual and not hairy, none were hairy and not sexual. My correspondent remarks: "There may be women with scanty pubic hair possessing very strong sexual emotions. My own experience is quite the opposite." He has also independently reached the conclusion, arrived at by many medical observers and clearly suggested by some of the facts here brought together, that profuse hair frequently denotes a neurotic temperament.

It may be added that Mirabeau, as we learn from an anecdote told by an eye-witness and recorded by Legouvé, had a very hairy chest, while the same is recorded of Restif de la Bretonne.

It is a very ancient and popular belief that if a hairy man is not sensual he is strong: *vir pilosus aut libidinosus aut fortis.* The Greeks insisted on the hairy nates of Hercules, and Ninon de l'Enclos, when the great Condé shared her bed without touching her, remarked, on seeing his hairy body: "Ah, Monseigneur, que vous devez être fort!" It may be doubted whether there is any exact parallelism between muscular strength and hairiness, for strength is largely a matter of training, but there can be no doubt that hairiness really tends to be associated with a generally vigorous development of the body.

Although the observations concerning hairiness of body as an index of vigor, whether sexual or only generally physical, are so ancient, until recent years no attempts have been made to demonstrate on a large scale whether there is actually a correlation between hairiness and sexual or general development of the body. Some importance, therefore, attaches to Ammon's careful observations of many thousand conscripts in Baden. These observations fully justify this ancient belief, since they show that on the one hand the size of the testicles, and on the other hand girth of chest and stature, are correlated with hairiness of body.

Ammon's observations were made on nearly 4000 conscripts of the age of 20. From the point of view of the hairy system he divided them into four classes:—

I. To which 6.1 per cent. of the men belonged, with smooth bodies.

II. Including 25.3 per cent., only slight hairiness.

III. 53.8 per cent., more developed hairy system, but belly, breast and back smooth.

IV. 14.7 per cent., hair all over body.

V. 0.1 per cent., extreme cases of hairiness.

The beardless were 12.1 per cent., those with no axillary hair 9 per cent., those with no hair on pubis 0.4 per cent. This corresponds with the fact that hair appears first on the pubis and last on the chin.

In the first class 69 per cent. were beardless, 54 per cent. without any axillary hair and 6 per cent. without pubic hair. In the second class 24 per cent. were beardless, 17 per cent. without axillary hair. In the third class 3 per cent. were beardless and 3 per cent without axillary hair.

Below puberty the diameter of testicles is below 14 millimeters. There were 13 conscripts having a testicular diameter of less than 14 millimeters. These infantile individuals all belonged to the first three classes and mostly to the first. The average testicular diameter in the first class was nearly 24 millimeters, and progressively rose in the succeeding classes to over 26 millimeters in the fourth.

While there was not much difference in height, the first class was the shortest, the fourth the tallest. The fourth class also showed the greatest chest perimeter. The cephalic index of all classes was 84. (O. Ammon, "L'Infantilisme et le Feminisme au Conseil de Révision," *L'Anthropologie*, May-June, 1896.)

We thus see that it is quite justifiable to admit a type of person who possesses a more than average aptitude for detumescence. Such persons are more likely to be short than tall; they will show a full development of the secondary sexual characters; the voice will tend to be deep and the eyes bright; the glandular activity of the skin will probably be marked, the lips everted; there is a tendency to a more than average degree of pigmentation, and there is frequently an abnormal prevalence of hair on some parts of the body. While none of these signs, taken separately, can be said to have any necessary connection with the sexual impulse, taken altogether they indicate an organism that responds to the instinct of detumescence with special aptitude or with marked energy. In these respects observation, both scientific and popular, concords with the probabilities suggested by the three standards in this matter which have already been set forth.

No generalization, however, can here be set down in an absolute and unqualified manner. There are definite reasons why this should be so. There is, for instance, the highly important consideration that the sexual impulse of the individual may be conspicuous in two quite distinct ways. It may assume prominence because the individual possesses a highly vigorous and well-nourished organism, or its prominence may be due to mental irritation in a very morbid individual. In the latter case—although occasionally the two sets of conditions are combined—most of the signs we might expect in the former case may be absent. Indeed, the sexual impulses which proceed from a morbid psychic irritability do not in most cases indicate any special aptitude for detumescence at all; in that largely lies their morbid character.

Again, just in the same way that the exaggerated impulse itself may either be healthy or morbid, so the various characters which we have found to possess some value as signs of the impulse may themselves either be healthy or morbid. This is notably the case as regards an abnormal growth of hair on the body, more especially when it appears on regions where normally there is little or no hair. Such hypertrichosis is frequently degenerative in character, though still often associated with the sexual system. When, however, it is thus a degenerative character of sexual nature, having its origin in some abnormal fœtal condition or later atrophy of the ovaries, it is no necessary indication of any aptitude for detumescence.

Idiots, more especially it would seem idiot girls, tend to show a highly developed hairy system. Thus Voisin, when investigating 150 idiot and imbecile girls, found the hair long and thick and tending to occupy a large surface; one girl had hair on the areolæ of the mamma. (J. Voisin, "Conformation des organes génitaux chez les Idiots," *Annales d'Hygiène Publique*, June, 1894.) It should be said that in idiot boys puberty is late, and the sexual organs as well as the sexual instinct frequently undeveloped, while in idiot girls there is no delay in puberty, and the sexual organs and instinct are frequently fully and even abnormally developed.

Hegar has described an interesting case showing an association, of fœtal origin, between sexual anomaly and abnormal hairness. In this case a girl of 16 had a uterus duplex, an infantile pelvis, very slight menstruation and undeveloped breasts. She was very hairy on the face, the anterior aspects of the chest and abdomen, the sexual regions, and the thighs, but not specially so on the rest of the body. The hairs were of lanugo-like character, but dark in color. (A. Hegar, *Beiträge zur*

Geburtshülfe und Gynäkologie, vol. 1, p. 111, 1898.) Sometimes hiruties of the face and abdomen begin to appear during pregnancy, apparently from disease or degeneration of the ovaries. (A case is noted in *British Medical Journal*, August 2 and 16, pp. 375 and 436, 1902.) Laycock many years ago referred to the popular belief that women who have hair on the upper lip seldom bear children, and regarded this opinion as "questionless founded on fact." (Laycock, *Nervous Diseases of Women*, p. 22.) When this is so, we may suppose that the abnormal hairy growth is associated with degeneration of the ovaries.

There is another factor which enters into this question and renders the definition of a physical sexual type less precise than it would otherwise be. The sexual instinct is common to all persons, and while it seems probable that there is a type of person in whom sexual energies are predominant, it would also appear that the people who otherwise show a very high level of energy in life usually exhibit a more than average degree of energy in matters of love. The predominantly sexual type, as we have seen, tends to be associated with a high degree of pigmentation; the person specially apt for detumescence inclines to belong to the dark rather than to the purely fair group of the population. On the other hand, the active, energetic, practical man, the man who is most apt for the achievement of success in life, tends to belong to the fair rather than to the dark type.[1] Thus we have a certain conflict of tendencies, and it becomes possible to assert that while persons with pronounced aptitude for sexual detumescene tend to be dark, persons whose pronounced energy in sexual matters tends to ensure success are most likely to be fair.

The tendency of the fair energetic type, the type of the northern European man, to sexuality may be connected with the fact that the violent and criminal man who commits sexual crimes tends to be fair even amid a dark population. Criminals on the whole would appear to tend to be dark rather than fair; but Marro found in Italy that the group of sexual offenders differed from all other groups of criminals in that their hair was predominantly fair. (*Caratteri dei Delinquenti*,

---

[1] For some of the evidence on this point, see Havelock Ellis, "The Comparative Abilities of the Fair and the Dark," *Monthly Review*, August, 1901; *cf. id. A Study of British Genius*, Chapter X.

p. 374.) Ottolenghi, in the same way, in examining 100 sexual offenders, found that they showed 17 per cent. of fair hair, though criminals generally (on a basis of nearly 2000) showed only 6 per cent., and normal persons (nearly 1000) 9 per cent. Similarly while the normal persons showed only 20 per cent. of blue eyes and criminals generally 36 per cent., the sexual offenders showed 50 per cent. of blue eyes. (Ottolenghi, *Archivio di Psichiatria*, fasc. vi, 1888, p. 573.) Burton remarked (*Anatomy of Melancholy*, Part III, Section II, Mem. II, Subs. II) that in all ages most amorous young men have been yellow-haired, adding, "Synesius holds every effeminate fellow or adulterer is fair-haired." In folk-lore, it has been noted (Κρυπτάδια, vol. ii, p. 258), red or yellow hair is sometimes regarded as a mark of sexuality.

In harmony with this fairness, sexual offenders would appear to be more dolichocephalic than other criminals. In Italy Marro found the foreheads of sexual offenders to be narrow, and in California Drähms found that while murderers had an average cephalic index of 83.5, and thieves of 80.5, that of sexual offenders was 79.

On the other hand, high cheek-bones and broad faces—a condition most usually found associated with brachycephaly—have sometimes been noted as associated with undue or violent sexuality. Marro noted the excess of prominent cheek-bones in sexual offenders, and in America it has been found that unchaste girls tend to have broad faces. (*Pedagogical Seminary*, December, 1896, pp. 231, 235.)

It will be seen that, when we take a comprehensive view of the facts and considerations involved, it is possible to obtain a more definite and coherent picture of the physical signs of a marked aptitude for detumescence than has hitherto been usually supposed possible. But we also see that while the *ensemble* of these signs is probably fairly reliable as an index of marked sexuality, the separate signs have no such definite significance, and under some circumstances their significance may even be reversed.

THE PSYCHIC STATE IN PREGNANCY.

The Relationship of Maternal and Sexual Emotion—Conception and Loss of Virginity—The Anciently Accepted Signs of This Condition—The Pervading Effects of Pregnancy on the Organism—Pigmentation—The Blood and Circulation—The Thyroid—Changes in the Nervous System—The Vomiting of Pregnancy—The Longings of Pregnant Women—Maternal Impressions—Evidence for and Against Their Validity—The Question Still Open—Imperfection of Our Knowledge—The Significance of Pregnancy.

IN analyzing the sexual impulse I have so far deliberately kept out of view the maternal instinct. This is necessary, for the maternal instinct is specific and distinct; it is directed to an aim which, however intimately associated it may be with that of the sexual impulse proper, can by no means be confounded with it. Yet the emotion of love, as it has finally developed in the world, is not purely of sexual origin; it is partly sexual, but it is also partly parental.[1]

---

[1] See, e.g., Groos, *Æsthetische Genuss*, p. 249. "We have to admit," Groos observes, "the entrance of another instinct, the impulse to tend and foster, so closely connected with the sexual life. It is seemingly due to the co-operation of this impulse that the little female bird during courtship is so often fed by the male like a young fledgling. In man 'love' from the biological standpoint is also an amalgamation of two needs; when the tender need to protect and foster and serve is lacking the emotion is not quite perfect. Heine's expression, 'With my mantle I protect you from the storm,' has always seemed to me very characteristic." Sometimes the sexual impulse may undergo a complete transformation in this direction. "I believe there is really a tendency in women," a lady writes in a letter, "to allow maternal feeling to take the place of sexual feeling. Very often a woman's feeling for her husband becomes this (though he may be twenty years older than herself); sometimes it does not, remaining purely sex feeling. Sometimes it is for some other man she has this curious self-obliterating maternal feeling. It is not necessarily connected with sex intercourse. A prostitute, who has relations with dozens of men, may have it for some feeble drunken fool, who perhaps goes after other women. I once saw the change from sex feeling to mother feeling, as I call it, come almost suddenly over a woman after she had lived about four years

In so far as it is parental it is certainly mainly maternal. There is a drawing by Bronzino in the Louvre of a woman's head gazing tenderly down at some invisible object; is it her child or her lover? Doubtless her child, yet the expression is equally adequate to the emotion evoked by a lover. If we were here specifically dealing with the emotion of love as a complex whole, and not with the psychology of the sexual impulse, it would certainly be necessary to discuss the maternal instinct and its associated emotions. In any case it seems desirable to touch on the psychic state of pregnancy, for we are here concerned not only with emotions very closely connected with the sexual emotions in the narrower sense, but we here at last approach that state which it is the object of the whole sexual process to achieve.

In civilized life a period of weeks, months, even years, may elapse between the establishment of sexual relations and the oc-

---

with a man who was unfaithful to her. Then, when all real sex feeling, the hatred of the woman he followed, the desire he should give her love and tenderness, had all gone, came the other feeling, and she said to me, 'You don't understand at all; he's only my little baby; nothing he does can make any difference to me now.' As I grow older and understand women's natures better, I can see almost at once which relation it is a woman has to her husband, or any given man. It is this feeling, and not sex passion, that keeps woman from being free." Not only is there a sexual association in the impulse to foster and protect, there would appear to be a similar element also in the response to that impulse. Freud has especially insisted on the partly sexual character of the child's feelings for those who care for it and tend it and satisfy its needs. It is begun in earliest infancy; "whoever has seen the sated infant sink back from the breast, to fall asleep with flushed cheeks and happy smile, must say that the picture is adequate to the expression of the sexual satisfaction of later life." The lips, moreover, are the earliest erogenous zone. "There will, perhaps, be some opposition," Freud remarks (*Drei Abhandlungen zur Sexualtheorie*, pp. 36, 64), "to the identification of the child's feelings of tenderness and appreciation for those who tend it with sexual love, but I believe that exact psychological analysis will place the identity beyond doubt. The relationship of the child with the person who tends it is for it a continual source of sexual excitement and satisfaction flowing from the erogenous zones, especially since the fostering person—as a rule the mother—regards the child with emotions which proceed from her sexual life; strokes it, kisses it, rocks it, and very plainly treats it as a compensation for a fully valid sexual object." Freud remarks that girls who retain the childish character of their love for their parents to adult age are apt to make cold wives and to be sexually anæsthetic.

currence of conception. Under primitive conditions the loss of the virginal condition practically involves the pregnant condition, so that under primitive conditions very little allowance is made for the state, so common among civilized peoples, of the woman who is no longer a virgin, yet not about to become a mother.

There is some interest in noting the signs of loss of virginity chiefly relied upon by ancient authors. In doing this it is convenient to follow mainly the full summary of authorities given by Schurig in his *Barthenologia* early in the eighteenth century. The ancient custom, known in classic times, of measuring the neck the day after marriage was frequently practiced to ascertain if a girl was or was not a virgin. There were various ways of doing this. One was to measure with a thread the circumference of the bride's neck before she went to bed on the bridal night. If in the morning the same thread would not go around her neck it was a sure sign that she had lost her virginity during the night; if not, she was still a virgin or had been deflowered at an earlier period. Catullus alluded to this custom, which still exists, or existed until lately, in the south of France. It is perfectly sound, for it rests on the intimate response by congestion of the thyroid gland to sexual excitement. (*Parthenologia*, p. 283; Bièrent, *La Puberté*, p. 150; Havelock Ellis, *Man and Woman*, fourth edition, p. 267.)

Some say, Schurig tells us, that the voice, which in the virgin is shrill, becomes rougher and deeper after the first coitus. He quotes Riolan's statement that it is certain that the voice of those who indulge in venery is changed. On that account the ancients bound down the penis of their singers, and Martial said that those who wish to preserve their voices should avoid coitus. Democritus who one day had greeted a girl as "maiden" on the following day addressed her as "woman," while in the same way it is said that Albertus Magnus, observing from his study a girl going for wine for her master, knew that she had had sexual intercourse by the way because on her return her voice had become deeper. Here, again, the ancient belief has a solid basis, for the voice and the larynx are really affected by sexual conditions. (*Parthenologia*, p. 286; Marro, *La Puberté*, p. 303; Havelock Ellis, *op. cit.*, pp. 271, 289.)

Others, again, Schurig proceeds, have judged that the goaty smell given out in the armpits during the venereal act is also no uncertain sign of defloration, such odor being perceptible in those who use much venery, and not seldom in harlots and the newly married, while, as Hippocrates said, it is not perceived in boys and girls. (*Parthenologia*, p. 286; *cf.* the previous volume of these *Studies*, "Sexual Selection in Man," p. 64.)

In virgins, Schurig remarks, the pubic hair is said to be long and not twisted, while in women accustomed to coitus it is crisper. But it is only after long and repeated coitus, some authors add, that the pubic hairs become crisp. Some recent observers, it may be remarked, have noted a connection between sexual excitation and the condition of the pubic hair in women. (*Cf.* the present volume, *ante* p. 127.)

A sign to which the old authors often attached much importance was furnished by the urinary stream. In the *De Secretis Mulierum*, wrongly attributed to Albertus Magnus, it is laid down that "the virgin urinates higher than the woman." Riolan, in his *Anthropographia*, discussing the ability of virgins to ejaculate urine to a height, states that Scaliger had observed women who were virgins emit urine in a high jet against a wall, but that married women could seldom do this. Bonaciolus also stated that the urine of virgins is emitted in a small stream to a distance with an acute hissing sound. (*Parthenologia*, p. 281.) A folk-lore belief in the reality of this influence is evidenced by the Picardy *conte* referred to already *(ante,* p. 53), "La Princesse qui pisse au dessus les Meules." There is no doubt a tendency for the various stresses of sexual life to produce an influence in this direction, though they act far too slowly and uncertainly to be a reliable index to the presence or the absence of virginity.

Another common ancient test of virginity by urination rests on a psychic basis, and appears in a variety of forms which are really all reducible to the same principle. Thus we are told in *De Secretis Mulierum* that to ascertain if a girl is seduced she should be given to eat of powdered crocus flowers, and if she has been seduced she immediately urinates. We are here concerned with auto-suggestion, and it may well be believed that with nervous and credulous girls this test often revealed the truth.

A further test of virginity discussed by Schurig is the presence of modesty of countenance. If a woman blushes her virtue is safe. In this way girls who have themselves had experience of the marriage bed are said to detect the virgin. The virgin's eyes are cast down and almost motionless, while she who has known a man has eyes that are bright and quick. But this sign is equivocal, says Schurig, for girls are different, and can simulate the modesty they do not feel. Yet this indication also rests on a fundamentally sound psychological basis. (See "The Evolution of Modesty," in the first volume of these *Studies*.)

In his *Syllepsilogia* (Section V, cap. I-II), published in 1731, Schurig discusses further the anciently recognized signs of pregnancy. The real or imaginary signs of pregnancy sought by various primitive peoples of the past and present are brought together by Ploss and Bartels, *Das Weib*, bd. i, Chapter XXVII.

Both physically and psychically the occurrence of pregnancy is, however, a distinct event. It marks the beginning of a continuous physical process, which cannot fail to manifest psychic reactions. A great center of vital activity—practically a new center, for only the germinal form of it in menstruation had previously existed—has appeared and affects the whole organism. "From the moment that the embryo takes possession of the woman," Robert Barnes puts it, "every drop of blood, every fiber, every organ, is affected."[1]

A woman artist once observed to Dr. Stratz, that as the final aim of a woman is to become a mother and pregnancy is thus her blossoming time, a beautiful woman ought to be most beautiful when she is pregnant. That is so, Stratz replied, if her moment of greatest physical perfection corresponds with the early months of pregnancy, for with the beginning of pregnancy metabolism is increased, the color of the skin becomes more lively and delicate, the breasts firmer.[2] Pregnancy may, indeed, often become visible soon after conception by the brighter eye, the livelier glance, resulting from greater vascular activity, though later, with the increase of strain, the face may tend to become somewhat thin and distorted. The hair, Barnes states, assumes a new vigor, even though it may have been falling out before. The temperature rises; the weight increases, even apart from the growth of the fœtus. The efflorescence of pregnancy shows itself, as in the blossoming and fecundated flower, by increased pigmentation.[3] The nipples with their areolæ, and the mid-line of the belly, become darker; brown flecks (lentigo) tend to appear on the forehead, neck, arms, and body; while striæ—at first blue-red, then a brilliant white—appear on the belly and thighs,

---

[1] Esbach (in his *Thèse de Paris,* published in 1876) showed that even the finger nails are affected in pregnancy and become measurably thinner.

[2] C. H. Stratz, *Die Schönheit des Weiblichen Körpers,* Chapter VI.

[3] Iron appears to be liberated in the maternal organism during pregnancy, and Wychgel has shown (*Zeitschrift fur Geburtshülfe und Gynäkologie,* bd. xlvii, Heft II) that the pigment of pregnant women contains iron, and that the amount of iron in the urine is increased.

though these are scarcely normal, for they are not seen in women with very elastic skins and are rare among peasants and savages.[1] The whole carriage of the woman tends to become changed with the development of the mighty seed of man planted within her; it simulates the carriage of pride with the arched back and protruded abdomen.[2] The pregnant woman has been lifted above the level of ordinary humanity to become the casket of an inestimable jewel.

It is in the blood and the circulation that the earliest of the most prominent symptoms of pregnancy are to be found. The ever increasing development of this new focus of vascular activity involves an increased vascular activity in the whole organism. This activity is present almost from the first—a few days after the impregnation of the ovum—in the breasts, and quickly becomes obvious to inspection and palpation. Before a quite passive organ, the breast now rapidly increases in activity of circulation and in size, while certain characteristic changes begin to take place around the nipples.[3] As a result of the additional work imposed upon it the heart tends to become slightly hypertrophied in order to meet the additional strain; there may be some dilatation also.[4]

The recent investigations of Stengel and Stanton tend to show that the increase of the heart's work during pregnancy is less considerable that has generally been supposed, and that beyond some enlargement and dilatation of the right ventricle there is not usually any hypertrophy of the heart.

---

[1] Vinay, *Maladies de la Grossesse*, Chapter VIII; K. Hennig, "Exploratio Externa," *Comptes-rendus du XIIe. Congrès International de Médécine*, vol. vi, Section XIII, pp. 144-166. A bibliography of the literature concerning the physiology of pregnancy, extending to ten pages, is appended by Pinard to his article "Grossesse," *Dictionnaire encyclopédique des Sciences médicales*.

[2] Stratz, *op. cit.*, Chapter XII.

[3] W. S. A. Griffith, "The Diagnosis of Pregnancy," *British Medical Journal*, April 11, 1903.

[4] J. Mackenzie and H. O. Nicholson, "The Heart in Pregnancy," *British Medical Journal*, October 8, 1904; Stengel and Stanton, "The Condition of the Heart in Pregnancy," *Medical Record*, May 10, 1902 and *University Pennsylvania Medical Bulletin*, Sept., 1904 (summarized in *British Medical Journal*, August 16, 1902, and Sept. 23, 1905.)

The total quantity of blood is raised. While increased in quantity, the blood appears on the whole to be somewhat depreciated in quality, though on this point there are considerable differences of opinion. Thus, as regards hæmoglobin, some investigators have found that the old idea as to the poverty of hæmoglobin in pregnancy is quite unfounded; a few have even found that the hæmoglobin is increased. Most authorities have found the red cells diminished, though some only slightly, while the white cells, and also the fibrin, are increased. But toward the end of pregnancy there is a tendency, perhaps due to the establishment of compensation, for the blood to revert to the normal condition.[1]

It would appear probable, however, that the vascular phenomena of pregnancy are not altogether so simple as the above statement would imply. The activity of various glands at this time—well illustrated by the marked salivation which sometimes occurs—indicates that other modifying forces are at work, and it has been suggested that the changes in the maternal circulation during pregnancy may best be explained by the theory that there are two opposing kinds of secretion poured into the blood in unusual degree during pregnancy: one contracting the vessels, the other dilating them, one or the other sometimes gaining the upper hand. Suprarenal extract, when administered, has a vaso-constricting influence, and thyroid extract a vaso-dilating influence; it may be surmised that within the body these glands perform similar functions.[2]

The important part played by the thyroid gland is indicated by its marked activity at the very beginning of pregnancy. We may probably associate the general tendency to vaso-dilatation during early pregnancy with the tendency to goitre; Freund found an increase of the thyroid in 45 per cent. of 50 cases. The thyroid belongs to the same class of ductless glands as the

---

[1] J. Henderson, "Maternal Blood at Term," *Journal of Obstetrics and Gynæcology*, February, 1902; C. Douglas, "The Blood in Pregnant Women," *British Medical Journal*, March 26, 1904; W. L. Thompson, "The Blood in Pregnancy," *Johns Hopkins Hospital Bulletin*, June, 1904.

[2] H. O. Nicholson, "Some Remarks on the Maternal Circulation in Pregnancy," *British Medical Journal*, October 3, 1903.

ovary, and, as Bland Sutton and others have insisted, the analogies between the thyroid and the ovary are very numerous and significant. It may be added that in recent years Armand Gautier has noted the importance of the thyroid in elaborating nucleo-proteids containing arsenic and iodine, which are poured into the circulation during menstruation and pregnancy. The whole metabolism of the body is indeed affected, and during the latter part of pregnancy study of the ingesta and egesta has shown that a storage of nitrogen and even of water is taking place.[1] The woman, as Pinard puts it, forms the child out of her own flesh, not merely out of her food; the individual is being sacrificed to the species.

The changes in the nervous system of the pregnant woman correspond to those in the vascular system. There is the same increase of activity, a heightening of tension. Bruno Wolff, from experiments on bitches, concluded that the central nervous system in women is probably more easily excited in the pregnant than in the non-pregnant state, though he was not prepared to call this cerebral excitability "specific."[2] Direct observations on pregnant women have shown, without doubt, a heightened nervous irritability. Reflex action generally is increased. Neumann investigated the knee-jerk in 500 women during pregnancy, labor, and the puerperium, and in a large number found that there was a progressive exaggeration with the advance of pregnancy, little or no change being observed in the early months; sometimes when no change was observed during pregnancy the knee-jerk still increased during labor, reaching its maximum at the moment of the expulsion of the foetus; the return to the normal condition took place gradually during the puerperium. Tridandani found in pregnant women that though the superficial reflexes, with the exception of the abdominal, were diminished, the deep and tendon reflexes were markedly increased, especially that of the knee, these changes being more marked in primiparæ than in multiparæ, and more pronounced as pregnancy advanced, the normal condition returning with

[1] J. Morris Slemans, "Metabolism During Pregnancy," *Johns Hopkins Hospital Reports*, vol. xii, 1904.
[2] B. Wolff, *Zentralblatt für Gynäkologie*, 1904, No. 26.

ten days after labor. Electrical excitability was sensibly diminished.[1]

One of the first signs of high nervous tension is vomiting. As is well known, this phenomenon commonly appears early in pregnancy, and it is by many considered entirely physiological. Barnes regards it as a kind of safety valve, a regulating function, letting off excessive tension and maintaining equilibrium.[2] Vomiting is, however, a convulsion, and is thus the simplest form of a kind of manifestation—to which the heightened nervous tension of pregnancy easily lends itself—that finds its extreme pathological form in eclampsia. In this connection it is of interest to point out that the pregnant woman here manifests in the highest degree a tendency which is marked in women generally, for the female sex, apart altogether from pregnancy, is specially liable to convulsive phenomena.[3]

There is some slight difference of opinion among authorities as to the precise nature and causation of the sickness of pregnancy. Barnes, Horrocks and others regard it as physiological; but many consider it pathological; this is, for instance, the opinion of Giles. Graily Hewitt attributed it to flexion of the gravid uterus, Kaltenbach to hysteria, and Zaborsky terms it a neurosis. Whitridge Williams considers that it may be (1) reflex, or (2) neurotic (when it is allied to hysteria and amenable to suggestion), or (3) toxæmic. It really appears to lie on the borderland between healthy and diseased manifestations. It is said to be unknown to farmers and veterinary surgeons. It appears to be little known among savages; it is comparatively infrequent among women of the lower social classes, and, as Giles has found, women who habitually menstruate in a painless and normal manner suffer comparatively little from the sickness of pregnancy.

We owe a valuable study of the sickness of pregnancy to Giles, who analyzed the records of 300 cases. He concluded that about one-third of the pregnant women were free from sickness throughout pregnancy, 45 per cent. were free during the first three months. When sickness occurred it began in 70 per cent. of cases in the first month, and was most frequent during the second month. The duration varied from

---

[1] Tridandani, *Annali di Ostetrica*, March, 1900.

[2] R. Barnes, "The Induction of Labor," *British Medical Journal,* December 22, 1894.

[3] See, *e.g.*, Havelock Ellis, *Man and Woman*, fourth edition, pp. 344, *et seq.*

a few days to all through. Between the ages of 20 and 25 sickness was least frequent, and there was less sickness in the third than in any other pregnancy. (This corresponds with the conclusion of Matthews Duncan that 25 is the most favorable age for pregnancy.) To some extent in agreement with Guéniot, Giles believes that the vomiting of pregnancy is "one form of manifestation of the high nervous irritability of pregnancy." This high nervous tension may overflow into other channels, into the vascular and excretory system, causing eclampsia; into the muscular system, causing chorea, or, expending itself in the brain, give rise to hysteria when mild or insanity when severe. But the vagi form a very ready channel for such overflow, and hence the frequency of sickness in pregnancy. There are thus three main factors in the causation of this phenomenon: (1) An increased nervous irritability; (2) a local source of irritation; (3) a ready efferent channel for nervous energy. (Arthur Giles, "Observations on the Etiology of the Sickness of Pregnancy," *Transactions Obstetrical Society of London*, vol. xxv, 1894.)

Martin, who regards the phenomenon as normal, points out that when nausea and vomiting are absent or suddenly cease there is often reason to suspect something wrong, especially the death of the embryo. He also remarks that women who suffer from large varicose veins are seldom troubled by the nausea of pregnancy. (J. M. H. Martin, "The Vomiting of Pregnancy," *British Medical Journal*, December 10, 1904.) These observations may be connected with those of Evans (*American Gynecological and Obstetrical Journal*, January, 1900), who attributes primary importance to the undoubtedly active factor of the irritation set up by the uterus, more especially the rhythmic uterine contractions; stimulation of the breasts produces active uterine contractions, and Evans found that examination of the breasts sufficed to bring on a severe attack of vomiting, while on another occasion this was produced by a vaginal examination. Evans believes that the purpose of these contractions is to facilitate the circulation of the blood through the large venous sinuses, the surcharging of the relatively stagnant pools with effete blood producing the irritation which leads to rhythmic contractions.

It is on the basis of the increased vascular and glandular activity and the heightened nervous tension that the special psychic phenomena of pregnancy develop. The best known, and perhaps the most characteristic of these manifestations, is that known as "longings." By this term is meant more or less irresistible desires for some special food or drink, which may be digestible or indigestible, sometimes a substance which the

woman ordinarily likes, such as fruit, and occasionally one
which, under ordinary circumstances, she dislikes, as in one
case known to me of a young country woman who, when bearing
her child, was always longing for tobacco and never happy except when she could get a pipe to smoke, although under ordinary circumstances, like other young women of her class, she
was without any desire to smoke. Occasionally the longings lead
to actions which are more unscrupulous than is common in the
case of the same person at other times; thus in one case known
to me a young woman, pregnant with her first child, insisted to her sister's horror on entering a strawberry field and
eating a quantity of fruit. These "longings" in their extreme
form may properly be considered as neurasthenic obsessions,
but in their simple and less pronounced forms they may well be
normal and healthy.

The old medical authors abound in narratives describing the longings of pregnant women for natural and unnatural foods. This affection
was commonly called *pica*, sometimes *citra* or *malatia*. Schurig, whose
works are a comprehensive treasure house of ancient medical lore,
devotes a long chapter (cap. II) of his *Chylologia*, published in 1725, to
pica as manifested mainly, though not exclusively, in pregnant women.
Some women, he tells us, have been compelled to eat all sorts of earthy
substances, of which sand seems the most common, and one Italian
woman when pregnant ate several pounds of sand with much satisfaction. following it up with a draught of her own urine. Lime, mud,
chalk, charcoal, cinders, pitch are also the desired substances in other
cases detailed. One pregnant woman must eat bread fresh from the
oven in very large quantities, and a certain noble matron ate 140 sweet
cakes in one day and night. Wheat and various kinds of corn as well
as of vegetables were the foods desired by many longing women. One
woman was responsible for 20 pounds of pepper, another ate ginger in
large quantities, a third kept mace under her pillow; cinnamon, salt,
emulsion of almonds, treacle, mushrooms were desired by others. Cherries were longed for by one, and another ate 30 or 40 lemons in one
night. Various kinds of fish—mullet, oysters, crabs, live eels, etc.—are
mentioned, while other women have found delectation in lizards, frogs,
spiders and flies, even scorpions, lice and fleas. A pregnant woman,
aged 33, of sanguine temperament, ate a live fowl completely with
intense satisfaction. Skin. wool. cotton, thread, linen, blotting paper
have been desired, as well as more repulsive substances, such as nasal
mucus and feces (eaten with bread). Vinegar, ice, and snow occur in

other cases. One woman stilled a desire for human flesh by biting the nates of children or the arms of men. Metals are also swallowed, such as iron, silver, etc. One pregnant woman wished to throw eggs in her husband's face, and another to have her husband throw eggs in her face.

In the next chapter of the same work Schurig describes cases of acute antipathy which may arise under the same circumstances (cap. III, "De Nauseâ seu Antipathia certorum ciborum"). The list includes bread, meat, fowls, fish, eels (a very common repulsion), crabs, milk, butter (very often), cheese (often), honey, sugar, salt, eggs, caviar, sulphur, apples (especially their odor), strawberries, mulberries, cinnamon, mace, capers, pepper, onions, mustard, beetroot, rice, mint, absinthe, roses (many pages are devoted to this antipathy), lilies, elder flowers, musk (which sometimes caused vomiting), amber, coffee, opiates, olive oil, vinegar, cats, frogs, spiders, wasps, swords.

More recently Gould and Pyle (*Anomalies and Curiosities of Medicine*, p. 80) have briefly summarized some of the ancient and modern records concerning the longings of pregnant women.

Various theories are put forward concerning the causation of the longings of pregnant women, but none of these seems to furnish by itself a complete and adequate explanation of all cases. Thus it is said that the craving is the expression of a natural instinct, the system of the pregnant woman really requiring the food she longs for. It is quite probable that this is so in many cases, but it is obviously not so in the majority of cases, even when we confine ourselves to the longings for fairly natural foods, while we know so little of the special needs of the organism during pregnancy that the theory in any case is insusceptible of clear demonstration.

Allied to this theory is the explanation that the longings are for things that counteract the tendency to nausea and sickness. Giles, however, in his valuable statistical study of the longings of a series of 300 pregnant women, has shown that the percentage of women with longings is exactly the same (33 per cent.) among women who had suffered at some time during pregnancy from sickness as among the women who had not so suffered. Moreover, Giles found that the period of sickness frequently bore no relation to the time when there were cravings, and the patient often had cravings after the sickness had ceased.

According to another theory these longings are mainly a

matter of auto-suggestion. The pregnant woman has received the tradition of such longings, persuades herself that she has such a longing, and then becomes convinced that, according to a popular belief, it will be bad for the child if the longing is not gratified. Giles considers that this process of auto-suggestion takes place "in a certain number, perhaps even in the majority of cases."[1]

The Duchess d'Abrantès, the wife of Marshal Junot, in her *Mémoires* gives an amusing account of how in her first pregnancy a longing was apparently imposed upon her by the anxious solicitude of her own and her husband's relations. Though suffering from constant nausea and sickness, she had no longings. One day at dinner after the pregnancy had gone on for some months her mother suddenly put down her fork, exclaiming: "I have never asked you what longing you have!" She replied with truth that she had none, her days and her nights being occupied with suffering. "No *envie*!" said the mother, "such a thing was never heard of. I must speak to your mother-in-law." The two old ladies consulted anxiously and explained to the young mother how an unsatisfied longing might produce a monstrous child, and the husband also now began to ask her every day what she longed for. Her sister-in-law, moreover, brought her all sorts of stories of children born with appalling mother's marks due to this cause. She became frightened and began to wonder what she most wanted, but could think of nothing. At last, when eating a pastille flavored with pineapple, it occurred to her that pineapple is an excellent fruit, and one, moreover, which she had never seen, for at that time it was extremely rare. Thereupon she began to long for pineapple, and all the more when she was told that at that season they could not be obtained. She now began to feel that she must have pineapple or die, and her husband ran all over Paris, vainly offering twenty louis for a pineapple. At last he succeeded in obtaining one through the kindness of Mme. Bonaparte, and drove home furiously just as his wife, always talking of pineapples, had gone to bed. He entered the room with the pineapple, to the great satisfaction of the Duchess's mother. (In one of her own pregnancies, it appears, she longed in vain for cherries in January, and the child was born with a mark on her body resembling a cherry—in scientific terminology, a *nævus*.) The Duchess effusively thanked her husband and wished to eat of the fruit immediately, but her husband stopped her and said that Corvisart, the famous physician, had told him that she must on no

---

[1] Arthur Giles, "The Longings of Pregnant Women," *Transactions Obstetrical Society of London*, vol. xxxv, 1893.

account touch it at night, as it was extremely indigestible. She promised not to do so, and spent the night in caressing the pineapple. In the morning the husband came and cut up the fruit, presenting it to her in a porcelain bowl. Suddenly, however, there was a revulsion of feeling; she felt that she could not possibly eat pineapple; persuasion was useless; the fruit had to be taken away and the windows opened, for the very smell of it had become odious. The Duchess adds that henceforth, throughout her life, though still liking the flavor, she was only able to eat pineapple by doing a sort of violence to herself. *(Mémories de la Duchesse d'Abrantès*, vol. iii, Chapter VIII.) It should be added that, in old age, the Duchess d'Abrantès appears to have become insane.

The influence of suggestion must certainly be accepted as, at all events, increasing and emphasizing the tendency to longings. It can scarcely, however, be regarded as a radical and adequate explanation of the phenomenon generally. If it is a matter of auto-suggestion due to a tradition, then we should expect to find longings most frequent and most pronounced in multiparous women, who are best acquainted with the tradition and best able to experience all that is expected of a pregnant woman. But, as a matter of fact, the women who have borne most children are precisely those who are least likely to be affected by the longings which tradition demands they should manifest. Giles has shown that longings occur much more frequently in the first than in any subsequent pregnancy; there is a regular decrease with the increase in number of pregnancies until in women with ten or more children the longings scarcely occur at all.

We must probably regard longings as based on a physiological and psychic tendency which is of universal extension and almost or quite normal. They are known throughout Europe and were known to the medical writers of antiquity. Old Indian as well as old Jewish physicians recognized them. They have been noted among many savage races to-day: among the Indians of North and South America, among the peoples of the Nile and the Soudan, in the Malay archipelago.[1] In Europe they are most

---

[1] Ploss and Bartels, *Das Weib*, Chapter XXX.

common among the women of the people, living simple and natural lives.[1]

The true normal relationship of the longings of pregnancy is with the impulsive and often irresistible longings for food delicacies which are apt to overcome children, and in girls often persist or revive through adolescence and even beyond. Such sudden fits of greediness belong to those kind of normal psychic manifestations which are on the verge of the abnormal into which they occasionally pass. They may occur, however, in healthy, well-bred, and well-behaved children who, under the stress of the sudden craving, will, without compunction and apparently without reflection, steal the food they long for or even steal from their parents the money to buy it. The food thus seized by a well-nigh irresistible craving is nearly always a fruit. Fruit is usually doled out to children in small quantities as a luxury, but we are descended from primitive human peoples and still more remote ape-like ancestors, by whom fruit was in its season eaten copiously, and it is not surprising that when that season comes round the child, more sensitive than the adult to primitive influences, should sometimes experience the impulse of its ancestors with overwhelming intensity, all the more so if, as is probable, the craving is to some extent the expression of a physiological need.

Sanford Bell, who has investigated the food impulses of children in America, finds that girls have a greater number of likes and dislikes in foods than boys of the same age, though at the same time they have less dislikes to some foods than boys. The proclivity for sweets and fruits shows itself as soon as a child begins to eat solids. The chief fruits liked are oranges, bananas, apples, peaches, and pears. This strong preference for fruits lasts till the age of 13 or 14, though relatively weaker from 10 to 13. In girls, however, Bell notes the significant fact from our present point of view that at mid-adolescence there is a revived taste for sweets and fruits. He believes that the growth of children in taste in foods recapitulates the experience of the race. (S. Bell, "An Introductory Study of the Psychology of Foods." *Pedagogical Seminary,* March, 1904.)

---

[1] Thus, in Cornwall, "to be in the longing way" is a popular symonym for pregnancy.

The heightened nervous impressionability of pregnancy would appear to arouse into activity those primitive impulses which are liable to occur in childhood and in the unmarried girl continue to the nubile age. It is a significant fact that the longings of pregnant women are mainly for fruit, and notably for so wholesome a fruit as the apple, which may very well have a beneficial effect on the system of the pregnant woman. Giles, in his tabulation of the foods longed for by 300 pregnant women, found that the fruit group was by far the largest, furnishing 79 cases; apples were far away at the head, occurring in 34 cases out of the 99 who had longings, while oranges followed at a distance (with 13 cases), and in the vegetable group tomatoes came first (with 6 cases). Several women declared "I could have lived on apples," "I was eating apples all day," "I used to sit up in bed eating apples."[1] Pregnant women appear seldom to long for the possession of objects outside the edible class, and it seems doubtful whether they have any special tendency to kleptomania. Pinard has pointed out that neither Lasègue nor Lunier, in their studies of kleptomania, have mentioned a single shop robbery committed by a pregnant woman.[2] Brouardel has indeed found such cases, but the object stolen was usually a food.

A further significant fact connecting the longings of pregnant women with the longings of children is to be found in the fact that they occur mainly in young women. We have, indeed, no tabulation of the ages of pregnant women who have manifested longings, but Giles has clearly shown that these chiefly

---

[1] The apple, wherever it is known, has nearly always been a sacred or magic fruit (as J. F. Campbell shows, *Popular Tales of West Highlands*, vol. I, p. lxxv. *et seq.*), and the fruit of the forbidden tree which tempted Eve is always popularly imagined to be an apple. One may perhaps refer in this connection to the fact that at Rome and elsewhere the testicles have been called apples. I may add that we find a curious proof of the recognition of the feminine love of apples in an old Portuguese ballad, "Donna Guimar," in which a damsel puts on armour and goes to the wars; her sex is suspected and as a test, she is taken into an orchard, but Donna Guimar is too wary to fall into the trap, and turning away from the apples plucks a citron.

[2] A. Pinard, Art. "Grossesse," *Dictionnaire Encyclopédique des Sciences Médicales*, p. 138. On the subject of violent, criminal and abnormal impulses during pregnancy, see Cumston, "Pregnancy and Crime," *American Journal Obstetrics*, December, 1903.

occur in primiparæ, and steadily and rapidly decrease in each successive pregnancy. This fact, otherwise somewhat difficult of explanation, is natural if we look upon the longings of pregnancy as a revival of those of childhood. It certainly indicates also that we can by no means regard these longings as exclusively the expression of a physiological craving, for in that case they would be liable to occur in any pregnancy unless, indeed, it is argued that with each successive pregnancy the woman becomes less sensitive to her own physiological state.

There has been a frequent tendency, more especially among primitive peoples, to regard a pregnant woman's longings as something sacred and to be indulged, all the more, no doubt, as they are usually of a simple and harmless character. In the Black Forest, according to Ploss and Bartels, a pregnant woman may go freely into other people's gardens and take fruit, provided she eats it on the spot, and very similar privileges are accorded to her elsewhere. Old English opinion, as reflected, for instance, in Ben Jonson's plays (as Dr. Harriet C. B. Alexander has pointed out), regards the pregnant woman as not responsible for her longings, and Kiernan remarks ("Kleptomania and Collectivism," *Alienist and Neurologist*, November, 1902) that this is in "a most natural and just view." In France at the Revolution a law of the 28th Germinal, in the year III, to some extent admitted the irresponsibility of the pregnant woman generally,—following the classic precedent, by which a woman could not be brought before a court of justice so long as she was pregnant,—but the Napoleonic code, never tender to women, abrogated this. Pinard does not consider that the longings of pregnant women are irresistible, and, consequently, regards the pregnant woman as responsible. This is probably the view most widely held. In any case these longings seldom come up for medico-legal consideration.

The phenomena of the longings of pregnancy are linked to the much more obscure and dubious phenomena of the influence of maternal impressions on the child within the womb. It is true, indeed, that there is no real connection whatever between these two groups of manifestations, but they have been so widely and for so long closely associated in the popular mind that it is convenient to pass directly from one to the other. The same name is sometimes given to the two manifestations; thus in France a pregnant longing is an *envie,* while a mother's mark on the child is also called an *envie,* because it is supposed to be due to the mother's unsatisfied longing.

The conception of a "maternal impression" (the German *Versehen*) rests on the belief that a powerful mental influence working on the mother's mind may produce an impression, either general or definite, on the child she is carrying. It makes a great deal of difference whether the effect of the impression on the child is general, or definite and circumscribed. It is not difficult to believe that a general effect—even, as Sir Arthur Mitchell first gave good reason for believing, idiocy—may be produced on the child by strong and prolonged emotional influence working on the mother, because such general influence may be transmitted through a deteriorated blood-stream. But it is impossible at present to understand how a definite and limited influence working on the mother could produce a definite and limited effect on the child, for there are no channels of nervous communications for the passage of such influences. Our difficulty in conceiving of the process must, however, be put aside if the fact itself can be demonstrated by convincing evidence.

In order to illustrate the nature of maternal impressions, I will summarize a few cases which I have collected from the best medical periodical literature during the past fifteen years. I have exercised no selection and in no way guarantee the authenticity of the alleged facts or the alleged explanation. They are merely examples to illustrate a class of cases published from time to time by medical observers in medical journals of high repute.

Early in pregnancy a woman found her pet rabbit killed by a cat which had gnawed off the two forepaws, leaving ragged stumps; she was for a long time constantly thinking of this. Her child was born with deformed feet, one foot with only two toes, the other three, the os calcis in both feet being either absent or little developed. (G. B. Beale, Tottenham, *Lancet*, May 4, 1889).

Three months and a half before birth of the child the father, a glazier, fell through the roof of a hothouse, severely cutting his right arm, so that he was lying in the infirmary for a long time, and it was doubtful whether the hand could be saved. The child was healthy, but on the flexor surface of the radial side of the right forearm just above the wrist—the same spot as the father's injury—there was a nævus the size of a sixpence. (W. Russell, Paisley, *Lancet*, May 11, 1889.)

At the beginning of pregnancy a woman was greatly scared by being kicked over by a frightened cow she was milking; she hung on to the animal's teats, but thought she would be trampled to death, and was ill and nervous for weeks afterwards. The child was a monster, with a fleshy substance—seeming to be prolonged from the spinal cord and to represent the brain—projecting from the floor of the skull. Both doctor and nurse were struck by the resemblance to a cow's teats before they knew the woman's story, and this was told by the woman immediately after delivery and before she knew to what she had given birth. (A. Ross Paterson, Reversby, Lincolnshire, *Lancet*, September 29, 1889.)

During the second month of pregnancy the mother was terrified by a bullock as she was returning from market. The child reached full term and was a well-developed male, stillborn. Its head "exactly resembled a miniature cow's head;" the occipital bone was absent, the parietals only slightly developed, the eyes were placed at the top of the frontal bone, which was quite flat, with each of its superior angles twisted into a rudimentary horn. (J. T. Hislop, Tavistock, Devon, *Lancet*, November 1, 1890.)

When four months pregnant the mother, a multipara of 30, was startled by a black and white collie dog suddenly pushing against her and rushing out when she opened the door. This preyed on her mind, and she felt sure her child would be marked. The whole of the child's right thigh was encircled by a shining black mole, studded with white hairs; there was another mole on the spine of the left scapula. (C. F. Williamson, Horley, Surrey, *Lancet*, October 11, 1890.)

A lady in comfortable circumstances, aged 24, not markedly emotional, with one child, in all respects healthy, early in her pregnancy saw a man begging whose arms and legs were "all doubled up." This gave her a shock, but she hoped no ill effects would follow. The child was an encephalous monster, with the extremities rigidly flexed and the fingers clenched, the feet almost sole to sole. In the next pregnancy she frequently passed a man who was a partial cripple, but she was not unduly depressed; the child was a counterpart of the last, except that the head was normal. The next child was strong and well formed. (C. W. Chapman, London, *Lancet*, October 18, 1890.)

When the pregnant mother was working in a hayfield her husband threw at her a young hare he had found in the hay; it struck her on the cheek and neck. Her daughter has on the left cheek an oblong patch of soft dark hair, in color and character clearly resembling the fur of a very young hare. (A. Mackay, Port Appin, N. B., *Lancet*, December 19, 1891. The writer records also four other cases which have happened in his experience.)

When the mother was pregnant her husband had to attend to a sow who could not give birth to her pigs; he bled her freely, cutting a notch out of both ears. His wife insisted on seeing the sow. The helix of each ear of her child at birth was gone, for nearly or quite half an inch, as if cut purposely. (R. P. Roons, *Medical World*, 1894.)

A lady when pregnant was much interested in a story in which one of the characters had a supernumerary digit, and this often recurred to her mind. Her baby had a supernumerary digit on one hand. (J. Jenkyns, Aberdeen, *British Medical Journal*, March 2, 1895. The writer also records another case.)

When pregnant the mother saw in the forest a new-born fawn which was a double monstrosity. Her child was a similar double monstrosity (*cephalothora copagus*). (Hartmann, *Münchener Medicinisches Wochenschrift*, No. 9, 1895.)

A well developed woman of 30, who had ten children in twelve years, in the third month of her tenth pregnancy saw a child run over by a street car, which crushed the upper and back part of its head. Her own child was anencephalic and acranial, with entire absence of vault of skull. (F. A. Stahl, *American Journal of Obstetrics*, April, 1896.)

A healthy woman with no skin blemish had during her third pregnancy a violent appetite for sunfish. During or after the fourth month her husband, as a surprise, brought her some sunfish alive, placing them in a pail of water in the porch. She stumbled against the pail and the shock caused the fish to flap over the pail and come in violent contact with her leg. The cold wriggling fish produced a nervous shock, but she attached no importance to this. The child (a girl) had at birth a mark of bronze pigment resembling a fish with the head uppermost (photograph given) on the corresponding part of the same leg. Daughter's health good; throughout life she has had a strong craving for sunfish, which she has sometimes eaten till she has vomited from repletion. (C. F. Gardiner, Colorado Springs, *American Journal Obstetrics*, February, 1898.)

The next case occurred in a bitch. A thoroughbred fox terrier bitch strayed and was discovered a day or two later with her right foreleg broken. The limb was set under chloroform with the help of Röntgen rays, and the dog made a good recovery. Several weeks later she gave birth to a puppy with a right foreleg that was ill-developed and minus the paw. (J. Booth, Cork, *British Medical Journal*, September 16, 1899.)

Four months before the birth of her child a woman with four healthy children and no history of deformity in the family fell and cut her left wrist severely against a broken bowl; she had a great fright and shock. Her child, otherwise perfect, was born without left hand and wrist, the stump of arm terminating at lower end of radius and ulna. (G. Ainslie Johnston, Ambleside, *British Medical Journal*, April 18, 1903.)

The belief in the reality of the transference of strong mental or physical impressions on the mother into physical changes in the child she is bearing is very ancient and widespread. Most writers on the subject begin with the book of Genesis and the astute device of Jacob in influencing the color of his lambs by mental impressions on his ewes. But the belief exists among even more primitive people than the early Hebrews, and in all parts of the world.[1] Among the Greeks there is a trace of the belief in Hippocrates, the first of the world's great physicians, while Soranus, the mose famous of ancient gynæcologists, states the matter in the most precise manner, with instances in proof. The belief continued to persist unquestioned throughout the Middle Ages. The first author who denied the influence of maternal impressions altogether appears to have been the famous anatomist, Realdus Columbus, who was a professor at Padua, Pisa, and Rome at the beginning of the sixteenth century. In the same century, however, another and not less famous Neapolitan, Della Porta, for the first time formulated a definite theory of maternal impressions. A little later, early in the seventeenth century, a philosophic physician at Padua, Fortunatus Licetus, took up an intermediate position which still finds, perhaps reasonably, a great many adherents. He recognized that a very frequent cause of malformation in the child is to be found in morbid antenatal conditions, but at the same time was not prepared to deny absolutely and in every case the influence of maternal impression on such conditions. Malebranche, the Platonic philosopher, allowed the greatest extension to the power of the maternal imagination. In the eighteenth century, however, the new spirit of free inquiry, of radical criticism, and unfettered logic, led to a sceptical attitude toward this ancient belief then flourishing vigorously.[2] In 1727, a few years after Malebranche's death, James Blondel, a physician of extreme acuteness, who had

---

[1] See especially Ploss and Bartels, *Das Weib,* vol. i, Chapter XXXI. Ballantyne in his work on the pathology of the fœtus adds Loango negroes, the Eskimo and the ancient Japanese.

[2] In 1731 Schurig, in his *Syllepsilogia,* devoted more than a hundred pages (cap. IX) to summarizing a vast number of curious cases of maternal impressions leading to birth-marks of all kinds.

been born in Paris, was educated at Leyden, and practiced in London, published the first methodical and thorough attack on the doctrine of maternal impressions, *The Strength of Imagination of Pregnant Women Examined,* and exercised his great ability in ridiculing it. Haller, Roederer, and Sömmering followed in the steps of Blondel, and were either sceptical or hostile to the ancient belief. Blumenbach, however, admitted the influence of maternal impressions. Erasmus Darwin, as well as Goethe in his *Wahlverwandtshaften,* even accepted the influence of paternal impressions on the child. By the beginning of the nineteenth century the majority of physicians were inclined to relegate maternal impressions to the region of superstition. Yet the exceptions were of notable importance. Burdach, when all deductions were made, still found it necessary to retain the belief in maternal impressions, and Von Baer, the founder of embryology, also accepted it, supported by a case, occurring in his own sister, which he was able to investigate before the child's birth. L. W. T. Bischoff, also, while submitting the doctrine to acute criticism, found it impossible to reject maternal impressions absolutely, and he remarked that the number of adherents to the doctrine was showing a tendency to increase rather than diminish. Johannes Müller, the founder of modern physiology in Germany, declared himself against it, and his influence long prevailed; Valentin, Rudolf Wagner, and Emil du Bois-Reymond were on the same side. On the other hand various eminent gynæcologists—Litzmann, Roth, Hennig, etc.—have argued in favor of the reality of maternal impressions.[1]

The long conflict of opinion which has taken place over this opinion has still left the matter unsettled. The acutest critics

---

[1] J. W. Ballantyne has written an excellent history of the doctrine of maternal impressions, reprinted in his *Manual of Antenatal Pathology: The Embryo,* 1904, Chapter IX; he gives a bibliography of 381 items. In Germany the history of the question has been written by Dr. Iwan Bloch (under the psendonym of Gerhard von Welsenburg), *Das Versehen der Frauen,* 1899. *Cf.,* in French, G. Variot, "Origine des Préjugés Populaires sur les Envies," *Bulletin Société d'Anthropologie,* Paris, June 18, 1891. Variot rejects the doctrine absolutely, Bloch accepts it, Ballantyne speaks cautiously.

of the ancient belief constantly conclude the discussion with an expression of doubt and uncertainty. Even if the majority of authorities are inclined to reject maternal impressions, the scientific eminence of those who accept them makes a decisive opinion difficult. The arguments against such influence are perfectly sound: (1) it is a primitive belief of unscientific origin; (2) it is impossible to conceive how such influence can operate since there is no nervous connection between mother and child; (3) comparatively few cases have been submitted to severe critical investigation; (4) it is absurd to ascribe developmental defects to influences which arise long after the fœtus had assumed its definite shape[1]; (5) in any case the phenomenon must be rare, for William Hunter could not find a coincidence between maternal impressions and fœtal marks through a period of several years, and Bischoff found no case in 11,000 deliveries. These statements embody the whole of the argument against maternal impressions, yet it is clear that they do not settle the matter. Edgar, in a manual of obstetrics which is widely regarded as a standard work, states that this is "yet a mooted question."[2] Ballantyne, again, in a discussion of this influence at the Edinburgh Obstetrical Society, summarizing the result of a year's inquiry, concluded that it is still *"sub judice."* In a subsequent discussion of the question he has somewhat modified his opinion, and is inclined to deny that definite impressions on the pregnant woman's mind can cause similar defects in the fœtus; they are "accidental coincidences," but he adds that a few of the

---

[1] J. G. Kiernan has shown how many of the alleged cases are negatived by the failure to take this fact into consideration. (*Journal of American Medical Association*, December 9, 1899.)

[2] J. Clifton Edgar, *The Practice of Obstetrics*, second edition, 1904, p. 296. In an important discussion of the question at the American Gynæcological Society in 1886, introduced by Fordyce Barker, various eminent gynæcologists declared in favor of the doctrine, more or less cautiously. *Transactions of the American Gynæcological Society*, vol. xi, 1886, pp. 152-196.) Gould and Pyle, bringing forward some of the data on the question (*Anomalies and Curiosities of Medicine*, pp. 81, *et seq.*) state that the reality of the influence of maternal impressions seems fully established. On the other side, see G. W. Cook, *American Journal of Obstetrics*, September, 1889, and H. F. Lewis, *ib.*, July, 1899.

[3] *Transactions Edinburgh Obstetrical Society*, vol. xvii, 1892.

cases are difficult to explain away. At the same time he fully
believes that prolonged and strongly marked mental states of the
mother may affect the development of the fœtus in her uterus,
causing vascular and nutritive disturbances, irregularities of
development, and idiocy.[1]

Whether and in how far mental impressions on the mother can
produce definite mental and emotional disposition in the child is a
special aspect of the question to which scarcely any inquiry has been
devoted. So distinguished a biologist as Mr. A. W. Wallace has, however, called attention to this point, bringing forward evidence on the
question and emphasizing the need of further investigation. "Such
transmission of mental influence," he remarks, "will hardly be held to
be impossible or even very improbable." (A. W. Wallace, "Prenatal
Influences on Character," *Nature*, August 24, 1893.)

It has already been pointed out that a large number of cases
of fœtal deformities, supposed to be due to maternal impressions,
cannot possibly be so caused because the impression took place
at a period when the development of the fœtus must already have
been decided. In this connection, however, it must be noted
that Dabney has observed a relationship between the time of
supposed mental impressions and the nature of the actual defect
which is of considerable significance as an argument in favor
of the influence of mental impressions. He tabulated 90 carefully reported cases from recent medical literature, and found
that 21 of them were concerned with defects of structure of the
lips and palate. In all but 2 of these 21 the defect was referred to an impression occurring within the first three months
of pregnancy. This is an important point as showing that the
assigned cause really falls within a period when a defect of development actually could produce the observed result, although
the person reporting the cases was in many instances manifestly
ignorant of the details of embryology and teratology. There
was no such preponderance of early impressions among the defects of skin and hair which might well, so far as development
is concerned, have been caused at a later period; here, in 7 out

[1] J. W. Ballantyne, *Manual of Antenatal Pathology: The Embryo*,
p. 45.

of 15 cases, it was distinctly stated that the impression was made later than the fourth month.[1]

It would seem, on the whole, that while the influence of maternal impressions in producing definite effects on the child within the womb has by no means been positively demonstrated, we are not entitled to reject it with any positive assurance. Even if we accept it, however, it must remain, for the present, an inexplicable fact; the *modus operandi* we can scarcely even guess at. General influences from the mother on the child we can easily conceive of as conveyed by the mother's blood; we can even suppose that the modified blood might act specifically on one particular kind of tissue. We can, again, as suggested by Féré, very well believe that the maternal emotions act upon the womb and produce various kinds and degrees of pressure on the child within, so that the apparently active movements of the fœtus may be really consecutive on unconscious maternal excitations.[2] We may also believe that, as suggested by John Thomson, there are slight incoördinations *in utero,* a kind of developmental neurosis, produced by some slight lack of harmony of whatever origin, and leading to the production of malformations.[3] We know, finally, that, as Féré and others have repeatedly demonstrated during recent years by experiments on chickens, etc., very subtle agents, even odors, may profoundly affect embryonic development and produce deformity. But how the mother's psychic disposition can, apart from heredity, affect specifically the physical conformation or even the psychic disposition of the child within her womb must remain for the present an insoluble mystery, even if we feel disposed to conclude that in some cases such action seems to be indicated.

In comprehending such a connection, however at present undemonstrated, it may well be borne in mind that the relationship of the mother to the child within her womb is of a uniquely intimate character. It is

---

[1] W. C. Dabney, "Maternal Impressions," Keating's *Cyclopædia of Diseases of Children*, vol. i, 1889, pp. 191-216.

[2] Féré, *Sensation et Mouvement*, Chapter XIV, "Sur la Psychologie du Fœtus."

[3] J. Thomson, "Defective Co-ordination in Utero," *British Medical Journal*, September 6, 1902.

of interest in this connection to quote some remarks by an able psychologist, Dr. Henry Rutgers Marshall; the remarks are not less interesting for being brought forward without any connection with the question of maternal impressions: "It is true that, so far as we know, the nervous system of the embryo never has a direct connection with the nervous system of the mother: nevertheless, as there is a reciprocity of reaction between the physical body of the mother and its embryonic parasite, the relation of the embryonic nervous system to the nervous system of the mother is not very far removed from the relation of the pre-eminent part of the nervous system of a man to some minor nervous system within his body which is to a marked extent dissociated from the whole neural mass.

"Correspondingly, then, and within the consciousness of the mother, there develops a new little minor consciousness which, although but lightly integrated with the mass of her consciousness, nevertheless has its part in her consciousness taken as a whole, much as the psychic correspondents of the action of the nerve which govern the secretions of the glands of the body have their part in her consciousness taken as a whole.

"It is very much as if the optic ganglia developed fully in themselves, without any closer connection with the rest of the brain than existed at their first appearance. They would form a little complex nervous system almost but not quite apart from the brain system; and it would be difficult to deny them a consciousness of their own; which would indeed form part of the whole consciousness of the individual, but which would be in a manner self-dependent." It must, if this is so, be said that before birth, on the psychic side, the embryo's activities "form part of a complex consciousness which is that of the mother and embryo together." "Without subscribing to the strange stories of telepathy, of the solemn apparition of a person somewhere at the moment of his death a thousand miles away, of the unquiet ghost haunting the scenes of its bygone hopes and endeavors, one may ask" (with the author of the address in medicine at the Leicester gathering of the British Medical Association, *British Medical Journal*, July 29, 1905) "whether two brains cannot be so tuned in sympathy as to transmit and receive a subtile transfusion of mind without mediation of sense. Considering what is implied by the human brain with its countless millions of cells, its complexities of minute structure, its innumerable chemical compositions, and the condensed forces in its microscopic and ultramicroscopic elements—the whole a sort of microcosm of cosmic forces to which no conceivable compound of electric batteries is comparable; considering, again, that from an electric station waves of energy radiate through the viewless air to be caught up by a fit receiver a thousand miles distant, it is not inconceivable that the human brain may send off still more subtile waves to be accepted and interpreted by the fitly tuned receiving brain. Is it, after all, mere fancy that a mental atmosphere or effluence emanates from one person to affect another, either soothing sympathetically or irritating antipathically?" These remarks (like Dr. Marshall's) were made without reference to maternal impressions, but it may be pointed out that under no conceivable circumstance could we find a brain in so virginal and receptive a state as is the child's in the womb.

On the whole we see that pregnancy induces a psychic state which is at once, in healthy persons, one of full development and vigor, and at the same time one which, especially in individuals who are slightly abnormal, is apt to involve a state of strained or overstrained nervous tension and to evoke various manifestations which are in many respects still imperfectly understood. Even the specifically sexual emotions tend to be heightened, more especially during the earlier period of pregnancy. In 24 cases of pregnancy in which the point was investigated by Harry Campbell, sexual feeling was decidedly increased in 8, in one case (of a woman aged 31 who had had four children) being indeed only present during pregnancy, when it was considerable; in only 7 cases was there diminution or disappearance of sexual feeling.[1] Pregnancy may produce mental depression;[2] but on the other hand it frequently leads to a change of the most favorable character in the mental and general well-being. Some women indeed are only well during pregnancy. It is remarkable that some women who habitually suffer from various nervous troubles—neuralgias, gastralgia, headache, insomnia—are only free from them at this moment. This "paradox of gestation," as Vinay has termed it, is specially marked in the hysterical and those suffering from slight nervous disorders, but it is by no means universal, so that although it is possible, Vinay states, to confirm the opinion of the ancients as

---

[1] H. Campbell, *Nervous Organization of Man and Woman*, p. 206; cf. Moll, *Untersuchungen über die Libido Sexualis*, bd. i, p. 264. Many authorities, from Soranus of Ephesus onward, consider, however, that sexual relations should cease during pregnancy, and certainly during the later months. *Cf.* Brenot, *De l'influence de la copulation pendant la grossesse*, 1903.

[2] Bianchi terms this fairly common condition the neurasthenia of pregnancy.

to the beneficial action of marriage on hysteria, that is only true of slight cases and scarcely enables us to counsel marriage in hysteria.[1]   Even a woman's intelligence is sometimes heightened by pregnancy, and Tarnior, as quoted by Vinay, knew many women whose intelligence, habitually somewhat obtuse, has only risen to the normal level during pregnancy.[2]   The pregnant woman has reached the climax of womanhood; she has attained to that state toward which the periodically recurring menstrual wave has been drifting her at regular intervals throughout her sexual life[3]; she has achieved that function for which her body has been constructed, and her mental and emotional disposition adapted, through countless ages.

And yet, as we have seen, our ignorance of the changes effected by the occurrence of this supremely important event— even on the physical side—still remains profound.   Pregnancy, even for us, the critical and unprejudiced children of a civilized age, still remains, as for the children of more primitive ages, a mystery.   Conception itself is a mystery for the primitive man, and may be produced by all sorts of subtle ways apart from sexual connection, even by smelling a flower.[4]   The pregnant woman

---

[1] Vinay, *Traité des Maladies de la Grossesse*, 1894, pp. 51, 577; Mongeri, "Nervenkrankungen und Schwangerschaft," *Allegemeine Zeitschrift für Psychiatrie*, bd. LVIII, Heft 5.   Haig remarks (*Uric Acid*, sixth edition, p. 151) that during normal pregnancy diseases with excess of uric acid in the blood (headaches, fits, mental depression, dyspepsia, asthma) are absent, and considers that the common idea that women do not easily take colds, fevers, etc., at this time is well founded.

[2] Founding his remarks on certain anatomical changes and on a suggestion of Engel's, Donaldson observes: "It is impossible to escape the conclusion that in women natural education is complete only with maternity, which we know to effect some slight changes in the sympathetic system and possibly the spinal cord, and which may be fairly laid under suspicion of causing more structural modifications than are at present recognized."   H. H. Donaldson, *The Growth of the Brain*, p. 352.

[3] The state of menstruation is in many respects an approximation to that of pregnancy; see, *e.g.*, Edgar's *Practice of Obstetrics*, plates 6 and 7, showing the resemblance of the menstrual changes in the breasts and the external sexual parts to the changes of pregnancy; *cf.* Havelock Ellis, *Man and Woman*, fourth edition, Chapter XI, "The Functional Periodicity of Woman."

[4] Thus the gypsies say of an unmarried woman who becomes pregnant, "She has smelt the moon-flower"—a flower believed to grow on the so-called moon-mountain and to possess the property of impregnating by its smell.   Ploss and Bartels, *Das Weib*, bd. I, Chapter XXVII.

was surrounded by ceremonies, by reverence and fear, often shut up in a place apart.[1] Her presence, her exhalations, were of extreme potency; even in some parts of Europe to-day, as in the Walloon districts of Belgium, a pregnant woman must not kiss a child for her breath is dangerous, or urinate on plants for she will kill them.[2] The mystery has somewhat changed its form; it still remains. The future of the race is bound up with our efforts to fathom the mystery of pregnancy. "The early days of human life," it has been truly said, "are entirely one with the mother. On her manner of life—eating, drinking, sleeping, and thinking—what greatness may not hang?"[3] Schopenhauer observed, with misapplied horror, that there is nothing a woman is less modest about than the state of pregnancy, while Weininger exclaims: "Never yet has a pregnant woman given expression in any form—poem, memoirs, or gynæcological monograph—to her sensations or feelings."[4] Yet when we contemplate the mystery of pregnancy and all that it involves, how trivial all such considerations become! We are here lifted into a region where our highest intelligence can only lead us to adoration, for we are gazing at a process in which the operations of Nature become one with the divine task of Creation.

---

[1] This was a sound instinct, for it is now recognized as an extremely important part of puericulture that a woman should rest at all events during the latter part of pregnancy; see, e.g., Pinard, *Gazette des Hôpitaux*, November 28, 1895, and *Annales de Gynécologie*, August, 1898.

[2] Ploss and Bartels, *op. cit.*, Chapter XXIX; Κρυπτάδια, vol. viii, p. 143.

[3] Griffith Wilkin, *British Medical Journal*, April 8, 1905.

[4] Weininger, *Geschlecht und Charakter*, p. 107. I may remark that a recent book, Ellis Meredith's *Heart of My Heart*, is devoted to a seemingly autobiographical account of a pregnant woman's emotions and ideas. The relations of maternity to intellectual work have been carefully and impartially investigated by Adèle Gerhard and Helena Simon, who seem to conclude that the conflict between the inevitable claims of maternity and the scarcely less inevitable claims of the intellectual life cannot be avoided.

APPENDIX.

HISTORIES OF SEXUAL DEVELOPMENT.

HISTORY I.—The following narrative has been written by a university man trained in psychology:—

So far as I have been able to learn, none of my ancestors for at least three generations have suffered from any nervous or mental disease; and of those more remote I can learn nothing at all. It appears probable, then, that any peculiarities of my own sexual development must be explained by reference to the somewhat peculiar environment.

1 was the first child and was, naturally, somewhat spoiled—a process which tended to increase my natural tendency to sentimentality. On the other hand, I was shy and undemonstrative with all except my nearest relatives, and with them as well after my seventh or eighth year. And here it may be well to describe my "mental type," as this is probably the most important factor in determining the direction of one's mental development. Of mental types the "visual" is, of course, by far the most common, but in my own case visual imagery was never strong or vivid, and has constantly grown weaker. The dominant part has been played by tactual, muscular and organic sensations, placing me as one of the "tactual motor" type, with strong "verbal motor" and "organic" tendencies. In reading a novel I seldom have a mental picture of the character or situation, but easily imagine the sensations (except the visual) and feel something of the emotions described. When telling of any event I have a strong impulse to make the movements described and to gesticulate. 1 remember events in terms of movements and the words to be used in giving an account of them; and in thinking of any subject I can feel the movements of the larynx and, in a less degree, of the lips and tongue that would be involved in putting my thoughts into words. I am easily moved to emotion, even to sentimentality, but am seldom if ever deeply affected and am so averse to any display of my feelings that I have the reputation among my acquaintances of being cold, unfeeling and unemotional. I am naturally quiet and bashful to a degree, which has rendered all forms of social intercourse painful through much of my life, and this in spite of a real longing to associate with people on terms of intimacy. As a child I was sensitive and solitary; later I became morbid as well. In a character so constituted the feelings and impulses

(231)

of the moment are likely to rule, and such has been my constant experience, though a large element of obstinacy in my character has kept me from appearing impulsive, and slight influences will bring about reactions which seem out of all proportion to their cause. For instance, I cannot, even now, read the more erotic of Boccaccio's stories without a good deal of sexual excitement and restlessness, which can be relieved only by vigorous exercise or masturbation.

The first ten years of my life were passed on a farm, most of the time without playmates or companions of my own age.

As far back as I can remember I indulged in elaborate day-dreams in which I figured as the chief character along with a few others who were chiefly creatures of my imagination, but at times borrowed from reality. These others were always boys until I learned the proper function of the sexual organs, when girls usurped the whole stage in numbers beyond the limits of a Turkish harem. Even at school my day-dreams were scarcely interrupted, for my shyness and timidity made me very unpopular among my schoolmates, who tormented me after the fashion of small boys or neglected me, as the spirit moved them. To make matters worse, I was brought up under the "sheltered life system," kept carefully away from the "bad boys," which category included nearly all the youngsters of the community, and deluged with moral homilies and tirades on things religious until I was thoroughly convinced that goodness and discomfort, the right and the unpleasant, were strictly synonymous; and I was kept through much of the time facing the prospect of an early death, to be followed by the good old orthodox hell or the equal miseries of its gorgeous alternative. I may say in all seriousness that this is a conservative and unexaggerated account of one phase of my early life—the one, I think, that tended most strongly to make me introspective and morbid. Later on, when I was trying to abandon the habit of masturbation, this early training greatly increased the despair I felt at each successive failure.

The first traces of sexual excitement that I can now recall occurred when I was about 4 years old. I had erections quite frequently and found a mild pleasure in fondling my genitals when these occurred, especially just after waking in the morning. I had no notion of an orgasm, and never succeeded in producing one until I was 13 years of age. In the summer of my sixth year I experienced pleasurable sensations in daubing my genitals with oil and then fondling or rubbing them, but I abandoned this amusement after getting some irritating substance into the meatus. A year later my mother warned me that playing with my penis would "make me very sick," but since experience had taught me that this was not true, my conviction that what was forbidden must necessarily be pleasant, sent me directly to my favorite retreat in the barn loft to experiment. Since, however, I failed, in spite of persistent effort, to produce any such pleasant results as I had expected, I soon gave up my attempts for other kinds of amusement.

A few months after this, in midsummer, a very sensual servant girl began a series of attempts to satisfy herself sexually with my help. She came nearly every day into the loft where I was playing and did her best to initiate me into the mysteries of sexual relationships, but I proved a sorry pupil. She would rub my penis until it became erect and then, placing me upon her, would insert the penis in her vulva and make movements of her thighs and hips calculated to cause friction. At times she varied the program by lying upon me and embracing me passionately. I can remember distinctly her quick, gasping breath and convulsive movements. She generally ended the seance by persuading me to perform cunnilingus upon her. None of these performances were intelligible to me and I invariably protested against being compelled to leave my play to amuse her. Even her fondling of my genitals annoyed me; and, stranger still, I preferred satisfying her by cunnilingus to the attempts at coitus.

It was nearly a year later that I experienced the first unmistakable manifestations of the sexual impulse—erections accompanied by lustful feeling and vague desires of whose proper satisfaction I had no notion whatever. It never occurred to me to associate my experiences with the servant girl with these new sensations. The peculiar fact about them was that they were generally occasioned by the infliction of pain upon animals. I do not remember how I first discovered that they could be evoked in this way, but I can clearly recollect many of my efforts to arouse this pleasurable excitement by abusing the dog or the cats, or by prodding the calves with a nail set in the end of a broom handle. I seldom manipulated my genitals at this time, and when I did it was for the purpose of causing sexual excitement rather than allaying it.

During this same year I got my first idea of sexual intercourse by watching animals copulate; but my powers of observation must have been limited, for I supposed that the penis of the male entered the anus of the female. In watching the coitus of animals I experienced lively sexual excitement and lustful sensations, located not only in the genitals, but apparently in the anus as well. I often excited myself by imagining myself playing the part of the female animal—a peculiar combination of passive pederasty and bestiality. A servant girl put me to right on the error of observation just mentioned, but neglected to apply the principle to human animals, and I remained for another year in complete ignorance of the structure of woman's sexual organs and of the intercourse between man and woman. In the meantime I cultivated my fancies of intercourse with animals, often still perversely imagining myself taking the part of the female; and the notion of such relationships gradually became so familiar as to seem possible and desirable. This is especially significant in view of later developments.

Up to my eleventh or twelfth year the erotic element in my daydreaming varied with the seasons. In the summer it played a dominant part, while in the winter it was almost entirely absent, owing, it may be, to the fact that most of my time was spent indoors or on long, tiresome tramps to and from school, and the further fact that during the winter I saw but little of the animals which had acted as a stimulus to sexual excitement. So little was I troubled in winter and so ignorant was I of normal intercourse that sleeping with a cousin, a girl of about my own age (7 or 8 years), resulted in no addition to my knowledge of things sexual.

It was early in my ninth year that I first learned something of the anatomical difference between man and woman and of the functions of the sexual organs in coitus. These were explained to me by a young male servant, who, however, told me nothing of conception or pregnancy. At first I was very little interested, as it did not immediately occur to me to associate my own erotic experiences with the matter of these revelations; but under the faithful tuition of my new instructor I soon began to desire normal coitus, and my interest in the sexual affairs of animals weakened accordingly. His teachings went still further, for he masturbated before me, then persuaded me to masturbate him, and finally practiced coitus inter femora upon me. He also tried to masturbate me, but was unable to produce an orgasm, though I found the experiment mildly pleasurable.

Early in my eleventh year we left the farm and lived in the city for several months. In the meantime there had been no developments in my sexual life beyond what has already been indicated. In the city I found so much to interest and amuse me that I almost entirely forgot my erotic day-dreams and desires. Though my chief playmates were two girls of about my own age I never thought of attempting sexual intercourse with them, as I might easily have done, for they were much wiser and more experienced in these things than myself. Shortly before the end of our stay in town an older schoolmate explained to me as much of the process of reproduction as is usually known by a precocious youngster of 12 years, but I firmly refused to credit his statements. He adduced the fact of lactation in proof of the correctness of his views, but I had been too thoroughly steeped in supernaturalism to be very amenable to naturalistic evidence of this sort and remained obdurate. But the suggestion stayed with me and perplexed me not a little; when we returned to the farm I began to watch the reproductive process in animals.

The following two years were decidedly unpleasant. I was growing rapidly and was sluggish, awkward and stupid. At school I was more unpopular than ever and seemed to have a positive genius for doing the wrong thing. On the rare occasions when my companions admitted me to their counsels I was a willing dupe and catspaw, with the result that I was much in trouble with my teachers. Being morbidly sensitive I suffered keenly under these circumstances and, as my health was not at all good, I often made of my frequent headaches excuses to stay at home, where I would lie abed brooding over my small troubles or, more often, dreaming erotic day-dreams and making repeated attempts to produce an orgasm. But though these efforts were accompanied by the most lustful thoughts and my imagination created situations of oriental extravagance, I was 13 years old when they first met with success. I remember the occasion very distinctly, the more so because I thought of it much and bitterly when shortly afterwards I tried to abandon a habit which the family "doctor book" assured me must result in every variety of damnation. At the moment, however, I was greatly surprised and gratified and tried at once to repeat the delightful sensation, but was unable to do so until the following day. From that time to the present I think I have masturbated an average of ten times per week, and this is certainly a very conservative estimate; for though up to my sixteenth year I could seldom produce an orgasm more than once a day I have often, during the last four or five years, produced it from four to seven times per day without difficulty and this for days and even weeks in succession. During these periods of excessive masturbation very little liquid was ejaculated and the pleasurable sensations were slight or entirely lacking.

From the time when I began masturbating regularly practically my whole interest centered in things pertaining to sex. I read the chapters of the family "doctor book" which treated of sexual matters; my day-dreams were almost exclusively erotic; I sought opportunities to talk about sex-relationships with my schoolmates, with whom I was now slowly getting on better terms; I collected pictures of nude women, learned a great number of obscene stories, read such obscene books as I could obtain and even searched the dictionary for words having a sexual connotation. Up to my fifteenth year, when ejaculation of semen began, there was a strong sadistic coloring to my day-dreams. Through this period, too, my bashfulness in the presence of the opposite sex increased until it reached the point of absurdity.

When fifteen years old I began to practice coitus inter femora on my brother and continued it intermittently for about two years. The experience was disappointing, for I had confidently expected a great increase of pleasure over masturbation in this act; and in casting about for some stronger stimulus I recurred to the forgotten idea of intercourse with animals. I promptly tried to put the idea to a test, but failed several times, and finally succeeded, only to find that the result fell far short of my expectations. Nevertheless I continued the practice irregularly for about three years—or rather through that part of the three years that I spent at home, for while I was at school opportunity for such indulgence was lacking. Long familiarity with the idea of intercourse with animals had made it impossible for me to feel the disgust with the practice which it inspires in most people; and even the perusal of Exodus xxii: 19 failed to make me abandon it. Firmly as I believed in the Mosaic law the supremacy of the sexual impulse was complete.

As early as my sixteenth year I tried to abandon "self-abuse" in all its forms and have repeatedly made the same effort since that time but never with more than very partial success. On two or three occasions I have stopped for periods of several weeks, but only to begin again and indulge more recklessly than before. The deep depression which followed each failure, and often each act of masturbation, I attributed solely to the loss of semen, leaving out of account the fact that I expected to feel depressed and the utter discouragement and self-contempt which accompanied the sense of failure and weakness when, in the face of my resolution, I repeatedly gave way and yielded to the temptation to an act whose consequences I firmly believed must be ruinous. I am now convinced that by far the greater part of this depression was due to suggestion and the humiliating sense of defeat. And this feeling of moral impotence, this seeming helplessness against an overpowering impulse which, on the other hand, seemed so trivial when viewed without passion, eventually weakened my self-control to a degree guessed by no one but myself and sapped the foundations of my moral life in a way which I have constant occasion to deplore.

The foregoing paragraphs give, I think, a fair idea of my condition when I left home for a boarding school at the beginning of my seventeenth year. From this time my experiences may be said to have run on in two distinct cycles—that of the summer months when I was at home, and that of the remainder of the year when I was at school. This fact will make some confusion and apparent inconsistency in the rest of this "history" unavoidable. When I left home I was shy, retiring, totally ignorant of social usage, without self-confidence, unambitious, dreamy, and subject to fits of melancholy. I masturbated at least once a day, though I was in almost constant rebellion against the habit. In my more idle moments I elaborated erotic day dreams in which there was a peculiar mixture of the purely sensual and the purely ideal element; which never fused in my experience, but held the field alternately or mingled somewhat in the manner of air and water. One person usually served as the object of my ideal attachment, another as the center round which I grouped my sensual dreams and desires.

At school I found more congenial companions than I had fallen in with elsewhere, and the necessary contact with people of both sexes gradually wore off some of the rougher corners and brought a measure of self-confidence. I had two or three incipient love affairs which my backwardness kept from growing serious. Out of this change of environment came a sense of expansion, of escape from self, which was distinctly pleasant. I still masturbated regularly, but no longer experienced the former depression except when at home during vacation. Relatively to the past, life was now so varied and interesting that I had less and less time for melancholy; and the discovery that I could lead my classes and hold my own in athletic sports seemed to indicate that my past fears had been exaggerated. Nevertheless I was never reconciled to the habit and often rebelled at the weakness that kept me its slave.

When I entered the university the effects of my useless struggle with the practice of masturbation were pretty well developed. I could no longer fix my attention steadily upon my work and found that only by "cribbing" and "bluffing" could I keep my place at the head of my classes. I was troubled not a little by the shoddiness of my work, and tried again and again during the course of the two years spent at this college to shake off the habit. At the university I was introduced gradually to a wider social circle and so far outgrew my bashfulness that I began to seek the society of the opposite sex assiduously. As I gained self-confidence I became reckless, getting at one time into serious trouble with the authorities which came near resulting in my expulsion. I became one of the more popular members of the clique to which I belonged—much to my surprise and even more to that of my acquaintances. The physical culture craze attacked me at this time and my pet ambition was the attainment of strength and agility. My bump of vanity also grew apace, but an unmeasured hatred of all kinds of foppishness kept me on the safe side of moderation in my dress and behavior.

During my second year of university life I had two love affairs in the course of which I found that my interest in any particular member of the fair sex disappeared as soon as it was returned. The pursuit was fascinating enough, but I cared nothing at all for the prize when once it was within reach. I may add that the interest I had in the girls was purely ideal. While at this school I do not think I masturbated half as often as while at the preparatory school.

When I left this college for —— University I took with me a formidable catalogue of good resolutions, first among which was the determination to abandon all kinds of "self-abuse." I think I kept this one about a month. As I had gone from a comparatively small school to one of the largest of American universities the change was great and the revelations it brought me frequently humiliating. I was lonesome, home-sick, and my bump of self-esteem was woefully bruised; and not unnaturally I soon began to seek a partial solace in day-dreams and masturbation. After I had become somewhat adapted to my new environment I indulged less frequently in either, and from that time to the present I have masturbated very irregularly, sometimes but little and again to excess.

Not long after I came to this place I met a young lady with whom I soon became quite intimate. For over a year our friendship was strictly platonic and then swung suddenly around to a sexual basis. We were ardent lovers for a few weeks, after which I tired of the game as I had before in other cases, and broke off all relations with her as abruptly as was possible. Since then I have almost wholly withdrawn from the society and companionship of women and have almost entirely lost whatever tact and assurance I once possessed in their company. Things pertaining to sexual life have interested me rather more than less, but have occupied my attention much less exclusively than before this episode. Though I have never intended to marry, my breaking off relations with this girl affected me much. At any rate it marked an abrupt change in the character of my sexual experiences. The sexual impulse seems to have lost its power to rouse me to action. Hitherto I had practiced masturbation always under protest, as it were—as the only available form of sexual satisfaction; while now I resigned myself to it as all that there was to hope for in that field. Of course I knew that a little effort or a little money would procure natural satisfaction of my sexual needs, but I also knew that I would never, under any ordinary circumstances, put forth the necessary effort, and fear of venereal disease has been more than enough to keep me away from houses of prostitution.

Some months ago I refrained from masturbation for a period of about six weeks and watched carefully for any change in my health or spirits, but noticed none at all. The only impulse to masturbate was occasioned by fits of restlessness accompanied by erections and a mildly pleasurable feeling of fullness in the penis and scrotum. I think that over 75 per cent. of my acts of masturbation are provoked by these fits of restlessness and are unaccompanied by fancy images, erotic thoughts, lustful desires, or marked pleasure. At other times the act is occasioned by erotic thoughts and images, and is accompanied by a considerable degree of lustful pleasure which, however, is never so intense as in my earlier experiences and has steadily decreased from the first. Usually the orgasm is accompanied by a strong contraction of all the voluntary muscles, particularly the extensors, followed by a slight giddiness and slight feeling of exhaustion. If repeated several times in the course of a single day the acts are followed by dullness and lassitude; otherwise the feeling of exhaustion passes away quickly and a sense of relief and quiet takes its place. So natural or rather habitual has this resort to masturbation as a means of relief from nervousness and restlessness become that the act is almost instinctive in its unconsciousness.

I am extremely sensitive to all kinds of sexual influences, and have an insatiable curiosity regarding everything that pertains to the sexual life of men or women. I am not, however, excited sexually by conversation about sexual facts and relationships, no matter what its nature, though in reading erotic literature my excitement is often intense.

The tendency to day dream has never left me, but there are no longer any elaborate scenes or long-continued "stories," these having been replaced by vaguely imagined incidents which are usually broken off before they reach a satisfactory climax. They are always interrupted by the intrusion of other matters, usually of more practical interest; and the long-continued habit of satisfying myself by masturbation has made erotic dreams rather tantalizing than pleasurable. I dream very seldom at night—at least I can scarcely ever remember any dreams upon waking—and practically never of sexual relations. I have not had a nocturnal emission for over three years, and probably not more than twenty-five in my life.

In my "love passages" with girls there has been no serious thought of coitus on my part, and I have never had intercourse with a woman—unless my early experiences with the servant girl be called such. Like all masturbators I always idealized "love" to the utter exclusion of all sensual cravings; and the notion that the physical act of coitus was something degrading and destructive of real love rather than its consummation was, of all prejudices I have ever formed, the most difficult to escape—a circumstance due, I suppose, to the fact that all I had ever been taught on the subject tended to the complete divorce of what was called "love" from what was stigmatized as a "base sensual desire." Judging from my own experience and observation I should say that "ideal love" is a mere surface feeling, bound to disappear as soon as it has gained its object by arousing a reciprocal interest on the part of the one to whom it is directed. So little did I "materialize" the objects of my "love" that I have never cared for kissing or the warm embraces in which lovers usually indulge. I have never kissed but one girl, and her with far too little enthusiasm to satisfy her. My last sweetheart was a very passionate girl, the warmth of whose embraces was somewhat torrid and, to me, both puzzling and annoying. The intensity of feeling which demanded such strenuous expression was beyond my knowledge of human nature. A somewhat peculiar circumstance in connection with these experiences is the fact that I often found myself trying to analyze my emotions with a purely psychological interest while playing the part of the intoxicated lover in his mistress's arms.

There is but little left to say on the subject of my sexual development. During the last two or three years my knowledge of the facts of the sexual life has been very greatly increased, and I have become acquainted with phases of human nature which were wholly unknown to me before. The part played by things sexual in my life is still, I suppose, abnormally large; it is undoubtedly the largest single interest, though my outer life is determined almost wholly by other considerations.

Of course I know nothing of the effect which long-continued masturbation may have had on my ability to perform normal coitus. I do not think I am subject to any kind of sexual perversion, for all my indulgence has been *faute de mieux* and, at least since I beagn masturbation, all my desires and erotic day-dreams have had to do only with normal coitus. The mystery which surrounds the sexual act seems at times to be regaining its former influence and power of fascination. I have no doubt, however, but that I should be greatly disillusioned should I ever perform coitus; and I greatly regret that I have not been able to test this conviction and so round out and complete this "history."

It may be worth while to say a word about my religious experiences, as, in many cases, they are closely bound up with the sexual impulse. I was never "converted," but on a dozen or more occasions approached the crisis more or less closely. The dominant emotion in these experiences was always fear, sometimes with anger and despair intermixed in varying proportions. A complete analysis of these experiences is, of course, impossible, but the various pleasurable feelings of which converts spoke in the revivals which I attended were a closed book to me. Following my revival-meeting experiences came a few days spent in a sort of moral exaltation during which I eschewed all my habits of which conventional morality disapproved, save masturbation, and felt no small satisfaction with my moral conditions. I became a first-rate Pharisee. Toward the women who had figured in my day dreams I suddenly conceived the chastest affection, resolutely smothering every sensual thought and fancy when thinking of them, and putting in place of these elements ideal love, self-sacrifice, knightly devotion—Sunday-school Garden-of-Eden pictures with a mediæval, romantic coloring. These day-dreams were always sexual, involving situations of extreme complexity and monumental silliness. Masturbation was always continued and usually with increased frequency. The end of these periods was always abrupt and much like awaking from a dream in which the dreamer has been behaving in a manner to arouse his own disgust. They were followed by feelings of sheepishness and self-contempt mingled with anger and a dislike of all things having to do with religion. My inability to pass the conversion crisis and a growing contempt for empty enthusiasm finally led me to a saner attitude toward religion. from which I passed easily into religious scepticism; and later the study of philosophy and science, and particularly of psychology, banished the last lingering remnant of faith in a supernatural agency and led me to the passion for facts and indifference to values which have caused me to be often called "dead to all morality."

HISTORY II.—C. A., aged 25, unmarried; tutor, preparing to take Holy Orders:—

My paternal ancestry (which is largely Huguenot) is noteworthy for its patriotism and its large families. My father, who died when I was a year old, is remembered for the singular uprightness and purity of his life from his earliest childhood. The photograph which I have shows him as possessed of a rare classic beauty of features. He was an ideal husband and father. At the time of his death he was a Master of Arts and a school principal. My mother is an extraordinarily neurotic woman, yet famed among her friends for her great domesticity, attachment to her husbands, and an almost abnormal love of babies. She has nobly borne the ill-treatment of her second husband, who for several years has been in a state of melancholia. My mother has been "highly-wrought" all her life, and has suffered intensely from fears of all kinds. As a young girl she was somnambulistic, and once fell down a stair-head during sleep. In spite of her bodily sufferings with indigestion, eye-strain, and depression she retains her youthfulness. She has slight powers of reasoning. She has had times of unconsciousness and rigidity. I have never heard any mention of epilepsy. She has a horror of showing prudishness in regard to the healthful manifestations of sex life, and is always praising examples of what she terms "a natural woman."

I have heard that during my first year my mother detected my nurse in the act of putting a morphine powder on my tongue for the purpose of keeping me quiet. I was subject to convulsions at this period, and narrowly escaped a permanent hernia. My family tell me that from the beginning I was a well-developed and boyish boy, full of mischief, impulsive, good to look upon, unusually affectionate, beloved by all.

In my third year I took pleasure in crawling under the bed with my boy-cousin, who was nine months my senior, and after we had taken down our drawers, in kissing each other's nates. I do not remember which of us first thought of this pastime.

At the age of 4 I gave myself a treat by gazing upward through a cellar window at the nates of a woman who was defecating from several feet above into a cesspool that lay beneath. It was during this summer also that I frightened myself by pulling back my prepuce far enough to disclose the purple glans, which I had never seen before. But this act gave me no desire to masturbate.

When 5 years old, and living in a great city, I drew indecent pictures in company with a little girl and her younger brother. These pictures represented men in the act of urinating. The penes were drawn large, and the streams of urine plainly indicated. One afternoon I induced the boy to go to the bath-room, lie on his back, and allow me to perform *fellatio* on him. I did not ask him to return the favor. I remember the curious tar-like smell of his clothing and the region about his genitals. It is possible that I gained my knowledge of *fellatio* from an unknown boy of 10, who had induced me, during the preceding summer to enter a sandy lot with him, watch him urinate, and then, kneeling before him, commit *fellatio*. A year later, as I was walking home in the rain to our summer cottage, with an open umbrella over my shoulder, a boy of 15, who was leaning against our fence, exhibited a large, erect penis, and when l had passed him urinated upon me and my umbrella. I never saw the boy again. I felt peculiarly insulted by his act. Back of the house there lived a 12-year-old boy who invited me to watch him defecate in the out-door privy, and during the act told me a number of indecent stories and words which I cannot remember.

About this time I fell in love with a little Jewish boy next door. Often I cried myself to sleep over the thought that perhaps he was lying on a sofa alone and crying with a stomach-ache. I longed to embrace him; and yet I saw little of him, and made little of him when I was with him.

Living in a Western city a few months later, some girls of 12 and 14 led me to their barn, where they dressed themselves in boys' clothing and made believe that they were cowboys. One of them told me to "shut my eyes, open my mouth, and get a surprise." When I opened my eyes once more a piece of hen-dung lay in my mouth. I have a vague remembrance of one of the girls asking me to enter a water-closet with her. She uttered some indelicate phrase, but I performed no act with her. In the house where I lived I once entered the bedroom of a half-grown girl while she was dressing. She knelt to kiss me innocently enough, and I, by a sudden impulse, ran my hand between her bare neck and her corset as far as l could reach. Apparently she took no notice of my movement. Although I did not masturbate, yet during this winter I experienced a tickling sensation about my genitals when I placed my hand beneath them as I lay on my stomach in bed. One evening I pulled up my night-dress and, holding my penis in my hand, I danced to and fro on the carpet. I imagined that I was one of a line of naked men and women who were advancing toward another similar line that faced them. I imagined myself as pleasurably coming in contact with my female partner who possessed male genitals.

The following summer I lived in the woods. My next-door playmate was a little girl of my own age—6 years. She sat down before me in the barn and exposed her genitals. This was the first time I had seen female organs, or had thought for a moment that they differed from

my own. In great perplexity I asked the little girl: "Has it been cut
off?" She and I defecated in peach baskets that we found in the upper
part of the barn.

When I was 7 years old and back in the Eastern city I lived in the
house of a physician. Alone with his 3-year-old daughter one day, I
showed her my erect organ, and felt a delicious gratification when she
stroked it with the words: "Nice! Nice!" I confessed my fault to
my guardian that night after I had said my prayers. I had complained
to my mother a year before of the inconvenience I found in my penis
being "so long sometimes." She said that she would "see about having
the end taken off." But I was never circumcised. Her words gave me
the doubly unpleasant impression that my *glans* was to be cut off.

There came occasionally to the kitchen of Dr. W.'s house a foul-
mouthed Irish laundress who used coarse language to me concerning urination. I loathed the woman, and yet one night I dreamed that I was
embracing her naked form and rolling over and over with her on the bed;
and in spite of my sight of female genitals a few months before, I
thought of her as having organs of my own kind and size. At my first
school I watched a red-haired boy of 12 expose the penis of a 7-year-old
boy as he lay on his back in the bath-room. I do not remember that the
sight gave me sexual pleasure.

I spent the summer before I was 8 in a double house. The adopted
daughter of our neighbor (a neurotic, retired physician) was a girl of
13 who had been taken from a poor laboring family. She got me to show
her my parts, touched them, and asked whether I urinated from my
scrotum. She also induced me to play with her genitals as we sat on a
sofa in the twilight, and to spank her naked nates with the back of a
hair-brush as she lay on a bed; but from none of these performances did
I derive physical satisfaction. The girl E. and I took delight in "talking
dirty secrets," as she expressed it. Her young cousin H. (nephew of her
adopted mother) never heard me use the word "thing" without sugges-
tively smiling. E. recalled the pleasant hours that she had spent with
her cousin when they were in their night-gowns. She did not particu-
larize these sexual relations. Under the board-walk the boy H. and I
once defecated in bottles. Some little girls who lived opposite us pulled
up their dresses one night and "dared" each other to dance out beyond
the end of the house, in full view of the road. We boys merely looked
on.

I now fell passionately in love with a remarkably handsome little
boy of my own age. I longed to kiss and hug him, but I did not dare
to do so, for he was haughty and intolerant of my attentions. I even
allowed him to stand with one foot on me and remark in a loud tone:
"I am Conqueror!" I endured no end of petty insults and much ill-
treatment from this boy. I reached the height of my passion on the

night that he appeared at our cottage in a tight-fitting suit of pepper-and-salt. I gloried in his perfect legs and besought my guardian that she would buy me a similar suit of clothes.

For the summer after I was 8 years old I lived in a cottage in a country town. The servant maid M. was a young girl of 16 who listened eagerly to my accounts of the "secrets" and actions in which the girl E. and I had taken delight a year before. I think that M. arranged a meeting between a little black-haired girl and me in order that we might take a walk and play sexually with each other. Just as we were starting on our walk one of my relatives said that I must not leave the yard.

The little girl and I had see-sawed together and I had been interested in her legs as she rose in the air. (When I was 13 years old and see-sawing at a picnic with a stout girl, the motion of the board and the sight of her straddled form filled me with longing to embrace her sexually.) One afternoon M. took me to the house of an acquaintance of hers. M.'s brother was in the room and made a number of unremembered remarks which struck me as being rather "free," and M. told me later that she and the girl once dressed as ballet dancers and danced before M.'s brother. I felt that he was lascivious. I was always remarkably intuitive.

I fell in love with a handsome, stout, black-haired boy who lived on a farm; but he was not a "farmer's son" in the common sense of the word. I visited him for two or three days, and we slept with each other, to my boundless joy. For his freckled girl cousin I did not care the turn of my wrist, although she was a nice enough little thing. One night when we three lay on a bed in the dark, and neither of us boys had eyes or words for her, she silently left us. He and I never committed the slightest sexual fault. I left him with tears at the summer-end, and I often kissed his photograph during the following winter.

In the flat-house where I began to live when I was 8 years old, I once practiced mutual tickling of a very slight character with a boy of my own age. We sat on chairs placed opposite to each other and we inserted our fingers through the openings in our trousers. Just as we were beginning to enjoy the titillation we were interrupted by the approach of one of my family who, however, was not quick enough to discover us. Down cellar I often saw the genitals of the janitor's little girls—they were fond of lifting their skirts and they did not wear drawers—but I had no desire to attempt conjunction. I once caught an older friend of mine (he was 13) in the act of leaving one of the girls. The pair had been in a coal-compartment. The boy was buttoning his trousers and I guessed what he had been doing. When I began to sleep alone in my tenth year I had no desire to masturbate, and was loath to do so by reason of ample warnings given me by my guardian and by the family physician. One afternoon a stunted friend of mine sat down in the back yard and astonished me by tying a piece of string to his penis. At a large private school which I now attended I made the acquaintance of the principal's son, and wondered why he had such a fancy for dressing his 5-year-old sister in boy's clothes. He closed the door on me while he was thus engaged. At my house we went to the bath-room together, and he showed me his circumcised and much-ridged penis. Neither of us made any mention of masturbating.

At this period I fell slightly in love with a 5-year-old boy with intensely black eyes. I would kiss him whenever we were alone, but I had no wish to seduce him. I was always interested in watching the urination of younger children. When I was 5 years old I went on my knees to a strange little boy in order to whisper in his ear an inquiry as to whether he wanted to urinate. I experienced a pleasurable thrill when I was 10 years old in leading a small girl cousin to the outdoor privy, in helping her on and off the open seat, in buttoning and unbuttoning her drawers, and in gazing at her vulva.

The summer before I was 10 I lived a wild life in the mountains. My companions were a negro girl, the two daughters of a clergyman, the two sons of a questionable woman hotelkeeper, and the daughter of the Irish scavenger. All of these children were extraordinarily sensual. Their leading pastime, from morning until night, was varying forms of indecency, with the supreme caress—which they termed "raising dickie" —as the most frequent enjoyment. The 5-year-old daughter of the scavenger explained to us how she had seen her father approaching her stout mother with an erect penis, the pair standing up before the lamplight during the act. This curly-headed, rosy-cheeked child handled her genitals so much that they were inflamed. I once saw her sitting in the road and rubbing dust against her vulva. I saw little of the elder daughter of the minister (she was 12 years old). She persuaded me to expose myself before her in the cellar of a partially-built house. In return for my favor she allowed me to look at her genitals. She did not ask for *conjunctio*. The two younger daughters were my intimates. With the middle one I was forever performing a weak conjunction that consisted in the laying of my member against her vulva. Notwithstanding all the entreaties of my little friend, I could not be persuaded to protrude my penis against her vagina; and not on one occasion can I remember obtaining an erection or extreme pleasure. Up in the garret she straddled slanting beams with her genitals exposed, and I followed her example. The negro girl and my little friend both urinated on a tent floor at my request. I did not fancy the odor of a girl's genitals, nor the appearance of the vulva when the labia were held apart.

The following summer, when I was almost 11, I took a long walk one day with my old friend, the girl E. We entered a patch of woods and ate our lunch, but no sense of sexual drawing toward the girl came over me and she did not offer to entice me. I slept with her boy-cousin one night, and her neuropathic aunt, a retired lady physician, bothered us by repeatedly creeping into our room. I felt intuitively that she was watching to see whether we would commit mutual masturbation—which we had no thought of doing. Three years before I had opened the door of her bedroom suddenly and saw E.'s naked form. The physician had been examining her, E. told me later. My guardian also annoyed me by repeated warnings not to play with myself.

Just before I turned 11 I was sent to a small and so-called "home" boarding-school. Eight of us lived in the smaller dormitory. The matron roomed downstairs. There was no resident master—a serious error. We small boys were told to strip one evening. We were then tied neck-to-neck and made to dance a "slave-dance," which was marked by no sexuality. A boy of 15, R., one afternoon gave me the astonishing information that my father had taken a part in my procreation. Up to this moment I had known only of the maternal offices, information of which had been beautifully supplied to me by my guardian when I was 7 years old. At that time I talked freely about the coming of a baby brother in a distant city; I watched the construction of baby clothes; I named the newcomer, and I was momentarily disappointed when he proved to be a girl. This same R., a strong boy with a large penis, got into the custom of lying in bed with me just before lights were put out. He would read to himself and occasionally pause to pump his penis and make with his lips the sound of a laboring locomotive. I felt impelled to handle his organ, for I was fascinated by its size, and stiffness, and warmth. Rarely he would titillate my then small and unerect penis. R. never ejaculated when he was with me; hence not until my third year was I acquainted with the appearance of a flow of semen. Sometimes R. would stop during his dressing to manipulate his penis, but was such a picture of rosy health that I doubt whether he brought himself often to ejaculation. R. told me that he had been to a brothel where his genitals were examined to determine whether they were large enough and not diseased. He also related how he "played cow" with a girl of his own age, she consenting to perform *fellatio* upon him. A dark-skinned, unwashed, pimpled but fairly vigorous boy of 16, with an irritable domineering manner, told me the delights of coitus with a girl in a bath-house, and I overheard his conversation with another "old" boy concerning the purchase of a girl in a big city for the sum of five dollars. No details were given.

I will now pass to my third year, when I was 13 years old. A large, well-set-up boy of 16, A., became my idol. His toleration of my presence in his room filled me with endless love. When I lied about a matter in which he was concerned, his denunciation of me brought me to a state of shuddering and weeping unspeakable. When our relations were established again A. allowed me to creep into his bed after the lights were out, and there I passionately embraced him, but without performing any definite act. When I turned over on my side with my back to him he drew my prepuce back and forth until I experienced orgasm, but not ejaculation. I would return his favor by pumping his erect penis, but with no ejaculation on his part. He did not propose *fellatio*, and I did not think of it. One night when he was in my bed I began to masturbate very slightly, whereupon he laughed, saying: "So that is the way you amuse yourself!" As a matter of fact the habit was not fastened upon me. He always laughed when the rubbing of his finger on my exposed glans caused me to shrink. Another boy, H., now began to show me his erect penis and we practiced mutual manipulations. A. laughingly told me how me had caught H. in the act of masturbating as he stood in the bath-tub. A. told me a number of sexual stories—how he enjoyed coitus in the bushes with a girl on the way home from entertainments; how half a dozen boys and girls stripped in the basement of a church and performed coitus on the velvet chairs which stood behind the pulpit; and how he and a younger boy, who camped out together, played with each other's genitals. F., a boy of 11, was highly nervous, subject to timidity and tears on the slightest provocation, often morose, and under treatment for kidney trouble. His penis was erect whenever I saw him undress. He told me that a partially idiotic man taught F. and his companion how to masturbate. The man invited the boys to his tent and there pumped his organ until "some white stuff came out of it." F. also told me that an Indian princess in his part of the country would permit coitus for fifty cents. A. sometimes slept with F., and I could imagine their embraces. S., a secretive, handsome boy of 13, wetted his bed with urine every night. The only sign that he gave of an interest in sexuality was his laughing remark concerning the coupling of rose-bugs. Of his chum, my beloved C., I will speak later. My small room-mate handled himself only slightly. I never had a desire to lie with him, since I disliked him, nor with my first room-mate, a "chunky," fiery boy of 10, whose penis interested me merely because it was circumcised and almost always erect. His masturbation was also so slight as not to attract any particular attention. A lusty German boy, B., showed no signs of sexuality until his third year, when he laughed about his newly-appearing pubic hair, and told several of us openly of how he enjoyed to play "a drum-beat" on his penis before going to sleep. "I don't do it too much, though," he explained. He showed a mild curiosity when I gave him the resumé of a book on cohabitation which contained illustrations of the erect penis and the female organs. I had found this book in the woods and I read it eagerly during my third year.

I came to the point of agreeing with A., who said: "Everyone is smutty." Indeed I lived in a lustful world, and yet my mind was bent also on books, and writing, and the outdoor world. I was overgrown and splendidly developed, with a medium-sized penis and a scant growth of pubic hair. My face wore a somewhat infantile expression. My mouth was a perfect "Cupid's bow," my hair thin and light. I was troubled about my snub-nose, which gave the boys a great deal of amusement. As a matter of fact I exaggerated its upward tendency out of my morbid self-consciousness and cowardice. My imagination was extraordinarily intense, as it had always been. I was sensitive to smells and sounds and colors and personalities, and to the subtle influence of the night. I was timid and easily moved to tears, but not from any physical weakness until after. At the lower house there was the boy Z., famed for his large penis; and the older G., a boy of 15, who was the leader in sexuality at his dormitory. Z. showed me his penis and exposed his glans often enough, but we did not manipulate each other. G. told us to notice how large a space his penis occupied in his trousers, and laughed over Z.'s custom of masturbating by means of a narrow vase. G.'s special lover was a nervous boy of ten. It is remarkable that none of us mentioned *fellatio* or *pœdicatio*. These acts may have occurred at school, but not to my knowledge. We did not have much to say sexually about the girls. We heard rumors of a 16-year-old, V., who had been sent away from school for coitus; and my first room-mate was said to have obtained *conjunctio* with a girl under cover of the chapel shed. Once A. and I pointed a telescope at the open windows of the girls' domitory, but we saw nothing to interest us. A day-scholar, J., a pale, nervous, bright boy of 13, took me into the study of his uncle-physician and together we gloated over pictures of the sexual organs. A. was with us on one occasion. J. told me how he liked to roll over and over in bed with his hand placed under his scrotum. This act, he said, made him imagine that he was obtaining coitus. He advised me to slide my penis back and forth in the vagina whenever I should actually obtain coitus. In my room at school J. once drew an imaginary map of a bagnio, in which the water-closet was carefully displayed *en suite* with the bedrooms. J. and I never masturbated together. Indeed, I cannot remember seeing his organ. A hulking boy of 16, who lived opposite the school-grounds, became intimate with J., and we three went on a walk up the railroad track. The big boy, W., tried to inflame my passions by telling me how he and J. had had coitus with a handsome black-haired widow in town, but I remained cold.

During this year I fell in love with C., a popular, talkative, witty boy of my own age, or perhaps a year younger. He fancied me and we slept together one night under the most innocent circumstances. I never dreamed of having sexual relations with him, and yet I fairly burned with love for him. My stay at his beautiful home over Sunday while his parents were away was one long delight. We slept in each other's arms, but there was no sexuality. En route to C.'s home he pointed with a glove to a little working-girl, saying he would like to have intercourse with her, but this was the only remark of the kind that ever passed his lips in my presence. When undressed save for his undershirt, he laughingly held his unerect organ in his hand and made the motions of obtaining conjunction with an imaginary partner. Once we spoke of masturbation (I could recite the information of my good physician with a marvelous show of virtue), and C. remarked: "Yes, doing that makes boys crazy." C. finally grew tired of my deceptive, babyish nature and ultra-interest in books and puzzles, but I cherished an undiminished affection for him, and when he was detained at home for a fortnight with a broken arm, I wrote him a passionate letter, which I sobbed over and actually wetted with my tears. But the fervor of my passion died at the close of the year. I consider this unsullied friendship to be the only redeeming feature of my sensual days at school.

Versed as I was in the warnings against masturbation, I found pleasure one afternoon when I was alone in slipping my penis through the open handle of a pair of scissors and in violently flapping my partially erect organ until a strange, sweet thrill crept over me from top to toe and a drop of clear liquid oozed from my member. But I gave up the manipulation with scissors, finding a greater-satisfaction in masturbating while I was defecating or just after it. I either pumped my organ by slipping the prepuce back and forth, or I grasped the organ at its root and violently jerked it back and forth. I soon began to masturbate not only every time that I defecated, but also at night just before I went to sleep, and sometimes early in the morning. On the whole I preferred the jerking just described. I always brought about ejaculation after perhaps five minutes of violent exertion.

My penis became chafed at the root, but I did not especially care. I remember the afternoon that I masturbated for the first time while I was defecating in the school water-closet. I cannot recall that at first I thought of coitus while I masturbated. On one occasion I masturbated over the *vase de nuit* after a delightful afternoon of tobogganing exploration up and down the mountain.

During this first year of abuse, I felt no ill effects whatsoever, although I realized, in an unthinking way, that I was doing wrong. But sexuality had assumed the proportion of a regular feature of our school life. It was difficult for me to place a "universal" view in its true perspective. I used to smile at the glazed, dull morning eye of poor H., who was a stunted boy of 15, and thus could not endure his losses so well as I could endure them. The qualms of conscience which I suffered were lost in my delight in my dawning sexual life. Sometimes I lay on my stomach in bed, and by placing my hand under my scrotum, according to the directions of J., brought up a pretty girl to mind. Just before Sunday school G., our chief reprobate, and the rest of us would hunt out what we considered to be nasty texts of Scripture. The chapter concerning the whoredoms of Aholah and Aholibah gave me an especial pleasure. T. mentioned the giggling that occurred at prayers in the lower dormitory when the details of Esau's birth were read out. A few days before G. was expelled—for exactly what cause I do not know—he told me of how greatly he enjoyed coitus on his grandmother's sofa with a girl of fifteen. When I went home on the boat for holidays I noted the large, black-haired penis of the strong boy of our school. He occupied a state-room with me, but made no sexual overtures.

Since my twelfth year I had been wrapped up all summer long in a boy who was six months my senior. We slept together constantly, but not once did we think of obtaining mutual gratification. On the contrary, we held up high ideals to each other and frowned on masturbation. I took delight in saying that I never had handled myself, and never would do so. Even at the height of my "auto-erotic" period, I skillfully concealed my habits from all my boy friends. A neurotic solo choir boy friend once spoke of obtaining ejaculation, whereupon I expressed utter ignorance of such an act, little hypocrite that I was. This boy told how the house servants joked with him about coitus and made laughing lunges at his organs.

But much as I loved my chum, my most passionate regard went out in my thirteenth year to N., a chubby, blue-eyed, choir-boy of 12. He was a pretty boy to any eye. He was not gifted, except in watersports, and anything but popular either with girls or with boys; yet I grew warm at the mention of his name. He did not care a fig for me. From first to last I had no consciousness of the sexual nature of my passion, and the thought of doing more than embrace and kiss him in an innocent manner never crossed my mind. For two summers I had nights of tossing on my bed (although I almost never was sleepless for any cause) when I would see his dear face and form, in and out of the swimming pool, or engaged perhaps in singing or in showing his beautiful teeth. I seldom was smitten with little girls, and I found myself embarrassed in their company after my ninth year; yet I thought well enough of their looks and ways to enjoy their company at dances. The girls liked me in a platonic way, for I was accounted a good, big, kind, blundering boy with a helping hand for the smallest fry.

During the summer after I was 13, I imagined myself in the early morning, when I was half awake, as persuading my wife to have coitus with me. In the course of my spoken words I kept my hand under my scrotum.

A plump girl-cousin of my own age was visiting at my uncle's during the summer after I was 13. With her I greatly desired to satisfy myself, but I could not be sure that my boy cousin (5 years old) might not find us out, even though she should consent. Once when we three were in the hay-loft a wave of lust rolled over me, but I made no proposal. Night and gaslight greatly increased my *libido*. On one occasion my aunt had gone to the village for ice-cream, and L. and I were left alone in the dining-room. I took her on my lap and had a powerful erection. I almost asked her to play sexually with me in the barn, but instead I spoke of an imaginary girl, the first letters of whose successive names spelled an indecent word for coitus—a word known to almost every Anglo-Saxon child, I fear. L. laughed, but gave no sign of assent. For a neighboring girl of 15 I felt such a drawing that early in the morning I would roll on the floor with my erect organ in my hand in riotous imagining of coitus with her. I walked with her in the woods and sat at her feet, but although I felt instinctively that she would satisfy me without much persuasion, yet I *could not* ask her. One night I started to church in order to walk home with her, and lead her (if possible) to a field where we might gratify ourselves (I picked out the exact grassy spot where we might lie); but when I was almost at the church door my "moral sense" (if that is what it was) rose and dragged me home again.

During the swimming hour I watched the genitals of the boys, comparing them carefully in the most minute details. Circumcised organs affected me as being disagreeable, and men's hairy, coarse genitals I abhorred.

When 13 I became acquainted with the new mail-boy at the inn. He was a city "street-boy," and got me into smoking cigarettes occasionally. I did not definitely take up smoking until I was 16. He told me that a mason once offered him ten cents if he would masturbate the man in a cellar. The boy said that he refused. I slept a few times with an ill-favored boy of fine parentage. He was of my own age, and I had played with him in a natural way for several years, but my increasing sexual desires led me to mutually masturbate with him, and even unsuccessfully to attempt with him mutual *pædicatio*. On the morning after our nights of sensuality I felt "gone" and miserable, but not repentant. By afternoon I was myself again. My relations with G. were purely animal, for I disliked his jealous disposition, his horse-laugh, his features, his form, his withdrawn scrotum and his under-sized penis. At home in the evening I often found myself inflamed with a mental picture of active *fellatio* with him, but I never performed this act, so far as I remember.

One of my great sexual desires was to walk along a fence on which a girl was seated. In order that I might feast my eyes on her pudenda she must not wear drawers.

When I turned 14 I had been, from my unusual size, in long trousers for several months. I entered a private day-school and progressed brilliantly in my studies. I kept up masturbation almost daily, sometimes twice a day, both in the water closet and in bed. I can remember ejaculating before urination in the school *cabinet*. At night I often found myself longing for the return of my sister, seven years my junior, in order that I might embrace her in bed and fondle her genitals. I had done these things during my Christmas vacation of the year before. I mildly reproached myself for such incestuous desires, but they recurred continually. I dreamed little. And I cannot remember the character of my dreams. My waking *libido* spent itself mostly in longings to embrace (without lustful acts) the forms of little boys of exquisite blonde beauty and thick hair. Narcissism may have been present, for in my twelfth year I had been told that at the age of 5 and 6 I was an extraordinarily beautiful little creature with long, lint-white hair. The preferable age was from 6 to 9. My eye was alert on the streets for boys answering to this description, and a street boy with long, white hair so won my passion that I followed him to his home and asked his mother if he might call on me and "play some games." As I did not even know the boy's name and had never seen him before, I was wonderingly refused. I sought in vain to find the whereabouts of another long-haired street boy whom I burned to embrace and load with benefits. I had a boundless desire for such a boy as this to idolize me—to look into my face out of big eyes and lose himself in love for me—to call me by endearing pet names—of his own accord to throw his arms around my neck. This second actual boy disappeared from my horizon by presumably moving away from the vast city neighborhood. I took a fancy to a small boy at school, who possessed the requisite delicacy, timidity, and sweetness, if not the physical requisites, of my beau ideal. I walked with him in the park and planned to have him at the house; but the matter was not arranged. At boarding-school I had associated much with younger and weaker boys, and had been ridiculed much for my cowardice in sports, but at the city school I moved with my equals and won their recognition. Our gymnasium director was middle-aged and of an indolent disposition. He liked to recall his youthful erections and to answer my sexual queries too fully, and cheerfully volunteered information on brothels. Yet I doubt whether he had an evil purpose in conversing with me. I thought I should never dare or want to enter one. I always conjured up the picture of a row of naked women from whom I could take my pick, and the smell of the women I imagined to be identical with the smell of my big friend A. at boarding-school. When I was traveling down town on an elevated train one afternoon the brakeman asked me whether I had ever been in a brothel, and told me that disorderly houses abounded in my neighborhood. "I have had connection with women," said this red-haired young man, waving his hand in greeting to a woman who nodded at him from a window, "since I was 15 years old. Not long ago a fine-looking, young woman in black offered to pay all my expenses if I would live with her and connect with her."

When a girl of perhaps 7, a distant cousin of mine, visited us for a few days, I gratified my lust by placing my hand under her genitals and swinging her to and fro. She giggled with pleasure. That summer I began to experience the evil effects of the masturbation which I had practiced daily for a year and a half. Pimples began to break out on my chin (my complexion up to this time had been white and delicate). The family ascribed my condition to digestive difficulties. In playing with the boys and girls I found myself seized with a terrible shyness and a tendency to look down and weep. I had lost all the courage I had—it had never been great—in the presence of a crowd of children. I was fairly at ease with a single companion. My self-consciousness was something more painful to me than I can convey in words. At home I wept in my room and cursed myself for a baby. I little realized the cause of my nervous collapse. Yet I had too robust a frame not to be able to sleep and to play hard. The sympathetic pleasure which I had found in swinging my girl-cousin to and fro I now doubled by letting a 7-year-old boy ride cock-horse on my feet. I experienced an erection during the process, and I almost induced ejaculation when I tickled the boy with my feet in the region of his genitals. To see his shrinking, giggling joy gave me an exquisite sexual thrill. I longed to sleep with the boy, but I was afraid of causing comment. At the new and large boarding school which I entered in the fall my most lustful dreams and ejaculations were concerned with standing this little boy on the footboard of a bed, taking down his knickerbockers, and performing *fellatio* on him. But I dreamed also of natural coitus. I fell in love with the handsome, 12-year-old son of the aged headmaster. The boy, O., sat next me at the table, and I never tired of gazing at him. It gave me a special sense of pleasure to look at him when he wore a certain flowing, scarlet, four-in-hand necktie. But O. was not attracted to me—for one thing I was in a disagreeably pimpled condition—and I could not induce him to linger in my room nor to sleep with me. My passion for O. did not diminish, and it rose to its supremacy on the evening when he appeared in our hallway (he roomed on the girls' side of the house and hinted at the sexual sights that he saw) in a costume of white satin, lace, and wings. He was ready for a costume party.

I now masturbated less frequently, for I was beginning to appreciate the horrible consequences of my indulgence. I had frequent pollutions, with dreams. My day was one long agony of fear. How I dreaded to go to sleep in the same bed with my older chum, who never made any advances beyond embracing me passively *cum erectione* while he was asleep. My day was one long agony of fear. At meal time my feet constantly writhed in agony for fear that the headmaster's grown up young ladies should make fun of me, or that my lack of facial composure and my inability to look people in the eye might be commented upon. I tingled with apprehension, especially in the region of my stomach. Every nerve was taut in the effort I made to appear composed. I masturbated with erections over nothing. Greek recitations were for me an *auto da fe*. My heart beat like a trip-hammer at the thought of getting up to recite, and once on my feet my voice shook and my mind wandered. I hated the thought of people behind me looking at me. I rarely summoned the courage to turn my head either one way or the other. I vastly admired the "bravery" of the small, 15-year-old boy who recited so calmly and so well. I was too cowardly to play foot-ball and base-ball, and I dreaded even my favorite tennis because the spectators put me in a state of scared self-consciousness. Knowing my own condition, I was yet so blind to it most of the time, and such a Jekyll-and-Hyde, that I actually pitied a boy of 19 who was an eccentric and a scared victim of masturbation. But in spite of my neuropathic condition I developed intellectually. I do not touch upon this aspect of my life, however, because I am trying to limit myself strictly to sexual manifestations. At the present time I have not the courage to continue the narrative.

HISTORY III.—The following narrative is written by a clergyman, age 40, unmarried:—

My childhood and early boyhood were unmarked by sexual phenomena, beyond occasional erections, which commenced when about 5 years of age, without any exciting causes. These were accompanied by some degree of excitement, of the same nature as that which I experienced in later years. I was absolutely ignorant of sexual matters, but always had an idea that the essential difference between man and woman was to be found in the genital organs. This was sometimes a matter for thought and curiosity.

Being for many years an only child I saw little of other children, and formed the habit of amusing myself with making things—boats, houses, etc.—and acquired a taste for science. When I could read I preferred biography, history. and poetry to anything else.

When I was 13 years old and at a large school I heard for the first time of coitus, but very imperfectly. For a few days it filled my thoughts and mind, but feeling it was too engrossing a subject and one which took me off better things, I put it out of my mind. Later, another boy gave me a fuller description of the matter, and I began to have a great desire to know more and to be old enough to practice it. I also discovered that boys masturbated, and about a year after tried the experiment for myself. This vice was largely indulged in by my school-fellows. It never occurred to me that it was sinful, until I was nearly 16, when I came across a passage in Kenns's *Manual of School-boys*, in which it was hinted such things were wrong morally and spiritually. Previously I had felt it was an indelicate and shameful thing, and bad for health. This last idea was held as a solemn fact by all my boy friends. Gradually religion began to exert an influence over my sexual nature, obtaining as years passed a greater and greater restraining power. It is simply impossible for me to write a history of my sexual development without also describing the action which Christianity has had in determining its growth. The two have been so intimately bound together that my life history would not be a faithful record of facts if I left religion out of it.

At school I took part, with great keenness, in cricket and football, and was very ambitious to excel in everything in which I took an interest, but I always had other tastes as well, which were more precious to me, for example, the love for science, history, and poetry. Until I was past 16 years my desire was simply for coitus, girls and women attracted me only as affording the means of gratifying this desire; but when I was nearly 17 I began to regard girls as beautiful objects, apart from this, and to desire their love and companionship. At the same time it dawned upon me that life held much of joy in the love of women and in domestic life—so henceforth I regarded them in a higher and purer light, and apart from sexual gratification. In fact, from this period till I was over 20, this idea so dominated my whole being that the lower side of my nature was entirely held in subjection and abeyance by it. It was rather repulsive to think of girls as objects of lust. This state of mind was not brought about by any romantic attachment or through any acquaintance or through circumstances. I was living in great seclusion and had no girl friends. After this period the lower side of my nature woke up as a giant refreshed with wine, and I underwent for many years a constant struggle with my nature, in which religion always triumphed in the end. I never fell into fornication, though sometimes into the vice of masturbation. These outbursts of desire were periodic, about ten or fourteen days apart, and would last several days. I must record also the fact that from the time this awakening took place my ideal views of woman no longer seemed incompatible with sexual relations. I noticed that at about 27 there was a lessening of the desire, but that may have been due to overwork and consequent nervous exhaustion. I had a good deal of worry and studied daily for about eight hours. In any case the impulse was strongest during the years above mentioned. A little later in life, for a time, I became attached to a girl, and eventually engaged. I then observed, greatly to my sorrow and annoyance, that whenever I met this lady, or even thought of her, erections took place. This was particularly painful to me, as my thoughts were not of a lustful or impure character. Sometimes sitting by her at a religious service this would occur, when certainly my mind was far away from anything of the kind. That was the first woman ever kissed by me, except of course members of my immediate family circle. Later on my thoughts turned to marriage, and there was a great longing at times for this event to take place. However, as this attachment afterward became the great sorrow of my life for years, it needs no more comment. This closes one chapter of my history, and at present I do not propose to add another, as in a great measure it is only partly written. It may be well here to state that there has never been in me the slightest homosexual desire; in fact it has always appeared as a thing utterly inconceivable and disgustingly loathsome. I am fond of the society of both men and women, but on the whole prefer the latter. I have had several warm and intimate though platonic friendships, and get on exceedingly well with the other sex, although not a good-looking man. I have always been attracted to women by their spiritual or mental qualities, rather than by physical beauty, and feel strongly that the latter alone would never cause me to desire coitus. Unless there was an attraction other than that of the flesh, I should feel that I was following simply a brute instinct, and it would jar with my higher nature and cause revulsion. This was not the case in my earlier years to the same extent. I have often wondered whether the sexual impulse was strong in me or not, but if not, there is nothing in my physical state or family history to account for it. I am fairly cognizant with the lives of my ancestors, being descended from two old families. The sexual instinct was certainly not weak or abnormal in them. Personally, I am tall and healthy, well built, but sensitive and highly strung. Smell has never played any part in my life as a stimulant of sexual desire, and the mere thought of body odors would have a very decided effect in the opposite direction. Touch and sight appeal to me strongly, and of the two the former most.

I am convinced, after many years careful thought, that sexual vice and perversion could be greatly reduced if the young were instructed in the elements of physiology as they bear on this question. Personally, had I been thus enlightened much sin would have been avoided in my schoolboy days, and a perverted view of sexual matters would never have arisen in my mind. It took years to overcome the feeling that all such things were unclean and defiling. Eventually light came to me through reading a passage in a tractate on the Creed by Rufinus. He was defending the doctrine of the Incarnation against the pagan objection that it was an unclean and disgusting idea that God should enter the world through the womb of the Blessed Virgin Mary, and he meets it by showing that God created the sexual organs, therefore the objection is invalid—otherwise God would not be clean or pure, having Himself designed them and their functions. This passage is slight in itself, but gave birth to a line of thought which has influenced me profoundly. I no longer regard sexual matters as disgusting and unholy, but as intensely sacred, being the outcome of the Divine Mind. Further, the Incarnation of the Saviour has not only sanctioned motherhood and all that is implied by it, but has eternally sanctified it as the means chosen for the manifestation of God to the world. I should not obtrude my theological conceptions, but for the fact that they have determined my life-history in that aspect.

HISTORY IV.—When I was 9 years old a boy at the preparatory school, which I attended, showed me the act of masturbation, which he said he had practiced for a long time, and which he urged me to imitate, if I wished to become a father when I grew up, and married! Boy-like I believed him and tried, but the sensation obtained was not a pleasant one (I suppose that I was too rough with myself) and I desisted.

When I was about 12 years old, a schoolfellow told me that he had seen his nurse copulating with the groom, and he and I used to haunt the woods in the hope that we might see an amorous couple so engaged, but without success. We often talked of the act, as to how it was done. Neither he nor I had any clear ideas on the subject, save as to the organs involved. I was about 15 when a maidservant of the house in which I was a boarder, came to my bedroom one night and taught me how to masturbate her. She said that this was a good thing for me to do, and warned me never to "play with myself" as it would kill me, or drive me mad. I told her that I had tried it, but could not bring on a pleasurable feeling, so she did it to me, and although I did not have an emission, I derived great pleasure from the act. She told me that it never did a boy any harm to let a girl play with his parts, and promised that if I would keep the secret, she would often do this for me. Naturally I promised to say nothing, and she often came up to my room. Later on she used to insert my penis into her vulva, while she was rubbing it, at the same time giving me a pigeon kiss. This *modus operandi* was much appreciated by me. One night, after we had been together thus, I dreamt of her and her maneuvers and had my first emission. I was very proud of this, as I considered that I had at last attained to man's estate, and told her of it. She never allowed me to insert my penis into her vulva after that, alleging that she did not want to have a baby.

I was about 16½ years old when I had my first real coitus, my partner in the act being a girl some two years older than I, who lived near us. I enjoyed the act very much, as she permitted, nay insisted on, emission *intra vaginam*, and told her that this was much nicer than my amours with the maidservant which of course I had confided to her. She laughed, and said: "Of course." We often copulated, as long as I was at home, and then I lost sight of her. Of all the women with whom I have had to do, save one, she had the most copious secretion of mucus, which in those days I believed was the woman's semen. Her thighs used to be wet with it.

At the University I had regular relations with women of all sorts, rarely missing a week. Two of them were married women, one the wife of a solicitor, the other of a doctor. How proud I felt of my first intrigue with a married woman! I felt that I was really a man of the world now!

But though my friends used to tell me all about their love affairs, and I longed to confide in them, I did not do so. This was because when I went up to the University, my uncle said that he would give me a word of advice and hoped that I would follow it—never to give away a woman, and never to refuse to respond to a woman's advances, whoever she were. To neglect this advice would, he said, be foolish, and to break the rules "damned ungentlemanly." I wish I had always followed advice proffered, as closely as I have followed this. One night, when I was somewhat disguised in liquor, as our grandfathers would have put it, I picked up a girl, who was a private prostitute, if the phrase be permissible. She declined copulation, and proposed other means of satisfaction. I insisted, being stubborn in my cups. Had I been sober I should have done as she suggested, for I have always made it a point to allow the woman to choose the method of gratification, and not to demand, or even suggest, anything myself. I like to please women, and I have always been curious as to their wants and desires, as revealed, without outside influence, by themselves. The result of my refusing all methods of gratification save the most ordinary was that the girl, who must have known that she was not all right, but shrank from saying so in so many words, gave me a gonorrhœa, which lasted nine weeks and much interfered with my amours, as I naturally declined to run the risk of infecting my partner, a risk which to my certain knowledge many a young fellow has run, with disastrous consequence to the confiding woman. As it was due to my tipsy obstinacy, I could not blame the girl, but resolved never to drink too much again, a resolve which I have kept, save once, unbroken. In those days we youngsters thought that it was manly to be able to carry one's liquor well, and did all in our power to attain to the seasoned head; but I considered that the risks entailed were too serious to be neglected.

I was well on in my 26th year when I met a widow with whom I fell in love, with the result that I married her. She is a most sensible woman, and it was her intellectual gifts which were the attraction to me. In my amours intellect has never played a part. She has all along been cognizant of, and lenient to, my polygamous tendencies; for she recognizes the fact that whatever *fredaine* I may have on hand makes not the slightest difference in my love and respect for her. Were she a more sensual woman, perhaps things would be different.

In all I have had to do with 81 other women, of whose special characteristics I kept a careful note at the time. Twenty-six were normal women with whom my *liasons* have lasted long, so I know more about them than I do about the other fifty-five, who were prostitutes, and with some of whom my dealings were but for an afternoon.

The races represented have been these, for I have seen a bit of the world: English, Scotch, Irish, Welsh, French, German, Italian, Greek, Danish, Hungarian, Roumanian, Indian, and Japanese. Taking them all round, the only difference that I found between old and young women is that the older ones are less selfish, and more complaisant, and less inclined to resent one's being unable to attain to the height of their desire, for from time to time I have been unable to "come up to the scratch" after a heavy night's labor, or when I was afraid of being caught in the act of coition, a fear which, in my experience, acts as a stimulus to desire in women, unlike its action in men. Of all the women with whom I have had to do the nicest in every way have been the French women. The English women of the town drink too much, and are far too keen on getting as much money as they can for as little as they can, to please me. Were the London girls to recognize that men do not like a tipsy woman, and that where there is so much competition the person who is most skillful and most polite gets the most custom, the alien invasion in Regent street would soon come to an end.

Of the fifty-five prostitutes: eighteen informed me that they were in the habit of masturbating; eight of their own free will, without asking for reward, did *fellatio*; six asked me to do *cunnilingus*, which I naturally declined to do; three proposed anal coitus. Of those who did *fellatio*, two (one French and one German) told me that they had taken to it because they had heard that human semen was an excellent remedy against consumption, which disease had carried off some of their relatives, and that they had gradually come to like doing it. All who told me that they masturbated, asked me whether I did so too, and two desired me to show them the act, one alleging that she liked to see a man do it; she had been married late in life, after a "stormy youth" and had had, she said, a large experience of the male sex. They all seemed to think that however much the practice of self-excitement might hurt a man, and all thought that it would hurt him, a woman might masturbate as often as she liked, failing better means of satisfaction, as she had no such loss of substance as a man.

Of the twenty-six normal women, whom I knew more intimately than I did the fifty-five prostitutes, thirteen, without being questioned be me, blurted out the fact that they were habitual masturbators, apparently all required to think of the loved person to obtain full satisfaction. *Fellatio* was proposed, and fully performed, by nine, of whom three experienced the orgasm as soon as they perceived that I had attained to it. All were more or less excited while doing it. One proposed anal coitus, "just to see what it was like;" and three proposed *cunnilingus*, one having been initiated by a girl friend, and one by her husband. The third had, I believe, evolved the act out of her own inner consciousness in her desire to experience pleasure with me. My relations with one of the twenty-six were confined to my masturbation of her, the while she did *fellatio*, as she said that she "had no feeling inside down there."

With two exceptions my partings from these normal women have not been tragic and all whom I have met in after life (seven) have been very ready to resume relations with me, four of them having made the proposal themselves.

One thing has struck me, and that is the, often great, difference that exists between what a woman's looks lead one to think she is, and what she is when one becomes her lover; the most sensual woman that I have met might have sat for her portrait as the Madonna, and she was the only one who took pleasure in hearing and relating "smoking-room stories," a form of amusement which, perhaps from their want of appreciation of humor and wit, women do not indulge in—at least in my experience.

HISTORY V.—(A continuation of History III in Appendix B to the previous volume.)

As I became better I commenced to dream of true love. I wondered, too, if my horrible past really could be lived down and a young woman come to love *me*. I took pleasure in reading love poems, especially Browning's, and illustrated some with little water-colors. . . .

I was sitting in the stalls one night seeing a performance by a company of English actors when one of them played so badly that I thought to myself: "Why, hang it, I could play it better myself!" The next minute another thought followed: "Why not try?" I came out of the stalls the proverbial stage-struck youth. I was sitting in the same place another night when the young man next to me entered into conversation. By a strange coincidence he knew a few young men, amateurs, who were going to form a company, give up their situations and travel, if they could induce a few more to join them and put a little money in. I made an appointment for the following evening. . . .

There were lots of meetings in bedrooms and rehearsals between the beds, but ultimately I was told a school-room had been engaged and a professional actress, A. F. I went to the school-room and found all the boys there, and a young woman with a pale, rice-powder complexion. On introduction she gazed at me as if struck dumb. If she had been better-looking (I thought her vulgar and puffy) I would have been flattered. I was disappointed, but rather frightened (she had a stage presence) of her professional ability, especially when we commenced to rehearse. I had to make love to her, too, which embarrassed me. She had a good profile, I noticed, and would have been better looking, I thought, if she were in better condition, for she was young, about my own age, twenty-three or four. We were all young—enjoyed our rehearsals, and had lots of fun—but I did not respond to the advances A. was evidently making to me. Finally we started on our tour. As the weeks went on A. F., like the others, improved wonderfully in health and appearance. If we had had anything like houses it would have been a pleasant trip. My strangeness did not escape the notice of the boys altogether, for I was still a bit strange in mind and nerves— and deeply religious, bowing my head before each meal and reading my little Bible and prayer-book at odd times. I drank no alcohol. I spent a good deal of time by myself or with my faithful companion A., who was nearly always at my side, she and her appealing eyes. I was surprised to see how quickly she had improved; she looked quite attractive and ladylike some evenings at meals, but I only tolerated her. I was selfish and conceited.

Things had been going on like this for a week—always playing to empty houses and our money lower and lower—when A. said to our other lady, Mrs. T., on a train in my presence: "I shall have to give him up, I suppose; he will have nothing to do with me." Mrs. T. said: "You give him up, do you?" and looked at me as if she were going to try her hand. A. said "Yes," and looked at me, smiling sadly. I don't know what motive prompted me—whether my vanity was alarmed at her threatened desertion or that she had really made some impression on me by her love, probably a little of both—but I said: "No, don't; come and sit down here," making way for her, and she joyfully came and nestled against me. From that time I ceased to treat her with ridicule, and kissed her at other times than when on the stage. I was subject still to black moods, and would not speak to her for hours sometimes, but she seemed content to walk with me and was infinitely patient. I had heard she was living with—if not married to—an actor. I asked her about him once, and she said she did not love him; she loved me and had never loved before. Her face had a touching sadness; her life had been unhappy and stormy, with no love and little rest in it. Her face, when she had lost her dissipated look and unhealthy pallor, was exquisite, delicate as a cameo. Love had improved her manners, too; she was more gentle and refined. I let things drift without thinking of the future, when one night after the performance—I was lying on the sofa and A. was sitting at my side, as usual—I suddenly thought, with the brutality that characterized me in these matters—"I will ask her to let me sleep with her." I still fought against any premonitory thought of self-abuse, but here, I thought to myself, is a chance of something better that will do me no harm and perhaps good. When she understood me she turned very red and walked away, shaking her head. But I let her understand that was the only way of retaining me, and finally, when they had all gone to bed, she gave herself to me, reluctantly and sadly; for she, too, had been drifting on without thinking of anything of this sort (she hated it at this time), but just living for her love of me, her first true love.

Before this occurred, I must tell you, I had been so much better that I sometimes felt capable of doing anything, a sense of power and grasp of intellect which was combined with delicacy of feeling and sensitiveness to beauty, to skies and clouds and flowers. I seemed to be awakening to true manhood, to my true self. And at meals, it is worth recording, I commenced to have a distaste for meat.

These glimpses of a better state of things left me on cohabiting with A., and for a time my gloom and black religious mania came on me once more. I now thought of my promise at confirmation, and it seemed to me I had offended beyond pardon. When we came to the next town, however, I openly slept with A. all night, leaving my own bed untouched. When we returned to Adelaide one of our party remarked: "The only man who had any success with the women on the tour was a Bible-reading, praying, and good, pious, confirmed Christian."

A.'s nascent beauty and delicacy and improvement were gradually impaired, too. My own conduct became so morose at times that, besides increasing her misery, I offended the others, and bickerings ensued. I heard the other actress say "He's mad; that what's the matter." And I was so wrapped up in myself and my religious mania that I did not mind their thinking so.

After the tour was over A. asked me to come and see her at her home, and as I missed her very much I went one night to tea. She had a room in her father's house to herself. A. was dressed in her best and we had an affectionate meeting. After tea I asked her if she were married to E. She said "No." Then I said: "Who are you married to?" She commenced to cry then, and told me something of her life, the saddest I ever heard. When only 17 she had been courted by a young man she did not care for, but who prevailed on her parents by pretending he had seduced her, but wished to marry her. Strange as it may seem, A. did not know what marriage meant, her mother being one of those silly women who don't like talking of these things and let their daughters grow up in ignorance, expecting they will learn from some one. In nine cases out of ten this happens, but A. was an exception. It was this, and the fact that she had not a particle of love for her husband, that gave her such a hatred of coition. When her mother saw the sheets the morning after the marriage she burst out crying; she did not like the young man and saw she had been deceived.

A.'s husband soon showed his true character; he was in reality a gaol-bird. He beat her, drank, and even wanted her to go on the streets to earn money for him. She left him and went home; it was then she began her theatrical career by entering the ballet. At intervals her husband, drunk and desperate, would waylay and threaten her in the street. One day after a rehearsal he attempted to stab her. She got on in spite of all, being a born actress, and played small parts in traveling companies. Then E., who had also gone on the stage, courted her and she listened to him, not because she cared for him, but he protected her and offered her a home. She joined him; but his drunkenness and sensuality were so gross that he ruined his health and he attempted to maltreat A. in a nameless way. And whenever she was in the family way he would leave her alone and half-conscious in the cellar for days. To add to her misery she had epileptic fits. Then sometimes they would be out of an engagement and starving. They had been so hungry as to steal raw potatoes out of a sack and eat them thus, having no fire. She would often have had engagements, but E. was jealous and would not let her act without him. And he beat her as her husband had done, and her health became undermined. It was just after one of the forced miscarriages that she joined our traveling company, and that accounted for her yellow and puffy appearance. E. was now away up-country with a circus, but was expected down any time. A. told me a good deal of all this, between her tears, while sitting at my feet, and her tone carried conviction. When I ought to have gone home I persuaded her to let me stay all night. We had been in bed some time when her mother knocked at the door and wanted to come in for something in a chest of drawers there. "Why don't you open the door, A.? Who have you got there? Hasn't that fellow gone?" A. was confused and told me to get under the bed, but I refused, and she covered me up with the bed clothes as well as she could and opened the door. She had hid my clothes, but missed one of my shoes, and her mother saw it. "Oh, A.," was all she said; "you've got that fellow in bed," and went out crying. "Well, Fred" (my stage name), "you've got me into a nice row," A. said. She gave me my breakfast in the morning and I walked out of the front door without being molested. Another night I entered her window by a ladder and stayed all night. In the middle of the night E. came home drunk. She would not let him in and told him she would have nothing more to do with him. He attempted to break in the door, when A. called to me, and hearing a man in the room he went away, saying, as he went downstairs: "Oh, A.! Oh, A.!" as if he thought she would not have done such a thing. He never molested us after that night.

I think it was my intention, at first, to break off with A. gradually. I found, however, I could not keep away from her, and it commenced to be evident to me that a bachelor's life in lodgings again would be dreary and lonely. And all this time the fear that I had offended God troubled me more than I have said, and it occurred to me (there may have been a touch of sophistry in this, or not) that if I were a true husband to her for the future—stuck to her and worked for her for the rest of my days —perhaps it would find favor in God's sight and be an atonement for my sin. Had she been free I would have married her, I believe. But she began to be harassed by her mother and bothered about my incessantly coming there and staying all night. It ended in my telling her I would be a husband to her, and she came and lived with me at my lodgings. We had one room and our meals cost us sixpence each. Cheap as it was, it was a struggle for me to earn money at all. I remember feeling ill and anxious once, and sustaining myself by the thought of my father wheeling the heavy truck up the street when he married my mother. And I decided to wheel my truck, too.

A. seemed happy and her love increased, if possible; at first, though, she must have found me a trying lover, for I made her kneel and pray with me two or three times a day, which she did with such a queer expression of face. Sometimes her feelings got the better of her, and she would say: "Oh, damn it, Fred, you are always praying." And then I would be shocked and she would be sorry. . . . Coitus was frequent; she commenced to like it now. . . .

A. was not looking well one evening when she came in, and lay down on the bed. Presently she commenced to make a strange noise, and I saw her eyes were closed and her hands clenched. "Ah," said the landlady, who came in to help me; "she has epileptic fits." When her convulsions were over she looked blankly at us, knitting her brows and evidently puzzling her poor brain to remember who we were. For many years it was my fate to see her looking at me thus, at first stony and estranged, like a dweller in another star, then half-recalling with extended hand, then forgetting again with hand to mouth, then the gradual dawn of memory and love, and final full recognition. "It's Fred, my Fred!" I never got used to it; it always moved me to tears. . . . It was not to be thought that we had no quarrels. I still had fits of bad temper, and sometimes they came into collision with A.'s temper. It hurt my vanity considerably to see how soon she relinquished the respectful, patient, spaniel-bearing she had when we were traveling. I said some cruel things to her and she retorted. One would have thought, to hear us, that all affection was over. But when the mood of rage wore itself out we would both be sorry and make it up with tears, and be very happy in spite of our poverty.

I think it was lust that prevented me from striving to fulfill my ambitions. A. let me do anything I liked, at all times of day or night, although she seemed surprised at my proceedings sometimes, for it was becoming a fever of lubricity with me. She still thought only of her love. I remember her coming in one day, tired, pale, perspiring, and worried—we had hardly anything in the house and she had been to the theater ineffectually—and when her eyes lighted on me the whole expression of her face changed, softened and brightened at once, and she came and kissed me and said: "It is so strange, I was thinking all sorts of nasty things coming along, but as soon as I see my pet's face I feel happy—I don't care for anything—I would sooner share a crust with him than have all the money in the world!"

I commenced to feel libidinous curiosity to examine her—this was mostly on Sundays—and she let me, blushing at first, but laughing. Then I would try new positions in coitus I had heard of. Still she did not enter into my mood.

She was engaged at this time to play in a pantomime and I commenced to lead a miserable, jealous existence. I heard scandal about her, baseless enough, but in the diseased, nervous, anxious state I had brought myself to it nearly drove me mad. I would go with her sometimes to visit her mother, whom I began to like. Her brother I still saluted coldly. It caused me horror and jealousy to see A. kissing him and letting him tickle her. In my rage, when we came home, I even said that perhaps she would let him do something else, naming it brutally and coarsely. I remember her shame, astonishment, indignation and tears. If ever a man tried a woman's love I did. But she forgave me, even that.

We went to live in a little cottage. It was in this cottage that A. first showed signs of lust, and in the diseased state of my mind, instead of regretting it, I encouraged her. She told me one day that the orgasm very often did not occur at the same time with her as with me, and that it would not unless I put my little finger into the anus. This her husband taught her, and she would rather have died than confess it to me when we first met. We would often devote our Sundays to having a picnic as we termed our lustful bouts, stimulating ourselves with wine. Her temper was not improved thereby (though her fits entirely stopped for a twelvemonth)—we had wordy warfares, but we made it up again always with tears. Nor did I allow myself to deteriorate without reactions and excursions into better things. I was always reading Emerson; it was he who rescued me from orthodox Christianity and taught me to trust in myself and in Nature. I have never ceased this struggle towards better things to this day. There, in a nutshell, is my life; I have always been defeated when temptation came, but I have never ceased to struggle. I determined to be more abstemious in sexual indulgence and asked her to help me. She agreed willingly, for she was easily led. Whenever we fell back again into excess it was my fault.

At a theatrical performance we first met a Miss T., a young German who sang. She was about 25, with modest, quiet and engaging manners. A. and she became very friendly. I liked her; she was tall, dark and lithe, but had bad teeth.

I had been ill and at this time A. and I had a quarrel, my temper suddenly breaking out in murderous frenzy. I called her names and finally put her outside the house, telling her to go to her mother: I suffered a very hell of remorse and misery. Everything in the quiet, lonely house reminded me of her, seemed fragrant of her; my anguish became so keen I could not stop in the house, though I was just as wretched walking about. I kept this up for two days, when I met her coming to look for me. One look was enough—"A.!" "Pet!" in broken sobs—and in tears we kissed and made it up. Miss T. was with her, and I greeted her, too, with happy tears in my eyes. Another time, when A. was giving way to *her* temper, and one would have thought all love was dead, I said "Don't you love me then?" and the word alone was a talisman, her face changed, she held out her arms and began to sob quietly. . . She accepted an offer to travel with a small theatrical company who were going up-country. She was not looking well when I left and after a time I received a telegram telling me to come to her at once as she was ill. Dreading all sorts of things I borrowed my fare and went to her. I knew nothing of women, of their point of view and different code of honor, and was very far from the attitude of Guy de Maupassant who said he liked women all the better for their charmingly deceitful ways. A. wanted to see me and had taken the surest means to ensure my coming. I was angry at first, but she looked so well and was so loving that I could not be angry long.

One day when I was working the landlady came in and began talking about A. and her conduct before I came. She had gone into the actors' rooms at all hours, the woman said, and drank and been as bad as the rest in her conversation. It was the second time a married woman had run her down to me, and I commenced to think there might be something in it, and suffered all my mad jealousy over again. Not knowing the freedom actors and actresses allow themselves on tour, without there being necessarily anything in it, I worried till I thought I had nothing to do but die. And then one of the great struggles of my life occurred. Walking the country roads, I asked myself: "If it *is* true, if she has been unfaithful, will you forgive her and help her to arrive at her best?" For a long time the answer was "No!" But perhaps my striving for unity with myself had done some good, and the final resolution was for forgiveness. I felt more peace of mind then, and when I told a dying consumptive lodger in the house what the land-lady had said, he replied, "Don't you believe a word of it. I know she loves you!" . . . .

After an absence I found myself one evening in a town where A. was performing. I went round to the back and they told me she had gone to a room in the hotel to change for another part. I followed and entered the room, with a glass of spirits I found that an effeminate young actor was bringing to her. She was half undressed, her beautiful arms and shoulders bare. My arrival was unexpected and she looked at me surprised, I thought coldly, as I reproached her for not keeping a promise she had made to me to touch no alcohol during the tour, but soon her arms were round my neck. She cried like a child. She was bigger and handsomer and healthier. There was not only an increased strength and size, but an increased delicacy and sweetness; her eyes and brows were lovely; there was an indescribable bloom and fragrance on her, such as the sun leaves on a peach; the traveling, country air, and freedom from coitus (had I known it) had enabled her to arrive at her true self, not only a beautiful woman, but a woman of fascination, of wit, vivacity and universal *camaraderie*. Her face was like the dawn; all my fears and jealousy left me like a cloud that melts before the sun. I remember the look on her face as she embraced me in bed that night. It had just the very smallest touch of sensuality, but was more like some beautiful child's who is being caressed by one she loves; this divine, drowsy-eyed, adorable look I had never seen on her face before—nor have I since.

We fell back into our old lustful ways. Later on A. became ill and the black devil of epilepsy returned. I became gloomy. . . A rest-lessness and selfish brutality came over me; our love and peace were gone. I persuaded A. to go to Melbourne and look out for an engage-ment. The day before she was to sail we went to Glenelg for a trip. The sea air, as often happened, precipitated A.'s fits. We had gone down to the pier and A. said she felt bad. I just managed to support her to the hotel before she became stiff, and I made some impatient remark (for she nearly dragged me down) which she heard, not being quite uncon-scious and said half incoherently and very pitiably: "Be kind, oh, be kind!" repeating it after consciousness left her. Her heart had been breaking all day at the prospect of parting, and also, I expect, because I was so ready to part with her. That moment was a crisis in my life. I was in a murderous humor, but she looked so unutterably wretched that it seemed impossible to be anything but kind. I made myself speak lovingly to her, in moments of partial consciousness, hired a room, car-ried her up, and nursed her and petted her all night. The act of self-control, and forcing myself to be kind whatever I felt, became a habit in time, a sort of second nature.

In a few days she sailed. When she had gone I was remorseful and mad with myself. How could I let her go by herself? I resolved to follow her as speedily as possible, and did so.

If I remember rightly I came to the conclusion about this time that we ought not to have coition unless we felt great love for each other. It seemed to corroborate this to a certain extent that A. always seemed more electric and pleasant to the touch when we had connection for love and not for lust. Leave it to Nature, I would say to myself. I began to feel how much my struggles, efforts and temperate living had improved me. I had more self-respect, though something of the old self-consciousness was still left. I did not get better continuously, but in an up-and-down zigzag. I still had moods of rage approaching madness and periods of neurotic depression. Long walks decidedly helped to cure me, and the sea, sun, wind, clouds and trees colored my dreams at night very sweetly. I frequently dreamed I was walking in orchards or forests, and a deeper, slightly melancholy but potent savor, as of a diviner destiny, was on my soul.

After a long absence, during which she had frequently been ill, A. joined me. I could see she was recovering from fits, which I began to realize that she had more frequently in absence from me, and also from drinking, perhaps. She was small and thin, but fresh and sweet as honey, and all signs of fits and tempers passed away from her face, so wonderful in its changes. I had become so healthy through my abstinence, temperance and long walks that our meeting was a new revelation to me of how delicate, fragrant and divine a convalescent woman may be. She was glad and surprised to see me looking so well, and if she put her hand on my arm I felt a joyous thrill. I was certainly a better man for abstaining and she a better woman and I determined not to have connection unless we were carried away by our love. As a matter of fact we did not give way to excess, though we were very loving. I tried to persuade myself that we had not gone back to our old ways, but I could not do so long.

Miss T. put in an appearance every day. She did not look so innocent, but as it was no business of mine I did not trouble. She seemed more attached to A. than ever. . . . A. was still very loving with me, but it was an effort to me to keep up to her pitch, and when A. proposed to go to Melbourne with Miss T. to sell off the furniture before settling in Adelaide, I was rather glad of the opportunity of abstaining from coitus and of watching myself to see if I again improved. When A. and Miss T. came to see me before going down to the steamer, A. was nearly crying and Miss T., changed from the old welcome friend, was not only pale and anxious, but looked guilty as if she had some treachery in her mind; she could not meet my eye. I thought less of it then than afterwards. And once more I took long walks at night and rose early to catch the freshness of the mornings.

Some time before this I had read a book advocating a vegetarian diet, and at this time I chanced to read Pater's beautiful "Denys L'Auxerrois," the imaginary portrait of a young vine-dresser, who was attractive beyond ordinary mortals and lived, until his fall and deterioration, on fruit and water. The words, "a natural simplicity in living" remained in my memory. I resolved to read more carefully the book on scientific diet. Who can say, I thought, what changes for the better may come to me if I live on a strictly scientific and natural diet?

I fasted one whole day, and then had a breakfast of cherries, in the middle of the day a meal of fruit, and walking in the afternoon—a gray, rainy day—I felt so light, so different, and the gray sky looked so sweet and familiar, that I was reminded of the luminous visions of my boyhood. It was a distinct revelation. This Pan-like, almost Bacchic feeling, did not last, however, nor was I always able to maintain my new method of diet, though I tried to do so. I made the attempt, however, but I imagine I was more than usually run down. I would walk miles in the hope of feeling less restless. One holiday I walked down to Glenelg, having only had grapes for my dinner, and lying on the beach I looked through a strong binocular glass I had borrowed at the girls bathing. And the beauty of their faces in their frames of hair, of their arms, of their figures, seen through their wet clinging dresses, satisfied me and filled me with joy, gave me for a short time that peace and content—in harmony with the strong sunlight on the waves and the rhythmic surf on the shore—I was seeking. The summer evenings on the pier or along the beach had a peculiar savor; one felt the youth and beauty there even on dark nights, the air was fragant with them, white dresses and summer hats disappearing down the beach or over the sand hills. It was easy—doubtless justifiable sometimes—to put a lewd construction on these disappearances; but I felt it need not have been so; that it was not necessary that youth and beauty, even the sexual act itself if led up to by love, should be a subject of giggling and sniggering. I always left the beach and its flitting summer dresses with a sigh.

A., after writing once, ceased writing at all and once more her mother and I were left in a state of anxiety and suspense. At last I determined to go to Melbourne to look for her, the only clue I had being a remark in her letter that a certain actor was giving her an engagement. In Melbourne I could not find any traces of her for some days and what traces I did find of her were not calculated to allay my anxious fears. One hotel-keeper told me that some one of A's name had stayed there with another hussy (giving Miss T's stage name): "There were nice carryings on with the pair of them." I thought of Miss T's strange looks, but could not imagine what hold she had on A., for A. loved me, I knew. I seemed to be in an inextricable maze. I could settle to nothing and was thinking of applying to the police when I heard that the actor A. had mentioned had taken his company to the Gippsland lakes. I followed to Sale, found the actor and was told that A. was not there. "She slipped me at the last moment," he said, "and remained in Melbourne." I returned to my lodgings, with my anxiety and nervous restlessness increased tenfold. But suddenly my fear and restlessness left me like a cloud. I felt quiet, young, peaceful, able to enjoy the country. A. was doubtless all right and would be able to explain her silence. I undressed leisurely and happily, thinking of the stars,

The next day, Sunday, I awoke refreshed and still at peace. After breakfast, hearing children's voices, I went out into the garden and there was a collision of souls who somehow were affinities. A young girl about twelve or younger with a fine presence and handsome face fixed her eyes on me for half a minute and then came and sat on my knee. She was one of those children I am accustomed to call "love-children," because they are so much brighter, healthier, larger and more loving than others. I always imagine more love went to their making. We fell in love and she said, stroking my beard, "Oh, you are pretty!" and I said, "And so are you!" We were so affectionate that the servant called the child away and I went for a walk, finding my little sweetheart waiting for me on my return. The touch of her hand was electric and her voice fresh and musical. I kissed her, but had become more self-conscious since the morning and wondered if her mother or the servant were looking, or even of they would appear. I was not so frank and natural as my little chum. I have often thought of her since. She had the breadth of forehead, the strength and yet lightness of limb, together with the hands and feet, not too small, that I always imagine the dwellers in Paradise will have.

I returned to Melbourne and continued trying to find A. At the same time I commenced in earnest to live on fruit and brown bread only, and enjoyed better tone and health every day, so that it was a joy to walk down the street in the sun and exchange glances with passengers à la old Walt. One day in the Botanical Gardens veils seemed to be lifted off my eyes. I could look straight at the sun and taking my note of color from that golden light I turned my eyes on the flowers, the mown grass, the trees, and for the first time perceived what a heavenly color green is, what divine companions flowers are, and what a blue sky really means. For half an hour I was in Paradise, and to complete my joy Nature revealed to me a new and unexpected secret.

I was lying on a bench, basking, and my silk shirt coming open the strong sun made its way to my breast and presently I felt a totally new sensation there. I had discovered the last joy of the skin. My skin, fed by healthy fruit-made blood, must have functioned normally under the excitation of the sun just then (for a brief space only, alas!). I cannot describe the joy, any more than I could describe the taste of a peach to one who has only eaten apples: it was satisfying, divine. I opened my shirt wider, but the feeling only spread faintly, and indeed this halcyon sunny hour terminated in a restlessness that sent me walking into town to look for A.

At last I heard, not of A., but of Miss T. She was in a ballet. I went round during rehearsal and while waiting entered into conversation with a little chorus girl with a good face, who was sewing. On my telling her whom I was seeking she stopped sewing and looked at me quickly: "Oh, are you her husband? I know her. *I have seen them together.*" She looked as if she were going to tell me something, but merely shook her old-fashioned head in a mournful, indescribable way, saying "Why don't you keep your wife with you?" I went to the door and presently saw Miss T. She tried to avoid me, I thought, and looked more vicious than ever, but after a minute's thought reluctantly told me where she and A. were staying. To hide my fears and suspicions I had assumed a careless demeanor, but I think I should have strangled her had she refused to tell me. I hastily went to the place indicated and going up the stairs (to the astonishment of the people) opened the door and found myself face to face with A.—but how changed! She had the hard, harlot, loveless look I detested. I felt for a few minutes that I did not love her, and she regarded me coldly too, but presently old habits reinstated themselves. She put out her hands, very pitiably, and then was sobbing in my arms. I could get nothing out of her but sobs, and to this day do not know where she spent all these weeks nor why she did not write. Miss T. came in after rehearsal, pale and hard-faced. I greeted her politely, but was watching her, trying to puzzle out why A. did not look as she usually did after long absence from coition. Miss T. took another room in the same house and was soon joined by another ballet girl, young and very pretty, who soon began to have fits. A. was always crying until Miss T. went away with her pretty friend. I knew nothing, could hardly be said to suspect anything definite, and yet I pitied that pretty girl whose eyes looked so helpless and appealing.

I set to work again. But I continued to live on fruit and bread, and taking off my clothes I would stand up at the window in the sun. A lot of prostitutes, however, who lived at the back saw me and were scandalized or shocked or thought me mad. The landlady heard of it and spoke to A. So I had to desist from my glorious sun-baths.

We slept on a single bed, and though I did my best to avoid coitus (I wanted to wait and think out some theory of it), A., who knew nothing of this, wanted to resume our old habits, and finally I surrendered. But my sufferings next day were intense, and I had the sense of having fallen from some high estate. My thoughts were divided between two theories: one that our misery was caused by our diet, more or less; the other that we had fallen into some error as regards coitus, and this was becoming almost a certainty with me.

There is one incident I think worthy of note which happened before the "fall" just mentioned and when I was living on fruit and in splendid health. At a performance I saw a girl on the stage with handsome legs in tights, and once as she straightened her leg the knee-cap going into position gave me such a strange and keen joy—of that quality I call divine or musical—that I was like one suddenly awakened to the divinity and beauty of the female form. The joy was so keen and yet peaceful, familiar, and subjective that I could not help comparing it to a happy chemical change in the tissues of my own brain. Like the unexpected functioning of my skin in the sun it was a sign of a partial return to a normal condition, another glimpse of Paradise.

I stuck to my new diet and gained a fresh elation and joy in life. Gradually clothes became insupportable, and I went down to the beach as often as possible to take them off, and at nights, beside the patient and astonished A., I would lie naked. One evening, passing some grass, I looked over the fence like a gipsy and felt a longing to take off my clothes and sleep in the grass all night. It was of course impossible. And A. looked unhappily in my face; she began to think her mother, who now thought I was mad, must be right.

That night I woke up and found myself having coition. I was angry and felt I had been put back in my progress, but a fever of lust now came over me. I would sit under the tap and let the cold water run over me to conquer the fever, but at the end of a week my hopes were frustrated and I even turned against my natural diet, on which I had made flesh. A., as I expected, went through her usual fits, and slowly recovered. (If we had connection only once she in about three weeks had a mild attack of fits; if we had coition more than once the fits were more severe.) I relapsed more than once and as a means of impressing my resolution for future abstinence I would walk for miles in the middle of pitch-black nights. . . .

Miss T. came over to Adelaide and as I knew nothing definite against her and heard that she was engaged, I thought perhaps my suspicions were unfounded and was friendly. But one day in town I saw her and A. on a tram going out to our cottage. Even then my suspicions might not have been awakened, but I saw Miss T. say something rapidly to A., and A. called out to me, "Will you be coming home soon?" And I answered "No." When the tram had gone on I found myself vaguely wondering what Miss T. wanted to know that for, for my perceptions were becoming acute enough to understand women's ways. In another minute I was walking rapidly home. When I came to the door it was locked. I knocked and knocked and no one came. I called out and threatened to kick in the door. Still no one came. Mad with rage I commenced to put my threat into execution, when the door was opened by Miss T., half-naked, in her petticoats, and pale as death, but no longer defiant. "So I've caught you, have I?" I *looked*, but could not trust myself to speak. Wondering why A. did not appear I went into the bedroom. She was lying on the bed, just as Miss T. had left her, on the verge of a fit, and on seeing me she held out her hands piteously, and when I stooped over her she whispered, "Send her away, send her away." Then she became unconscious and going into the next room I ordered Miss T. (who had managed to scramble on her dress) out of the house. I spoke scornfully as if addressing a dog, and she slinked out with a malignant but cowed look I hope never to see on a woman's face again. What they had been doing with their clothes off I do not know; women will rather die than confess. When A. had recovered from her fit she denied that there had been anything between them, and stuck to it doggedly, but with such a forlorn look I had not the heart to prosecute my inquiries.

For my part, all the efforts I had been making for so long seemed for a time to be in vain; for some weeks I sank into a sort of satyriasis, and even my anger against Miss T. turned to a prurient curiosity. At the same time I was not always able to adhere to my diet. But both as regards coition and diet I was still fighting, and on the whole successfully. My fits of temper, however, were excessive and my ennui became gloomy despair. One day I blasphemed on crossing the Park and spoke contemptuously of "God and his twopenny ha'penny revolving balls," referring to the planetary system. But for long walks I should have gone mad. A. was drinking in the intervals of her fits. I found half-empty bottles of wine hidden away. This did not improve my temper, and one day—this was when she was well and up—I struck her a heavy blow on the face, and she aimed a glass decanter at me. She went home to her mother and I lived alone in the cottage. I heard soon afterwards that her husband had come back and that they had made it up. Our parting was not, however, destined to be final.

Even out of that month's sufferings I made capital. I was better after my tendency to lubricity, my gloom, rage, restlessness and degradation. They had been but the irritations of convalescence.

INDEX OF AUTHORS.

INDEX OF SUBJECTS.

Abyssinians, coitus among, 163.

Acquired element in erotic symbolism, 28.

Acromegaly and sexual development, 186.

Alcohol, aphrodisiac effects of, 174.

Algolagnia, in relation to scatologic symbolism, 56; as a form of erotic symbolism, 106.

Anæsthesia, sexual, 186.

Anæsthetics in relation to sexual excitement, 156.

Anaphrodisiacs, 177.

Animal copulation, attraction of, 72.

Animals, detumescence in, 158, 160, 168.

Annamites, coitus among, 163.

Antipathies of pregnant women, 212.

Anus in relation to pubic hair, 128; as an erogenous zone, 133.

Apes, sexual organs of, 125, 127, 136, 165; sexual congress in, 144, 147.

Aphrodisiacs, 172 *et seq.*

Apples, longings of women for, 216.

Arabs, penis in, 122.

Artist, compared to lover, 108.

Associations of contiguity and resemblance in erotic symbolism, 3.

Australian method of sexual congress, 147, 148.

Auto-suggestions, longings of pregnancy as, 213.

Bartholin, glands of, 145.

Beard in relation to sexual development, 197.

Beauty, the objective element in, 107 *et seq.*

Bestiality, 77 *et seq.*

Bladder in relation to sexual excitement, 56, 154, 155.

Blood during pregnancy, 206.

Blood-pressure during detumescence, 151, 169.

Breasts, and erotic temperament, 188; during pregnancy, 206.

Bromide as an anaphrodisiac, 177.

Bulbo-cavernous reflex, 149, 157.

Camphor as an anaphrodisiac, 177.

Cantharides, effects of, 174.

Castration, results of, 180, 183.

Celery as an aphrodisiac, 174.

Children, attracted to foot, 16; to scatology, 53; to copulation of animals, 72; to hair, 74; food impulses of, 215.

Chinese, foot-fetichism of, 21.

Circulatory conditions during coitus, 151; during pregnancy, 207.

Clitoris, 118, 121, 126, 129 *et seq.*, 146.

Clothes, erotic fascination of, 45.

Coitus, the phenomena of, 111 *et seq.*; the methods of, 146 *et seq.*; ethnic variations in methods of, 147, 151; respiratory and circulatory conditions during, 151; interruptus as a cause of vasomotor disturbance, 152, 178; glandular activity during, 153; motor activity during, 153 *et seq.*; psychic state during, 157; serious effects of, 168.

Congenital element in erotic symbolism, 27.

Contiguity in erotic symbolism, associations of, 3.

Coprolagnia, 47, 62 *et seq.*

Coprophagia, religious and sexual, 57.

Courtship, 142.

Crystallization, Stendhal's, 9, 107.

Defile, the impulse to, 95.

Distillatio, 153.

Dog, human sexual intercourse with, 83.

Dynamometric experiments during sexual excitement, 154.

(281)

Reprint Publishing

For People Who Go For Originals.

This book is a facsimile reprint of the original edition. The term refers to the facsimile with an original in size and design exactly matching simulation as photographic or scanned reproduction.

Facsimile editions offer us the chance to join in the library of historical, cultural and scientific history of mankind, and to rediscover.

The books of the facsimile edition may have marks, notations and other marginalia and pages with errors contained in the original volume. These traces of the past refers to the historical journey that has covered the book.

ISBN 978-3-95940-261-3

Facsimile reprint of the original edition
Copyright © 2016 Reprint Publishing
All rights reserved.

Made in Germany

www.reprintpublishing.com

www.ingramcontent.com/pod-product-compliance
Lightning Source LLC
Chambersburg PA
CBHW080326270326
41927CB00014B/3110